Alan Champely
USA

COMPUTER CAPACITY
A Production Control Approach

COMPUTER CAPACITY

A Production Control Approach

by
Melvin J. Strauss

Vice President
The Chase Manhattan Bank, N. A.

VAN NOSTRAND REINHOLD COMPANY

NEW YORK   CINCINNATI   ATLANTA   DALLAS   SAN FRANCISCO
LONDON   TORONTO   MELBOURNE

Van Nostrand Reinhold Company Regional Offices:
New York Cincinnati Atlanta Dallas San Francisco

Van Nostrand Reinhold Company International Offices:
London Toronto Melbourne

Library of Congress Catalog Card Number: 81-260
ISBN: 0-442-26243-4

Manufactured in the United States of America

Published by Van Nostrand Reinhold Company
135 West 50th Street, New York, N.Y. 10020

Published simultaneously in Canada by Van Nostrand Reinhold Ltd.

15 14 13 12 11 10 9 8 7 6 5 4 3 2 1

Library of Congress Cataloging in Publication Data

Strauss, Melvin J
  Computer capacity.

  Includes index.
  1. Electronic data processing—Management.
I. Title.
QA76.9.M3S76   658.05   81-260
ISBN 0-442-26243-4   AACR1

To Sally,
my wife,

without whose encouragement and assistance this book could not have been completed.

The author wishes to acknowledge
the contributions of Charles B. Gibbs,
whose early work led to several of the
thoughts expressed in this text.

PREFACE

The integration of data processing into the mainstream of business is perhaps one of the most significant achievements in recent years. Unfortunately, "the computer" has proved to be one of the more difficult production facilities to manage. Why is this so?

It seems to me that few businessmen understand computer technology well enough to treat data processing in the same manner as they do any other segment of a corporation. At the same time, few people in data processing understand business and the language of business well enough to express data processing concerns in a way that business executives can understand and act upon.

Questions always seem to arise that never get answered to the mutual satisfaction of both the business manager and the data processing manager. The biggest question of all is:

- How is managing data processing different than managing any other production function?

Questions that seem enshrouded in computer technology arise:

- Should an application be run on a dedicated computer or on a utility?
- What size computers should be acquired—minis, large systems, extremely large systems?
- What constrains the use of computer capacity and how can these constraints be minimized?
- When you buy a computer, how do you know how much capacity to order?

Some questions that seem removed from the technology also remain:

- What is service, what do users perceive to be good service, how can good service be delivered, and how can users' perceptions be managed?
- Once computers are acquired, how many people must be hired to operate them?
- Is there a quantitative method of relating size of capacity and number of operations staff to service?

Financial questions seem to linger too:

- How do you determine the real cost of processing a job?
- How do you determine what to charge users for service? And, just as important, how do you anticipate the consequences of instituting a specific chargeback scheme?
- Of what use is the budgeting process, and how can it be easily implemented?

ix

In the pages that follow, I have addressed these questions by applying basic production control and accounting techniques to the areas of computer capacity planning, data center management, and computer chargeout. To those with experience in industrial engineering, *Computer Capacity* will be a fresh application of proven techniques. Readers without such experience will find the material takes a "common sense" approach to issues of production and cost accounting.

I have sought to remove computer jargon from data processing. This facilitates the understanding of data processing by nontechnical senior managers. It also facilitates effective communication of issues to senior managers by data center managers and capacity planning analysts.

When you finish reading *Computer Capacity,* you will have all the tools required to effectively operate a data center, to effectively plan capacity to meet future demand, and to understand your costs and financial risks. In short, you will be able to manage data processing in the same way that successful general managers run other businesses.

MELVIN J. STRAUSS

CONTENTS

COMPUTER CAPACITY

A Production Control Approach

1
INTRODUCTION

There is an old saying that goes like this:
"Never invest in anything that eats or can break."
Most of us seem to ignore this advice. What seems to cause most of
the problems is failure to heed the corollary:
"If you must invest in something that can break, make sure the
repairman speaks your language."

1.1 PURPOSE

The development of the data processing industry has generally centered about, and indeed often has been caused by, the need to solve technological problems that constrained the manipulation of information. At first, attempts to solve these problems resulted in the development of large pieces of hardware, often filling an entire room to accomplish simple addition, sorts, etc. The first large-scale development of solid state electronics eliminated the technological problems of power and heat dissipation and also provided a degree of miniaturization, thereby further permitting the development of larger-capability computing devices.

As engineering advances continued to create larger, more powerful devices, one of the next technological problems to be encountered was that of flexibility. The computational capabilities of existing computers had been a function of their physical hardware configuration, i.e., each function was hardwired into the computer. Each time a change in calculation was required, the engineer literally disconnected and reconnected wires, physically creating new logic circuitry. Then, a new type of engineer more oriented toward the mathematical sciences, appeared on the scene, and the computer industry witnessed the development of the operating system, a method of altering the flow of electrical currents within a more generalized set of computer electronics. The operating system permitted nonelectrical engineers to make rapid changes in computing logic. This new brand of engineer, who came to be known as a "programmer," flourished and came to equal, if not dominate, the electrical engineer.

Both programmers and electrical engineers remained immersed in their own sets of interrelated technological issues, often unconcerned or unaware of the financial implications of the systems solutions they provided for the corporations that employed them. The language of their new technology was markedly different that that used by marketing and other business counterparts, and the semitechnical jargon they used among themselves tended to isolate the ranks of data processing (DP) practitioners still further. In short, they became a subculture within the business community, not really understood but tolerated because their services seemed to provide substantial cost benefits. With few exceptions outside the world of data processing vendors, data processing professionals have not been elevated to positions of senior corporate responsibility, despite earlier industry predictions of rapid advancement.

The DP practitioner's approach towards his or her position in a corporation often ignores three basic concerns faced by all data center managers and their senior management, namely:

- managing existing computer capacity
- forecasting future capacity requirements, and
- communicating what are essentially technical matters to senior, often nontechnical corporate management.

Systems and data center managers, fondly looking back over years of promotions, tend to stay with the formulas that got them promoted: they continue to deal with the technological aspects of technological issues. Senior managers, recognizing that they have been wildly successful in life without ever having to learn what a tape drive is, also see no reason to change their modus operandi. Reluctant to invest precious time to understand the technological details of daily data processing problems, they see no reason to learn to converse in DP jargon when avoiding it has served them well.

While data processing practitioners and business people seem content to continue along their separate paths, their corporations are nevertheless adversely affected by the schism separating the two groups because gathering and digesting the data required to solve production and cost problems has become difficult.

The purpose of this text is to provide both senior management and the DP practitioner with a methodology for identifying and quantifying issues of capacity and demand within the data center without becoming entrapped by language problems. Enlarging upon this subject somewhat, the text takes the position that the data center is basically no different than any other type of line operation, although a little more surrounded by high technology than some and a little less surrounded than others. Input arrives and, through some process involving both human and machine interface, is converted to output. The techniques that the text offers are variations of those that have been used to manage other noncomputer-related types of capacity for many years.

While the techniques described throughout this text provide quantitative methods of dealing with capacity and economic issues, the language used has been selected to provide someone who has not grown up professionally in data processing with the techniques required to address issues of production and cost.

1.2 SCOPE

The discussions that follow can be divided into two major categories: first, *capacity* and *demand,* and, second, *economic considerations.* Chapters 2 through 5, as well as Chapter 8, consider issues of capacity and demand, while Chapters 6 through 8 discuss economics. However, each subject grouping should be considered as no more than a translation of the other since, in any business, capacity and economics are highly interwoven. Capacity describes alternative states of production, while economics describes corresponding alternative business scenarios.

The theme of communications between the general manager and the world of data processing runs throughout the text and is discussed in depth in Chapter 9. Following are brief outlines of each chapter.

CHAPTER 2—DEMAND

In data processing, the concept of "demand" is often confused with utilization. Thus, most DPers relate to such entities as EXCPs and CPU seconds when referring to demand. Software Physics is an extension of this concept. Still others in data processing relate to "jobs processed," "mix factors," and "throughput," though even here there are wide variations in the use of these terms.

Since computer operators rarely complain of a lack of available EXCPs, movable bytes, and so on, the chapter states that computer demands are demands for the allocation of devices, that when additional capacity is purchased, allocatable devices, not containers of EXCPs or CPU cycles, are delivered by the manufacturer. This is consistent with methodologies used in other industries to relate to resources with zero shelf lives.

In addition to the basic utility of this definition of the concept of demand, the discussion provides the DP practitioner with a supply/demand-type framework consistent with descriptions of other segments of the corporation that his superiors manage. Hence the DPer is provided with a communications technique while the senior manager receives a partial data center management/capacity planning framework.

With the definition of demand complete, Chapter 2 then addresses the issue of control over demand. In order to solve the problem of uncertainties over demand size, user expectations of service, and DPers' understanding of user satisfaction criteria, the concept of the data processing service agreement or contract is introduced. A description is offered of the contents of these agreements and the aspects of interpersonal behavior associated with implementing this technique. Service contracts provide the DPer with a mechanism to defend against user variances and the user with a means of assuring service in an environment he or she often can relate to only as a black box. They give the senior manager a tool for distinguishing real DP service problems from perceived difficulties and for determining the actual organization location of production problems.

CHAPTER 3—CAPACITY AND ITS CONSTRAINTS

A distinction is made between relating to capacity in the sense of planning to accommodate demand, as defined in Chapter 2, and relating to capacity for system-tuning purposes. Planning to accommodate demand, like macroeconomics, addresses the response and capabilities of the system as a whole; looking at capacity in terms of its various parts, like microeconomics, enables the fine tuning of overall predictions and some enhancement of the system as a whole. Making this distinction permits the senior manager to understand capacity/demand relationships within the data center without having to reduce himself to a discussion of technical items. At the same time, DPers are provided with a communications tool enabling them to convey their production concerns to management while maintaining a structure for managing technical concerns with their technicians.

The technique employed to quantify the usability of capacity is an extension of the technique used for quantifying demand given in Chapter 2. Constraints upon the use of computer capacity are described in terms of efficiency and of segmentation. This technique enables the senior manager and the DPer to deal with problems within the data center in terms of quantifiable risks to service versus production (service or capacity) alternatives. This is the basis for later discussion of processing costs and prices and dedicated facility/utility trade-off considerations.

CHAPTER 4—PERFORMANCE/EFFICIENCY

Computer capacity and its uses having been described in the last three segments, this chapter addresses the efficiency of the manual portion of the operation and the classical computer measurement approach to efficiency.

Since the central object of attention in the data center is generally the multimillion dollar machine, attention to problems and their solutions generally is focused on the input to, and receipt of outputs from, the hardware. This emphasis leads to the tendency of "optimizing" throughput of a single stage of what is in effect a multistage production process. To the detriment of the process as a whole, basic workflow analyses are ignored at the preceding and succeeding workstations. Furthermore, where these problems result in delays or backlog of input and processing, recovery procedures produce sharp temporary increases in computer utilization, i.e., utilization becomes greater than demand. When these situations are recurring and uncontrolled, the tendency is to perceive a demand higher than is actually the case and to acquire additional capacity. The cost implications of this state are described in a later chapter.

Chapter 4 also presents standard production-control techniques for tracking efficiency and basic techniques for analyzing and categorizing the occurrence of problems. Organizational aspects of analyzing efficiency and enforcing adherence to efficiency objectives are discussed.

An overview of classical computer performance measurement is provided, outlining the scope of issues addressed and comparing the major types of measurement tools available to the analyst, and, finally, a discussion of reliability and associated methods of increasing effective data center capacity is offered.

CHAPTER 5—STAFFING

While considerable effort is generally spent on addressing computer capacity requirements, little if any effort is devoted to determining adequate operations staff levels. The setting of staff levels usually is based upon past history or upon some DPer's intuition. Senior management's response to this method of staffing is generally a combination of anger and frustration. They tend to suspect that staff is too large, yet they are unable to penetrate the technical atmosphere to attack questions that essentially refer to standard issues of work methods.

The chapter examines the data center as a series of workstations, using standard industrial engineering concepts. This approach reduces the data center to a series of small, manageable centers, some of which may operate computer or other equipment, but which essentially convert raw input to finished output. Four techniques for setting manual production standards are discussed: MTM, standard data, time ladders, and linear programming techniques. Further discussions are provided that describe methods of selecting the appropriate technique as a function of workstation characteristics. This has particular significance for workstations with high variability, either in volume or in composition of input/output requirements. Examples of such variability are job setup functions where job inputs may vary widely from one job to another, tape mounting volume per hour, and so on.

Following the discussion of constructing manual work standards is a presentation of line balancing techniques. Finally, the behavioral and organizational problems of setting standards on a production line are addressed.

CHAPTER 6—BUDGETING

Intended as an overview or refresher on the budgeting process for the DPer, this chapter addresses the capability to adequately manage a budget and budgetary variances, a prerequisite to the cost/price discussion in Chapter 7 and the utility/dedicated-facility discussion of Chapter 8.

The topics in this chapter include the development of capital and expense budgets, depreciation methods, cost of funds, and lease versus purchase analyses.

CHAPTER 7—CHARGEOUT: COSTS VERSUS PRICES

Most data processing charging schemes merely separate total expense into a finite number of segments and then divide by an estimate of future average utilization. Since these schemes have the same bases as existing methods for relating to utilization (*not* demand) and capacity, the data center manager has the same problem with user charges as he does with service, while the user and senior management share the same credibility problem with data processing charges as they do with DP service and bottom-line expenses.

The chapter addresses this issue first by defining and differentiating between the terms "cost" and "price" and then by relating to data processing costs in the same context as the discussion of demand in Chapter 2 and of the budgeting process in Chapter 6. Several alternative pricing strategies are described, including price equals cost, full-service versus unbundled charges, and charges for dedication (staff or machines). The advantages, disadvantages, and behavioral effects of each strategy are discussed.

CHAPTER 8—THE UTILITY VERSUS DEDICATED-FACILITY DECISION

The economic, organizational, and technical considerations of this type of capacity decision are discussed at length. Economic issues presented include standard bottom-line comparisons, but more importantly, include several other topics essential to such decisions: differences between alternatives of treatment of unutilized capacity; the implications of imbalances between peak and average demand in relation to capacity segment size; the application of the concepts of marginalism and incrementalism; and the applicability of economics of scale. While some of these appear to be capacity/demand-oriented, they are also presented in terms of their strong economic impact.

Other issues covered include control over discretionary versus nondiscretionary processing; problems of nonstandardization of software and technical procedures, such as labeling conventions and naming conventions; the requirement to exchange data between different parts of the corporation; and the requirement to determine whether alternative capacity scenarios offer the same degree of support services, planning and technical staff, and back-up processing facilities.

CHAPTER 9—COMMUNICATING ISSUES

Since gaining management approval for a capacity acquisition decision is as much a function of the ability to communicate issues to senior management as it is a function of obtaining the correct technical solution to a problem, Chapter 9 concludes by offering a technique for structuring decision data. Recognizing the uncertainty inherent in presenting any type of decision data to a corporation's senior management, a layered approach to preparing the presentation, whether in tabular or graphical format, is outlined. The theme of language using terms consistent with those that the intended audience understands and is used to dealing with is stressed.

2
DEMAND

In this chapter, we examine problems with existing definitions of demand; offer an alternative based on standard industrial engineering techniques; and provide a mechanism to allow the data center to exercise a degree of control over user demands.

2.1 INTRODUCTION

It was once observed that demand, like beauty, is in the eye of the beholder. Put another way, the perception of demand is no more than an individual's perception of another's requirements. And since perceptions vary from one individual to another, the lack of a universally accepted definition of data processing demand has led historically to multitudes of conflicting views of both the qualitative and quantitative aspects of data center services. This state of affairs is generally responsible for many issues or problems related to data center performance and end-user satisfaction.

In general, we are faced with the dilemma of requiring that demand be defined in a manner consistent with the day-to-day computer operation and, it is hoped, in a manner consistent with other non-data processing definitions. Surprisingly, the young DP industry has had difficulty meeting this first requirement. Finding a widely understood manner of expressing data center demands would greatly reduce problems that most DP managers experience in communicating with their senior management, who are often not data processing–oriented. A common language for both parties would be more comfortable and therefore more acceptable to senior managers than the semitechnical jargon now used. As we shall see in ensuing chapters, an exceptionally good definition of data center demands would additionally serve the dual purposes of reducing operational problems (or, at the very least, surprises) and of providing accurate, reliable forecasts of future demand levels.

2.2 DEFINITION OF DEMAND

The prime requisites for successful servicing of any type of demand and in this specific case of computer demand, are a successful structure or format for relating to demand and a firm knowledge of the quantity and timing of the segments of demand that are expected. Although this is obvious, it has not been easy for the data processing industry to achieve, probably for reasons that are more historical than anything else.

The I/Os and EXCPs Among Us

Typically, data processing has chosen to represent demand in terms of dynamic entities, usually I/Os performed and compute seconds consumed. In IBM parlance, these terms are EXCPs and CPU seconds. Burroughs users refer to them as I/Os and CPU seconds, DEC users as QIOS and CPU seconds, and so on. The list of names grows as one considers the seemingly endless number of minicomputers on the market.

What do these terms mean?

"CPU seconds" is obvious. It is the combined cumulative number of seconds that the application utilizes the compute circuitry—the add logic, multiplication logic, comparison logic, etc.

The manipulation or transfer of one packet or logical unit of information is defined as one I/O or one EXCP. The rationale behind this is that the computer system must execute a section of code a fixed number of times (generally once on many computers) to handle or control the movement of a packet of data. On IBM, this code is named Execute Channel Program, hence EXCP. To systems programmers, this scheme of defining things that go on inside the computer seems relevant. Much of their formal (professional) education has geared them to this type of thinking. And, in fact, they have no choice but to deal with these entities if they are to implement new systems successfully or improve the efficiency of existing ones. (This topic is discussed further in Chapter 4.)

Furthermore, when DPers first became interested in measuring what was occurring within the computer, of the many variables that were of interest, I/Os and CPU seconds were among the few that the existing technology could measure and count. Thus, the applicability of EXCPs as a measure of computer demand was first recognized by the systems types that developed third-generation computers and has been propagated by the throngs of professionals to whom we give thanks for the daily maintenance and development of our computerized systems.

Example 2.1

The XYZ Corporation's payroll system maintains information on each of its 5000 employees. Running on a large mainframe, the system processes against a 1000-character record for each employee once per week. How does the I/O-CPU method state demand?

This type of process is relatively standard, yet the answer can vary depending on the data-handling conventions used by the programmer.

Each access to a group (or block) of data results in one I/O or EXCP. If the programmer has kept the 1000-character records logically intact, accessing an employee record once results in one I/O. If for other system-performance reasons breaking the record into two 500-character blocks was deemed appropriate, each access then results in two I/Os, and so on. Thus, 10 accesses to each record result in a total I/O load of either 5000 or 10,000 I/Os.

CPU requirements arise from execution of the application code as well as servicing I/Os. Therefore, if the application code required 300 seconds of CPU time and each I/O requires 1 millisecond, the demand due to running payroll is either:

305 CPU seconds and 5000 I/Os

or

310 CPU seconds and 10,000 I/Os, etc.

Obviously, programming conventions do not change daily, so that once a new application has stabilized, the load or perceived demand for computer resources remains constant for a given set of input data.

Example 2.2

The Southern Credit Corporation and the Headway Acceptance Company have both purchased the Consumer Credit Analysis (CCA) system, a commercially available software package, to perform various demographic analyses on the consumer-credit data bases they maintain. In order to test an arrangement to mutually back-up their computer sites, Headway's data base is run against the package on Southern's computer. Both mainframes are identical except that Southern has 32 disk drives compared to Headway's 16. The input data and analysis performed on the Southern facility are kept identical to an earlier run on Headway's machine.

For performance reasons, Headway's data base is spread to the full 32 disk drives. This results in a decrease in the amount of elapsed (wall-clock) time required from 3 hours to 2.5 hours. What difference in demand is identified by the I/O-CPU method?

The answer here is none. With the input, application (package) code and number and type of calculations held constant, the CPU seconds and data accesses (I/Os) will similarly remain constant. [Purists will correctly argue that there would be a slight decrease in resource usage for the latter run, corresponding to decreased contention for (i.e., easier access to) data residing on disks. However, the difference generally would be imperceptible, a small fraction of a percent.]

Forecasting future demand with this methodology generally involves extrapolating CPU and I/O trend information.

While it is good that this method of accounting for demand is not sensitive to changes in the capacity of the host computer system, we shall see later in Chapter 7 that this presents some inconsistencies in costing (although not necessarily in pricing). Later in this chapter, it may also be observed that the data center manager has less leverage effecting application changes with this method than with other alternatives.

The Throughput Method

A second method of relating to computer demand concerns itself with what is referred to as "throughput" but is often no more than relative rates of activity. DPers who use this method primarily rely on trend direction. When presenting statistics to management, they seek to convey that increasing trends reflect increasing demand and vice versa. In reading the following paragraphs, the reader should note that this is a somewhat indirect method of demand accounting.

Multiprogramming
Level

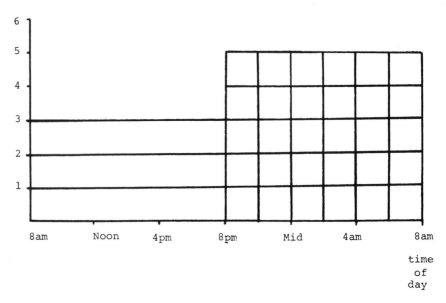

Figure 2.1. Multi-Programming Level Chart.

While there are variations in the definition of the term across the industry, "throughput" is generally defined as the total amount of useful processing carried out by a computer system in a given period of time. There is no universal agreement, however, on precisely what constitutes "useful processing." Often, one or more of a set of several terms are referenced. In many instances, the terms selected by the DPer for presentation to management do not refer to a unified value, and the senior manager is left with what he considers an abstruse array of numbers with little relevance.

The terms most often used in this scheme of demand definition are:

- **Multiprogramming level (MPL)**

  This is no more than the average number of application programs processed in the data center during some specified time interval. Assume, for example, as in Figure 2.1, that for 12 hours three on-line systems with one program each are run, and that for the next 12 hours thirty 2-hour batch programs are run. The MPL for the first 12 hours is 3, for the second 12 hours 5, and for the entire day 4.

  Note that which half of the day has the greater intensity of resource consumption cannot be determined since the statistic merely logs program residency and ignores all other processing characteristics. If, in 6 months, the MPL is measured at 6, one might correctly assume that demand had risen, but there would be no indication of the degree of the increase.

- **Elapsed processing hours**

  The total number of (wall) clock hours for each processed job is referred to as "total elapsed processing hours." If three jobs take 12 hours each to process, the elapsed hour total is 36. This term, then, is no more than the multiprogramming level multiplied by the appropriate time interval, usually 24 hours. If, through some efficiency problem, jobs that used to take 12 hours to process now take 15, the throughput method would portray an increase in demand.

- **Number of jobs**

This statistic merely tracks the number of jobs executed during the reporting period and assumes that, if there is a positive or negative trend, then demand is following a similar trend and that, if the numbers are sufficiently large, the magnitude of the increase in demand will approach the magnitude of the increase in number of jobs.

- **Output volume**

An index that assumes productive computer processing is represented by printed reports delivered to users, "output volume" is generally either the number of lines or the number of pages of print produced during the measured time interval.

- **Kernals, or standard jobs processed**

"Kernals" are generally defined as small packets of demand that represent the ratio in the whole workload of I/Os to CPU seconds. Restated, they are the least common denominators that characterize a workload's composition or blend of CPU seconds and I/Os. For example, if on an average day 40,000 CPU seconds and 800,000 I/Os were consumed, the kernal would be defined as 1 CPU second and 20 I/Os, or 100 CPU seconds and 2000 I/Os, etc.

Standard jobs, when related to the kernal concept, are average or expected values of job CPU and I/O requirements. The actual values are generally derived from simple averaging or from some form of modal analysis.

The throughput method considers trend information of this type of indicator.

- **Device utilization rates**

Device utilization rates are a group of statistics that refer to the average loading of each of several types of devices, generally CPU, I/O channels, tape drives, and/or disk drives. The idea here is that whatever demand is, its manifestation is the loading of the various subsystems that comprise the computer system as a whole.

Analysts that prefer throughput-based demand accounting schemes are usually primarily interested in trend information. This method has a distinct advantage over others in its class because it offers data in terms of capacity limitations for specific types of computer hardware.

- **Megabyte hours**

Perhaps the most confusing of all throughput statistics to the senior, nontechnical executive, "megabyte hours" refers to the amount and duration of main-storage residency for a program or group of programs.

This statistic had far greater usage in previous years when the operating systems for large-scale computers placed the requirement that a program remain stationary in core (main storage). In the trade, the requirement to

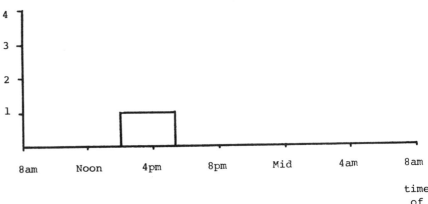

Figure 2.2. Multi-Programming Level Chart.

remain stationary was referred to as processing under a real (rather than virtual) operating system. Megabyte hours were primarily used as a statistic in IBM shops utilizing MVT and, to a lesser extent, MFT and DOS. These latter two operating systems, being somewhat more rigid that MVT, were associated with something called "region hours." Region hours reflected the fact that these operating systems segmented the computer into a fixed (contrasted with MVT's variable) number of regions or sectors, each region providing space for a program to reside while it is executed.

Since main storage has as its unit grouping something called the byte in many parlances, including IBM, if a program required 1 million bytes of main storage, it was said to require a megabyte. Two such programs, which required 90 minutes each to execute, would then be measured to consume 3 megabyte hours, etc.

Example 2.3

Headway's Consumer Credit Analysis (CCA) system, mentioned earlier, is composed of six programs, each taking 30 minutes to process and generally executed between 2 PM and 5 PM (This is described in multiprogramming-level format in Figure 2.2). The host computer is a 1000K (1-megabyte) main-storage machine configured with the same 16 disk drives mentioned earlier, four 9-track tape drives and two medium-speed printers. The only other application run on this computer is an on-line inquiry system, the Account Inquiry System (AIS), which allows Headway's field offices to inquire whether an account's status is delinquent. This system runs on-line from 9 AM to 5 PM and therefore is at times processing concurrently with CCA. The AIS data base is then updated, and several analyses are performed by three programs that run concurrently from 5 PM to 6 PM. A tape log of all inquiries is maintained as part of the on-line function.

Assume that each CCA job consumes 10 CPU minutes, 100K EXCPs split between two disk files and one tape file. For the sake of this example, assume the on-line portion of AIS results in the same CPU and I/O consumption as CCA: 60 minutes worth of CPU cycles and 500K accesses to data. The data center has received notice that transaction volume for each system is growing at the rate of 2% per month. How would the practitioner of the throughput method forecast demand at the end of six months?

This method dictates that the analyst construct a series of charts describing trends of each statistic belonging to the throughput method and then select those which, whether by intuition, past experience, or "professional judgment," he or she believes best describe the coming demand state. Figure 2.3a shows the average multiprogramming level for month 1 over a 24-hour day. Assuming transaction volume increases will take proportionally higher computer resources, each program will either consume a greater amount of resources per unit time or, if resource utilization is nearing capacity, will take longer elapsed time to process. The on-line system, by its very definition, operates only from 9 AM to 5 PM. Therefore, while it will consume more computer resources, increased transaction volume will not result in an increase to the multiprogramming level. The other four batch programs, however, can be assumed to elongate with volume increases. Figure 2.3b illustrates monthly trend data. Note that the average multiprogramming level for month 1 is 0.583 (5 hours of 1, 3 hours of 2, 1 hour of 3, and 15 hours of 0). Although some practitioners would argue against including 15

a) Multiprogramming
   Level

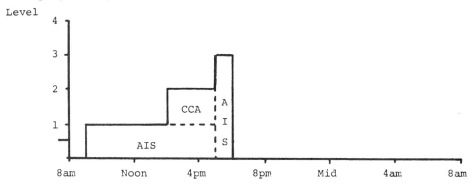

b) Multiprogramming
   Level

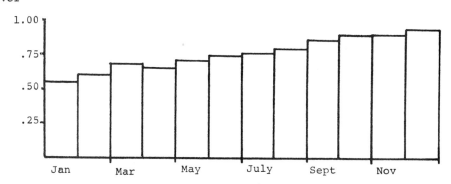

Figure 2.3. Throughput Method Demand Chart.

c) Number of jobs
   processed monthly

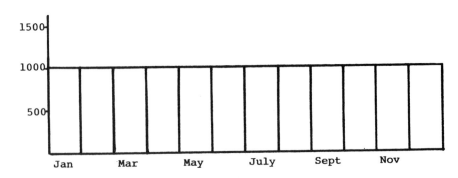

d) Kernals
   (millions per day)

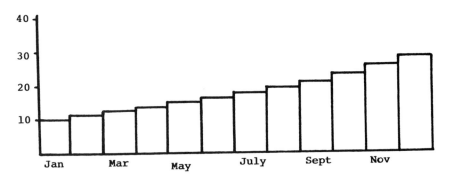

Figure 2.3. Throughput Method Demand Chart. (*continued*)

hours of zero in the answer, we shall observe in later chapters that to so delete would introduce profound errors into unit-production-cost calculations. Indeed, a deletion of this type would upset the underlying cost basis for dedicated-facility versus utility decisions. And one can observe that it would even upset the multiprogramming level statistic. It is left for the reader to calculate that each 10% increase to transaction volume in this example results in an increase to elapsed time of 0.6 hour. This translates to an increase in the multiprogramming level of 0.025, or only 4.3%, even though consumed computer resources have been increased by 10%.

Since the elapsed-hour statistic is merely the multiprogramming level multiplied by the reference period (24 hours), a graphical trending of this statistic would have a shape identical to Figure 2.3b but a vertical magnitude 24 times greater. The number of jobs statistic (Figure 2.3c) erroneously shows the workload remaining flat. Since virtually all printed output is generated by the batch jobs, the output volume trend would closely resemble Figure 2.3b.

Figure 2.3d increases at the rate of 10% per month to reflect the close relationship between input volume and resources consumed. This would be appropriate for graphing the trend of the kernal statistic. Since device utilization statistics relate to several types

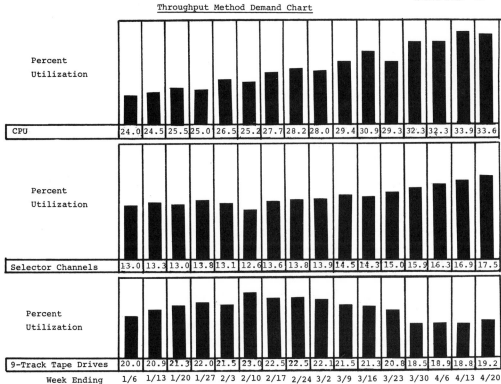

Figure 2.3(e). Throughput Method Demand Chart. (*continued*)

of computing equipment, several trend graphs would be required, as in Figure 2.3*e*. Since the megabyte-hour statistic represents the duration of core allocation, it would have a trend with shape similar to the multiprogramming statistic of Figure 2.3*b*.

In the example, the performance analyst would prepare a demand forecast for senior management by selecting a group of these graphical trends that, in his opinion provides a well-rounded representation of the demand state 6 months hence. The senior manager, who regularly deals with problems relating to return ratios, debt structuring, market penetration, and legal entanglements has finally been presented with the opportunity to brush away these issues for an evening in order to ponder the implications of rising megabyte-hour and selector-channel consumption in contrast with a markedly flat multiprogramming level.

Although somewhat exaggerated, the example underscores that while the throughput method attempts to be quantitative, it is actually highly qualitative and often confusing to its ultimate audience.

Software Physics

In response to the ambiguities, apparent inconsistencies, and frequently erroneous conclusions resulting from the previous two demand-accounting schemes, a methodology called software physics was developed. Its conceptualization is attributed to Kenneth W. Kolence, a widely respected early practitioner of software monitors.

The methodology that constitutes software physics is patterned after Isaac Newton's Third Law of Motion and has special significance for ardent fans of that law. Software physics seeks to quantify computer demand in terms similar to the Newtonian relationship of force, mass, distance, and time, $\mathbf{F} = m\mathbf{a}$. Software physics has as its basic variables software work, time, and storage occupancy. The methodology places prime emphasis on the term *software work,* which it defines as the movement or transformation of data. For example, the movement of a 500-byte record from a disk drive to main storage represents 500 units of software work; the printing (via line printer) of a 132-character record is 132 units; reading an 80-column punched card (transferring 80 characters from the card reader to main storage) is 80 units; and so on.

Since any computer program presents demands for numerous resource types, software work presents itself as a multivariate function

$$\text{Work} = f(\text{CPU, tape, disk, printer,} \dots).$$

In order to facilitate making this "science" universal across all computer hardware, a vector concept is used. The application whose work is stated as $W = f(\text{CPU, tape, disk, printer,} \dots)$ is presented as a "vector array":

$$\mathbf{W}_i = \begin{bmatrix} \text{CPU work} \\ \text{tape work} \\ \text{disk work} \\ \text{printer work} \\ \cdot \\ \cdot \\ \cdot \end{bmatrix} \quad or \quad \begin{bmatrix} \mathbf{W}_{i1} \\ \mathbf{W}_{i2} \\ \mathbf{W}_{i3} \\ \mathbf{W}_{i4} \\ \cdot \\ \cdot \\ \cdot \\ \mathbf{W}_{ij} \end{bmatrix}$$

where $\mathbf{W}_{ij}$ represents the work performed on a particular equipment class or type of resource. Central to the software physics theme is the idea that this vector is invariant, i.e., $\mathbf{W}_i$ remains a fixed quantity regardless of the type of computing facility employed. Therefore, if job J_i is processed on an IBM 115, its software work $\mathbf{W}_i$ is the same as if it were processed on a 3033MP.

The reader should be careful when interpreting the meaning of the term *vector.* Software physics determines the magnitude of $\mathbf{W}$ by summing each of the parts. A vector such as

$$W = \begin{bmatrix} 1 \\ 2 \end{bmatrix}$$

would be said to have a magnitude of three, i.e., if there is one unit of CPU work and two of tape work, total software work is three units. By contrast, a mathematics text would represent the sum of such a two-variable vector as

$$W = \sqrt{C^2 + t^2 - 2Ct \sin \theta}$$

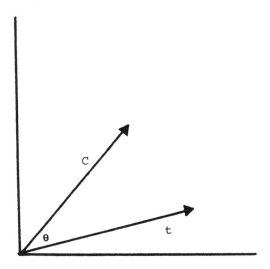

Figure 2.4. Vector Diagram.

as in Figure 2.4. However, the value θ, the angle between the two variables, has no meaning with respect to computer demand—there is no such directional relationship between consumed computer resources.

The manner in which that direction is defined is another difference between software physics vectors and those that mathematics texts discuss. Rather than defining a vector of size 2 and direction, e.g., of north by northwest, "the direction of a software force is defined to be the source-to-target container direction."[1] Thus, our vector of size 2 may have its direction stated as: from register 6 to tape drive 27. Further, while the reader will note that these "vectors" are written as arrays, "although vector arrays look like matrices, they neither follow matrix operation rules nor exhibit normal matrix properties."[2] Thus, while software physics defines what may be termed a resource space, the reader should maintain the distinction between the software physics concept of a vector and the traditional or standard concept.

Recognizing the existence of different speed devices of the same class (e.g., line printers), software physics borrows the concept of power from Newtonian mechanics by defining software power as:

Software power = (software work)/time.

The analyst who selects as a reference base a 1200 line per minute (lpm) printer would classify its power as 1.00, a 2000 lpm printer as 1.75, etc. A CPU with a cycle time of 1 million cycles per second would, all other factors being constant, have a power factor of 2.0 when compared to a CPU of speed 500,000

[1]K. W. Kolence, *The Meaning of Computer Measurement: An Introduction to Software Physics* (1976), p. 2–111., Institute for Software Engineering, Palo Alto, Calif.
[2]Ibid., p. 4–23.

Software work	$\mathbf{W} = \mathbf{W}_{CPU} + \mathbf{W}_{I/O}$ or $W = \begin{bmatrix} \text{CPU work} \\ \text{I/O work} \end{bmatrix}$	The sum of bytes of data transformed or moved from one device to another, including data passing through the CPU, system registers, main storage, and all I/O devices.
Throughput	$T = n/t$ or $\mathbf{T} = W/t\mathbf{W}$ $= 1/tW \begin{bmatrix} \text{CPU work} \\ \text{I/O work} \end{bmatrix}$	The number of jobs processed, n, per unit time, sometimes expressed as software work per unit time divided by the standard or average job.
Throughput power	$\mathbf{P} = \mathbf{W}/t$ $= 1/t \begin{bmatrix} \text{CPU work} \\ \text{I/O work} \end{bmatrix}$ or $\mathbf{P} = d\mathbf{W}/dt$	The rate at which software work is performed, either with respect to an entire configuration or, alternatively, individual device types. Restated, "throughput power" is a descriptor of the processing capability of a specific set of computer devices in terms of the speed of execution of a given workload.

Figure 2.5. Software Physics—Key Entities.

CPS, and so on. In this manner, a given level of work, for example, 1200 lines of print would be associated with equipment of power equal to

$$P = 1200/1200 \; or \; 1.00 \text{ on a 1200 lpm device}$$
$$or$$
$$P = 1200/(1200/1.75) \text{ or } 1.75 \text{ on a 2000 lpm device}$$

These terms are summarized in Figure 2.5.

These equations briefly describe software work and time, two of the three basic software physics variables. The third, storage occupancy, "is perhaps the most abstract concept in software physics, because it equates to the natural physics concept of existence."[3] It refers to the physical capacity of a device being used to house data, 3 million bytes in half full 6-megabyte main storage, 3 million bytes in a fully loaded 3-megabyte disk pack, etc.

It may be observed in Chapter 4 that elements of software physics are useful in simulating or modeling throughput and response-time capabilities of alternative computer configurations. Readers with further interest in software physics are referred to the Institute for Software Engineering.

The Allocation Method

In other disciplines, demands for resources are generally stated in terms consistent with the definition of those resources. The reader will note, however, that

---

[3]Ibid., p. 2–29.

the foregoing demand-accounting schemes do not follow this pattern—disk drives are not defined in terms of their EXCP capacity, mainframes are not defined in terms of their multiprogramming abilities, and so forth.

Using the airline industry as an example, consumer demand can be stated in terms of the allocation of certain key or critical resources, in this case, passenger-seat miles, the allocation of a seat, or physical space (load factor) for some distance. For the purposes of accounting of demand and capacity forecasting, the industry ignores such indices as engine operating hours, pounds of fuel consumed, and flight hours. Instead, it recognizes what is basically a two-tier approach to the analysis of its operating data.

The first tier concerns itself with the scheduling or deployment of resources to satisfy consumer demands for airline services. The second tier deals with streamlining or tuning the operating and delivery mechanisms for those services. We note that the airline industry's senior managers are concerned primarily with data relating to capacity and demand and are concerned with tuning data only insofar as it affects the so-called bottom line of the service-delivery mechanism. It is the streamliners—the industrial engineers or operations analysts—who are directly concerned with data regarding operations tuning or efficiency. While their activities affect capacity, the ability of capacity to satisfy demand, and the unit cost of capacity, one must maintain the distinction between these two classes of data and, more importantly, between these two classes of concerns.

A data processing operation bears striking similarities to the airline example. Both types of organizations are essentially service organizations whose products have shelf lives of zero—an unfilled seat at takeoff will never be booked, and an unused CPU cycle is lost forever. The allocation method defines demand (and also, as we shall observe in Chapter 3, capacity) in terms of types and quantities of equipment whose allocation is required in order for a given job to be processed. This takes the form given in Figure 2.6. A job starts at time t, requires the availability of l tape drives between t_1 and t_2, m disk drives, n percent of the available CPU cycles, etc. This is highly consistent with the control language conventions imposed by most major operating systems. As an example, IBM's control language, JCL, requires among other things a description of the type and quantity of tape and disk drives and core (real or virtual) region size.

The problem with which one is faced when using this scheme is one of detail. There are a large number of device types that could be required for any given job. In addition to the major categories described in Figure 2.6, there are channels, switches, controllers, printers, and terminals. Furthermore, each of these types of devices exists in a sizable number of variations. And there is a long list of data communications equipment that may be required in a seemingly infinite number of combinations.

Fortunately, this problem is circumvented by the "Critical Resource Concept." This concept recognizes that although there are literally dozens of types of devices on the computer room floor, it is possible to typify demand by referring to a few, generally on the order of three to six. Thus, while a program may require the use of three channels, two switches, three controllers, and six tape

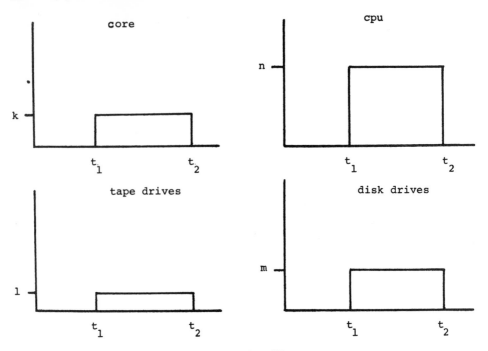

Figure 2.6. Allocation of Resources.

drives, for the most part all but the tape drives are transparent to both the program and the operations staff. All else may have operating system or tuning implications, but at the time of job processing, all that the computer operator is aware of is that the job has requested the allocation of six tape drives.

The allocation method treats CPU requirements in much the same manner, as the requirement to allocate a percentage of the available CPU cycles for some time interval $t_1 \rightarrow t_2$. Historically, the operator, has articulated this by describing jobs as either "heavy" or "light" consumers of CPU. Opponents of the allocation method contend that this scheme is insensitive to minute-to-minute fluctuations in requirements for CPU cycles, that 50% for a 2-minute duration may be an average of 0% and 100%. Allocation proponents argue that 1- or 2-minute spikes in consumption rarely affect computer output timeliness. They further argue that if this type of consumption spiking, or instability, is anything but a transient phenomena, then other, more serious problems exist.

The Allocation Method, then, calls for the observer to distinguish among perhaps dozens of resource types on the floor and the few that typify that multitude.

Example 2.4

Using the Allocation Method, describe the Headway Corporation's demand according to the information given in Example 2.3.

Figure 2.7 provides a brief graphic description. AIS on-line, with an expected consumption of 60 CPU minutes over an 8-hour period, is described as presenting demand for $60 \div 480$ or 12.5% of the available CPU cycles. The logging function, requiring the continuous availability of one tape, represents a tape drive demand of 1. Assuming for that performance reasons, disk-resident data are spread to two drives, disk demand is obviously 2. Demand for the remaining jobs is calculated in a similar manner.

Example 2.5

Acme Electronics, a West Coast retail audio and electronics distributor, maintains its inventory control on a medium-scale system, a DEF-10 with 1 million words of main storage, two line printers, four tape drives, and 44 megabytes of nonremovable disk

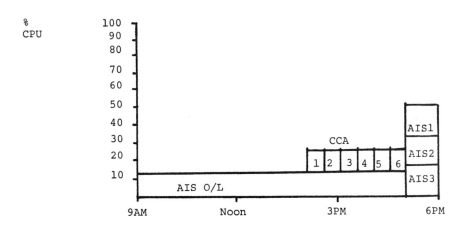

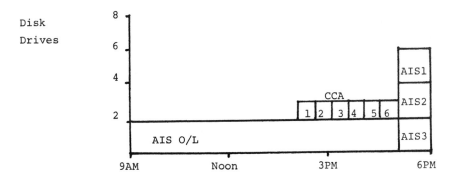

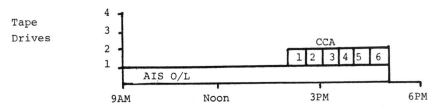

Figure 2.7. Statement of Demand.

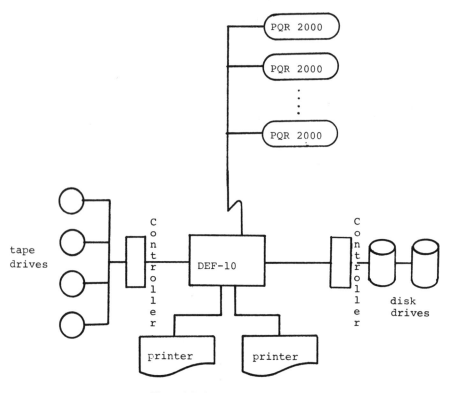

Figure 2.8. Computer Schematic.

storage. The system is accessed by one of two terminals residing in each of its 300 stores. Figure 2.8 describes this configuration along with the support equipment (i.e., channels, controllers, communications lines, etc.) required to run the system. The inventory system consists of three programs, input capture, file maintenance, and a report generator. Input capture runs between 9 AM and 10 PM and is merely a receiving mechanism for sales data logged the previous day by each store's PQR 2000 electric cash register and stored on a small diskette. An average of 1000 transactions per store are transmitted, each 100 characters in length, each consuming 0.0265 CPU seconds on the host CPU (DEF-10). The file maintenance program requires an hour of elapsed (wall-clock) time. Its logic is essentially a series of sorts and adjustments to inventory level records. Two tape drives are required to support the sort and CPU seconds required are 2550. The report generator prepares sales-trend and reorder data. Invariant to transaction data, this module runs between 11 PM and midnight, requires 5 minutes of CPU, and uses data resident on two tapes and 1 megabyte of disk storage. How is demand stated according to the allocation method?

This question will be examined from two viewpoints: first, that of the data center, and second, that of the user.

The data center, and in particular, the computer operator, approaches the application as if it were structured in the manner described in Figure 2.9. That is, the operator deals with a series of allocations that, when graphed, resembles a skyline. There is no need to become concerned with transaction information, characters of data moved across or between devices, and so on. Intentionally or not, when the user brought these three jobs into existence, it caused the data center to become concerned with device allocations.

Input capture requires 0.0265 × 1000 × 300, or 7950 CPU seconds. Over the 13-hour, 46,800-second execution period, this takes the form of 17% CPU allocation. Disk requirements are 100 × 1000 × 300, or 30 million characters, 68% of disk capacity. Similarly, the file maintenance requires 2550 ÷ 3600 or 71% of the CPU, 2 ÷ 4, or 50% of tape capacity and, assuming an additional 5 million characters of disk for sort work space, 35 million characters of disk capacity or four drives. Report generator demand is determined in the same manner.

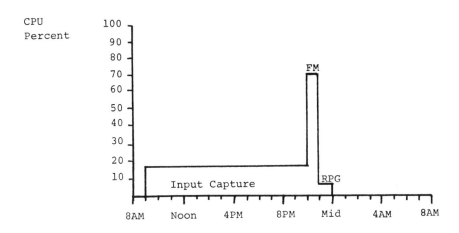

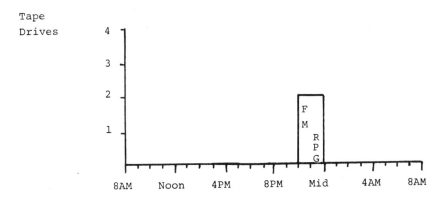

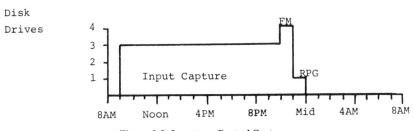

Figure 2.9. Inventory Control System.

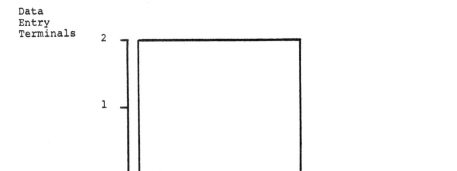

Figure 2.10. Users Perceived Demand.

Note that given the capacity requirements of Figure 2.9, so far as the production is concerned, the demand picture is complete.

The user's perception of demand bears little resemblance to the data center's. Users at the input stations in retail locations view demand in terms of the number of transactions they transmit during input capture. They view capacity as open ports or data conduits between 8 AM and 10 AM, and also as something else—a vaguely pictured "black box" of unknown dimensions that converts transactions to a set of printed outputs. Figure 2.10 describes the user's perception.

In summary, the Allocation Method, facilitates depicting computer demand in terms of a small number of critical resources. As we shall see in Chapter 3, this feature is particularly useful in quantifying capacity and the constraints on its use. The reader will note that the allocation method is key to the resolution of a number of issues discussed throughout this text, including that of quantifying demand.

2.3   QUANTIFICATION OF DEMAND

The trap that ensnares many corporate operations managers is variability. Dependencies on user input; output from other applications or other computer sites; reliability of computer hardware, computer (operating) software, and applications software; volume in the marketplace; and other changeable factors combine to cause havoc for schedulers, confuse line managers regarding what is expected of them, and frustrate and anger users, who simply want their reports on time. In many other professions outside data processing, the effects of these variable factors are commonly referred to as uncertainty.

Demand Versus Utilization

Generally, the major source of concern in any line function and, in this specific case, in the data center, is uncertainty. Unless serious problems exist regarding the integrity of capacity (see Chapter 4), if one can remove the uncertainty

SOURCE	CAUSE	EFFECT
User	Marketplace variances	Changes in driver demand (volumes) or input delay in marketplace resulting in change to computer demand
Other users	Relationships with other demand segments	Delay of input, volume variance of input resulting in extended or delayed processing
Data processing	Hardware/software reliability	Input delay, change to processing environment resulting in variance of utilization from demand

Figure 2.11. Variance of Utilization from Demand.

associated with demand, the stability of an operation is assured. This brings into focus the difference between demand and utilization, a concept generally ignored in data processing management.

"Demand" may be defined as the stated need for a particular volume of goods or services: the requirement for 100 seats on an airplane for next Tuesday's 11 AM flight from New York to London, the need for a ton of coal, or the request for two tape drives for 1 hour beginning at noon each Wednesday. These are fixed statements of consumer needs.

"Utilization," on the other hand, reflects actual usage: 110 passengers appeared at the plane's boarding gate, delivery of the coal was refused, or three tape drives were used for 45 minutes last Wednesday beginning at 12:30 PM.

The difference between demand and utilization is essential to the discussion of costs versus prices in Chapter 7, but, more importantly, the acknowledgment and the method of handling this difference is key to the establishment by the data center of control over how demand will be serviced and over how the shop will deploy its computer capacity.

Service Agreements

In other industries, the majority of firms conduct their business by using written agreements as the basis for defining deliverables or services to be performed as well as for stating anticipated prices. But in the environment of the corporate data center, this common practice is rarely implemented to full advantage.

The *"data processing service agreement,"* or contract, is a very simple but detailed tool that performs three functions. First, it specifies to the user when, under normal input conditions, he can expect to receive reports at a specified service level. That is, up to some threshold input time and input quantity (reels of tape, cards, transactions, or whatever else is meaningful to both the user and the data center), computer operations agrees to deliver the user's output at a specified hour of the day some percent of the time (for example, all products will be delivered at 10 AM on 90% of the days that the user complies with the previously outlined input arrangement).

Second, the contract specifies the types and quantities of computer resources required to produce the user's product. This may take the form of 1 hour of 100K bytes of core, 10% of available CPU cycles, one tape drive, or whatever entities line management requires to adequately schedule and reserve sufficient computer capacity. This component of the agreement often reflects predecessor/feeder relationships with other applications or corporate products. Note that the format of these descriptions is identical to the time-resource rectangles previously described by the allocation method.

Finally, the contract states in advance the actions that both parties can take when the above commitments cannot be met. This information often includes respecifications of output deadlines, instructions to process without certain inputs, or merely the phone numbers of responsible members of the organization to contact for further instructions.

The service contracts remove much of the uncertainty of service commitments that data processing line managers regularly face. Each contract separately quantifies the individual segments of demand; taken in total, the contracts quantify overall demand with which line managers must contend. The signatures both of the key user and the data processing management officials on the bottom of a contract that has been distributed to principal members of senior management help establish a clear-cut service environment free from the dangers of guesswork and misunderstanding. When all else fails, the contract also provides an organizational shield with which to explain past actions. A sample contract covering Example 2.4's AIS demand is provided as Appendix A. Appendix B offers an example of how one might structure a service agreement for testing or debugging.

The implementation of a series of service agreements is generally difficult but not because the contract mechanism is complex. The only technical requirement beyond access to a typewriter and paper is some kind of job-accounting package establishing a base line of demand on either a job or an application basis. Instead, the difficulty of implementing service agreements is rooted in behavioral and organizational issues. When faced for the first time with making written commitments to specific service requirements, the user or systems manager also realizes the accompanying loss of flexibility he or she will suffer. If users are responsible for timeliness or quality-control problems associated with input delivery, monitoring their actual performance against the contract specifications might identify (perhaps for the first time) that user problems are a source of data center service problems. If there are problems meeting systems development targets, monitoring the performance of providing capacity for systems testing and development may refute an otherwise unquantified, unsubstantiated corporate belief that the source of systems development delays is in data center performance. Similarly, data center management can find ways to resist using contracts if it believes that service difficulties are resulting from its own management problems, from instability in its capacity, etc.

For these reasons, the establishment of data processing service agreements can rarely result from a grass-roots movement. There is simply little incentive to establish contracts by the sector of the organization that perceives itself as a contributor to an existing negative service environment. Generally, if an area believes it is the recipient of undue criticism regarding service or output completion it can choose between two alternative courses of action. One is to overwhelm or "out gun" the opposition, with the risk that even if the strategy is successful, the fruits of victory may be outweighed by engendering sympathy for the loser and an attitude of skepticism toward the winner. The other alternative, whether through open negotiations with the "other side" or through direct discussion with senior management, is to elicit a top-down mandate, a directive from senior management that service contracts shall and must be established. Once an area openly offers to make a written commitment to specific deliverables at preset times and to establish bilateral measurements of performance at specific checkpoints, it becomes increasingly difficult to camouflage production or development problems in one area with unsubstantiated allegations regarding another area's service responsiveness.

2.4 SUMMARY

We see, then, that there are a number of methodologies used to describe needs for data processing services, and that each is meaningful to a specific audience.

- *The EXCP–CPU Second Method* has a great deal of meaning to the systems programmer, expressing computer usage in terms of the parameters of systems programming efforts.
- *The Throughput Method and Software Physics,* dealing heavily with processing rates, have strong followings among performance-measurement practitioners.
- *The Allocation Method,* with its emphasis on scheduling or allocating devices for specific users, has wide applicability to computer operations. This coupled with its recognition of the concept of the difference between demand and utilization enable it best to facilitate control over demand by using contracts data processing service agreements. Finally, the Allocation Method is the only method that enables data processing management to communicate with its senior management in language compatible with that of the other operating areas within the corporation and in terms to which non-DPers can relate.

3
CAPACITY AND ITS CONSTRAINTS

Chapter 3 applies the Allocation Method to the definition of capacity and seeks to quantify the amount of capacity that is available for use in a given computer configuration. A methodology is established to quantify the effect upon capacity of the three major classes of production constraints. A related discussion addresses the quantitative effect on user service of each class of constraint.[1]

3.1 INTRODUCTION

A distinction must be made between relating to capacity in the sense of planning to accommodate demand, as defined in Chapter 2, and considering capacity for system-tuning purposes. One perspective deals with the response and capabilities of the system as a whole, whereas the other enables fine tuning of predictions and minor enhancement of the whole system through analyzing the separate parts. A brief discussion of system fine tuning will be offered in Chapter 4. Our present concern is with the broader concept of this two-tier approach to treating capacity (see Figure 3.1)—focusing on a production facility called a computer rather than on a technological wonder consisting of hundreds of interrelating parts.

3.2 DEFINITION OF CAPACITY

One may take several approaches when formulating a definition of "capacity." Webster defines capacity as "active power" or ability. Other definitions include:

1. The throughput processing capability of a given machine
2. The number of jobs that can be processed in a given time interval

Were we to adopt the Allocation Method of demand accounting discussed in the previous chapter, one could argue that capacity should be defined no differently than demand; that is, capacity is nothing more than a device or group of devices that can be allocated for the purpose of satisfying specific demands. Thus, the complement of the demand for the allocation of, say, three tape drives

---

[1]M. Strauss, "Computer Production Control," presented at the European Computer Measurement Association (ECOMA) Conference, Paris, France, 1979.

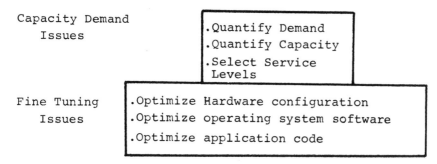

Figure 3.1. Separation of Capacity/Tuning Issues.

for 2 hours is capacity in units of tape drives. The complement of the demand for 15 minutes worth of CPU cycles over an hour of time is the capacity allocated in units of percent CPU. And so on.

Reviewing the rectangles that the Allocation Method uses to define demand in Figure 2.6, we note that the description of capacity in Figure 3.2 differs only by the description of a finite bound or limit to capacity by the vertical axis.

The Allocation Method, then, calls for one unit of measure for both defining and quantifying demand and capacity. This is particularly useful in comparison with the other demand-accounting methods. The CPU-I/O Method would have us treat a tape drive as a bucket of I/Os or EXCPs waiting to be sucked up by

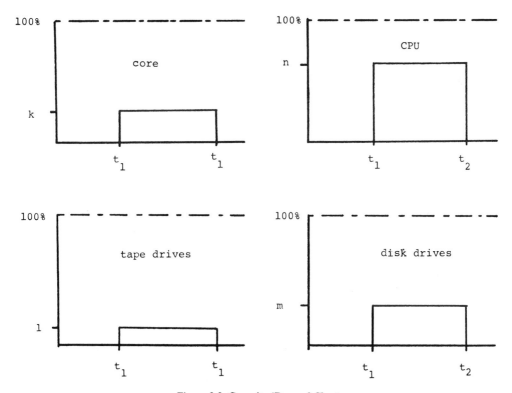

Figure 3.2. Capacity/Demand Chart.

a group of programs. It would force us to ask the question, "How many EXCPs are there in a model X tape drive constrained by a model Y channel constrained by a model Z CPU?"

The Throughput Method would have the programmer select a favorite subset of measures, graph them as in Figure 2.3, and then succumb to his or her best intuitive guess in order to determine at what level of utilization, megabyte hours per day, jobs processed, or whatever, the computer becomes saturated, and service begins to decline. This situation would be represented as in Figure 3.4.

The upper bounds, described by the dotted lines, can be penetrated (unless, of course, they are at 100%); they are often only guidelines selected by the analyst. We are, after all, dealing with a technology or processing environment that is more continuous than it is discrete. The CPU-I/O and Throughput Methods do not clearly articulate what is more of a service degradation zone (the area between the upper horizontal line and 100%) than a finite boundary. And they do not quantify the degree of service degradation one should expect at increasingly greater intrusion into the service risk zone.

The Allocation Method, however, is uniquely structured to facilitate the identification and analysis of computer capacity and its constraints while permitting the senior manager to understand capacity/demand relationships in the computer center without having to discuss technical items. It therefore provides the

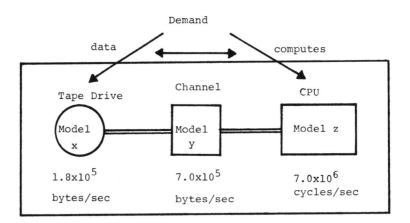

CPU demand: $c = f_1$ (computes, tape demand, time)

Tape demand: $t = f_2$ (data manipulations, CPU demand, time)

Tape Capacity $= g(f_1, f_2)$

Figure 3.3. Quantifying Capacity—CPU-I/O Method.

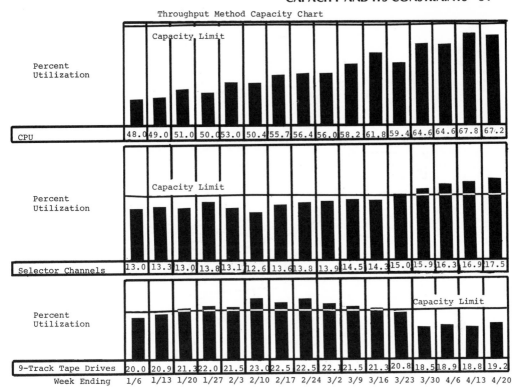

Figure 3.4. Throughput Method Capacity Chart.

analyst with a communications tool enabling him to convey production concerns to management while maintaining a structure for managing technical concerns with technicians.

The Critical Resource Concept

In Chapter 2, the Critical Resource Concept was introduced in order to reduce the number of types of resources with which one had to be concerned from up to several dozen to only three to five. This reduction facilitated the use of a set of boxes to describe only a few independent resources and their respective demands, as Figure 3.2 illustrates.

However, we recognize that these resources, each of these capacity/demand rectangles, are not truly independent—that we cannot make use of any one without being concerned with the availability and constraints of the others. We further recognize that we are dealing with the broader concept of capacity or with the upper level of a two-tier approach to capacity, and that ideally, we would rather discuss just one resource with senior management, i.e, "the computer." Few senior managers have the inclination, let alone the time, to deal with two kinds of printers, three kinds of disks, controllers, mass storage systems, CPUs, tape drives, drums, etc. They have become successful at what they do by being good at something other than data processing, and they perceive

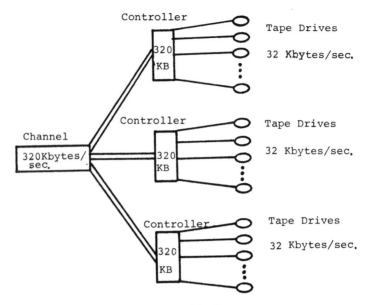

Figure 3.5. Constraining Resources.

that they can continue to be successful without having to become data processing professionals. Most would rather stay with the business end of the business instead of becoming involved in what is essentially a back-office operation. That being the case, if DPers could accurately relate most issues to management only in terms of "the computer" or "capacity," managers' lives would be made simpler and DPers would be a lot happier.

One might take a similar approach when describing the demand and capacity of, say, a steel mill. There are many types of resources necessary to manufacture the end product, yet the statement "the mill is at 85% of capacity" is well understood. Although there may be a large number of production constraints to be worked upon and a large-scale "tuning effort" required, the unitary measure conveys a meaningful message.

To reduce "the computer" to a single entity, we note that the "Critical Resource Concept" defines:

A critical resource as a generic type or class of capacity that is descriptive of, or symbolic of, the use of other resources and their constraints.

Thus, we were able in Chapter 2 to describe demands presented for data resident on tapes by just one unit—tape-drive allocation. The use of tape drives implies the use of channels and other supportive equipment. Furthermore, in this scheme, the tape drive itself is the constraining device; it has lower throughput capabilities than channels or controllers—a channel supports numerous tape drives as does a tape controller. Hence, the use of the tape drive is representative of the use of the other devices and, ignoring tuning issues, descriptive of the constraints or upper bound on throughput of the tape subsystem taken as a whole.

Extending this concept to the establishment of a unitary representation for all capacity, that is, for "the computer," one need only recognize that segmentation or sizing constraints of each resource type, to borrow a phrase, makes some critical resources more critical than others. This is best explained with the use of an example.

Example 3.1

Figure 3.6*a* describes a hypothetical system consisting of a CPU 10 units (each 10%) high and 10 units of I/O (each 1 drive high). If every job run on that system requires two units of CPU and one unit of I/O, the data center will run out of CPU before it runs out of I/O. Clearly, the constraining or most critical resource is the CPU. If each job required one unit each of CPU and I/O (Figure 3.6*b*), both resources would beome saturated at the same time. However, one, the CPU, is available only in large and relatively more expensive units. In such a case, CPU again is clearly more critical than I/O.

Figure 3.6*c* portrays a highly unusual case. In it, each job, or unit of demand, requires one unit of CPU and two of I/O, and I/O becomes saturated at only a 50% CPU load. Assuming, for the sake of the example, that each CPU has a physical limitation of 10 I/O attachments, I/O is seen to be the critical resource because it will constrain production long before the CPU will. This appears to be a case of the tail wagging the dog, and, indeed, it is: the most economically insignificant component controls or limits the most significant. In actual cases, when this type of CPU-I/O imbalance is great, it is often the symptom of a remarkably bad choice in selecting the host computer, or of an application requiring a special feature of an otherwise overpowered CPU.

Hence, we symbolize "the computer" by one capacity index, usually the CPU as in Figure 3.7. The index is no more than the most critical of the indices described by Figure 3.2's time-resource rectangles.

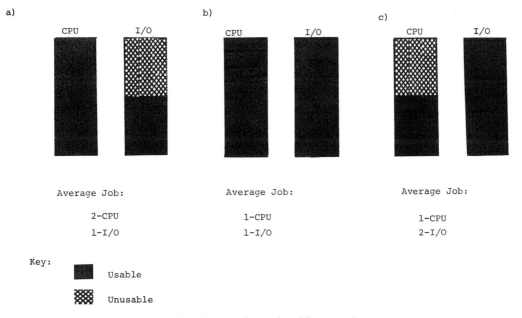

Figure 3.6. Capacity Constraint of Segmentation.

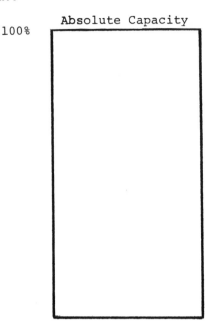

Figure 3.7. Capacity.

With capacity thus defined in terms of critical resources and their allocation, it remains to quantify the capacity made available by a given computer configuration.

3.3   DEFINING CONSTRAINTS

Obviously, no plant capacity, computers included, is expected to run at full throttle all of the time. While many classifications of constraints are possible, in general, constraints on the use of capacity may be grouped into three categories:

- Those that are a function of the capacity itself
- Those that are a function of the operation of capacity, i.e., of efficiency
- Those that are a function of demand

Capacity-Related Constraints

Constraints that are a function of capacity refer almost exclusively to the operating system. In a real, nonvirtual environment, the operating system usually resides in a fixed partition of main storage, as in Figure 3.8. Here, "Absolute Capacity" refers to 100% of the resources that physically comprise the computer. This is no more than the manufacturer's specifications of the machine's capability, generally bytes, words, or characters for main storage, cycle or instruction speed for CPU, etc. Since using the Allocation Method means dealing in terms of the percent of resource X or minutes of allocation, Absolute

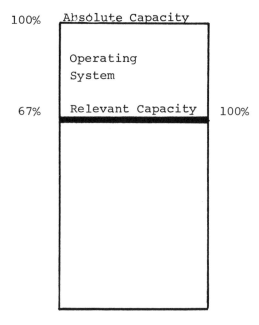

Figure 3.8. Capacity.

Capacity is referred to here as 100% of the box sitting on the data center floor. "Relevant Capacity" is defined as:

Relevant Capacity = Absolute Capacity − Operating System

For the sake of example, Figure 3.8 assumes the overhead of the operating system consumes approximately one-third Absolute Capacity. In practice, this is generally not far from reality.

In a virtual environment, it may be argued that, were there no demand, CPU utilization due to the operating system would in most cases be near zero. And, in fact, except for extremely low or extremely high application loads, utilization due to the operating system may, for the purposes here, be thought of as linearly proportional to application CPU, as the wedge in Figure 3.9 indicates. But, while it would at first glance appear that the operating system should be considered part of demand, in few cases (none for IBM of which the author is aware) can the computer's job-accounting system (SMF, RAWLOG, etc.) identify all operating system utilization to specific tasks or jobs.

Thus, there would be a measurement problem if, in an actual case, one were to try to categorize all resource usage, especially CPU, as purely application related. So, for practical purposes, we will maintain the distinction in representation of application state and operating-system state CPU utilization. Furthermore, since we are analyzing the upper bounds of capacity, we are concerned about heavily loaded systems (unloaded systems being relatively free of constraints). Our focus, then, is on the right side of Figure 3.9's wedge, where operating system consumption is large. Plainly, our conceptualization of the

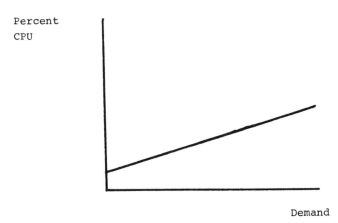

Figure 3.9. Virtual Operating System Overhead.

operating system, an overhead item, and of Relevant Capacity is the same for a virtual system as it is for real systems, and Figure 3.8 is representative of both.

Efficiency-Related Constraints

"Efficiency" is generally defined as:

the ratio of useful energy delivered by a dynamic system to the energy supplied to it.

In a computer environment this may be restated as the ratio of useful productive capacity to 100% relevant capacity. For our purposes, the complement of efficiency, "inefficiency," can be defined as:

the sum of all computer capacity lost for reasons of equipment downtime or error and spent on reexecuting jobs or portions of jobs.

Note that this definition of inefficiency refers only to matters related to the equipment and ignores the human element. (Staff efficiency is addressed in Chapter 4).

Conceptually, inefficiency can be treated either as a highly complex item or as a fairly simple one. For example, if the computer with all of its system data sets on a drum suddenly loses that drum for 4 hours, its performance obviously will drop somewhat. This decrease can be measured with various monitoring devices available on the market, or it can be estimated using a variety of models or simulators. The effect of this, however, is minimal over the long term, say over a week or a month. Furthermore, since we are developing a methodology here that seeks to reserve or identify capacity for contingencies, there is little more value to precisely quantifying the effect upon efficiency of the short-term loss of other than prime critical resources than there is to quantifying the number of systems programmers that can dance on the head of a pin. When considering equipment outages, it is generally sufficient to consider only those that have the effect of taking the entire system out.

Types of losses other than equipment failure include capacity required to reexecute jobs for reasons of operator error, minor equipment failure (disk drives fail in the middle of a job, tape problems occur, incorrect tapes are mounted, output in transit to the user is lost, etc.). These kinds of problems and their quantification and their control are covered further in Chapter 4. For the moment, it is sufficient to recognize that these problems do occur, that they can be quantified, and that, contrary to popular opinion, one can manage them to an objective or level with relative stability. This is represented in Figure 3.10. An assumed data center objective to manage efficiency to some level is reflected by a band of capacity held in reserve and equal to the complement of the efficiency objective plus any statistically insignificant variance. For example, if the objective was 92% and it was determined that 90% of the time daily efficiency varied by (i.e., its random walk was) no more than 2% from its average, the band size wound be 8% + 2% or 10%.

An important note. The implication of the band is not that the capacity it describes or holds in reserve for contingencies cannot be used. It only recognizes that, statistically, for some part of the time a chunk of capacity will not exist and, therefore, one cannot maintain an operating policy or schedule that presumes the entire system always to be available. Stated more simply, if a system is down 10% of the time, average demand is limited over time to 90% even though one might observe and even expect 100% utilization at any particular moment. Planning on using 100% of capacity at a specific time in the future

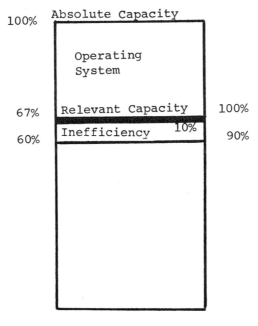

Figure 3.10. Capacity.

directly implies increased risk to maintaining a given level of service, that is, of maintaining contracted response times or output delivery schedules. Hereafter, this risk is referred to as "service risk." The theme of capacity, whose use may occur but whose availability should not be counted upon, continues in the discussion of other constraints to capacity.

Demand Related Constraints

At this point, a distinction must be made between the descriptions of constraints of nonvirtual, or discrete, computer systems and constraints on computers performing under virtual operating systems. The DPer is well aware of the different manifestations that constraints have in each type of capacity.

Real Systems

Often in nonvirtual systems, main storage—that, is what is often erroneously referred to as "core" or "core storage"—is the critical resource. Programs are loaded into the machine and reside checkerboard fashion in main storage as Figure 3.11 illustrates. The positioning of these programs is fixed, so that once loaded, their positions or, in DP terminology, their addresses, are not changed. This has an important implication.

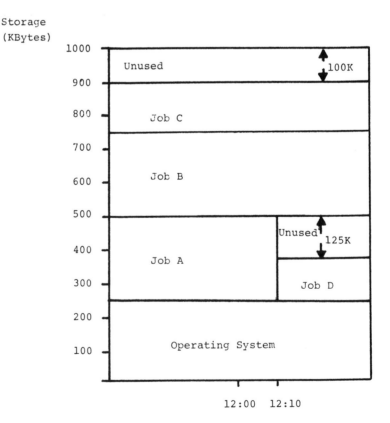

Figure 3.11. Storage Fragmentation.

Example 3.2

Assume, as in Figure 3.11, main storage is 1000K bytes or positions in size. The operating system resides in the first 250K. Job A resides from position 251 to 500, Job B from 501 to 750 and Job C from 751 to 900. At noon, Job A ends and Job D, 125K in size appears, ready to be run. The operating system, in its wisdom, loads D into the lowest available contiguous address space, positions 251–375. Ten minutes later, Job E appears, ready to be executed and requiring only 150K. The only problem is that while there are 225K storage positions idle or unused, they occur in segments smaller than the required 150K. The operating system, obviously an MVT type, does not know how to deal with split or segmented programs. It delays processing of Job E and 22½% of the system remains unused.

The discipline refers to this phenomenon as core fragmentation. It will be observed later that this is one manifestation of a larger phenomenon referred to as "unreachable capacity."

If instead the above example was an MFT or fixed-size region environment, the system, i.e., main storage, would be segmented into some number (*n*) of blocks (in IBM parlance referred to as regions) that, unless tampered with by the operator, do not vary in size. The region size would generally be selected to accommodate the largest program in a particular class; i.e., a 150K job cannot process in one or even three 50K regions and a contiguous region of at least 150K bytes is required.

Example 3.3

Assume that analysis of all jobs run during the day shift results in Figure 3.12, a frequency distribution of jobs by main-storage requirements. If the range of possible requirements (1K to 250K) is divided into three classes—1K to 100K, 101K to 150K, and 151K to 250K—it may be observed that each class is representative of approximately one third of all jobs. (We have assumed for the sake of example that CPU and

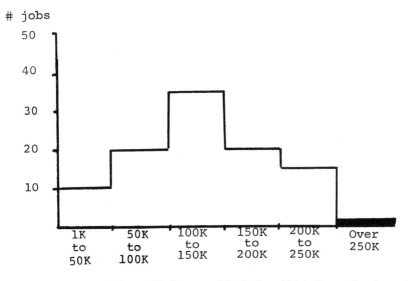

Figure 3.12. Frequency Distribution of Main Storage Requirements.

job elapsed times are roughly equivalent from one class to the next.) If the objective here is to maximize the number of jobs that can be processed, our first reaction is to create an equal number of 100K, 150K, and 250K regions. This would appear the best method of allocating CPU cycles uniformly across all regions.

However, with just one of each region size, only 100K + 150K + 250K, or 500K, of the 750K Relevant Capacity has been considered. There are several alternatives to segmenting the remaining 250K. The selection of the proper alternative is as much a function of operating priorities and job-arrival rates as of the availability of other resources.

If jobs arrive uniformly throughout the time period, and the objective is to utilize the equipment fully (an objective pursued almost zealously by many), then creating two additional regions, one of 150K and one of 100K would appear proper. If, however, on-line response time or batch job turnaround (elapsed time) is to be held to a minimum, one must then consider the effect of added CPU or I/O contention; that is, one must determine whether system response times or throughput are to define performance priorities. Clearly, if each job takes 25% of available CPU cycles, a multiprogramming level of 5 (defining five regions) would result in longer elapsed time. (Each job would require the same absolute number of CPU cycles but, since there is a limit of 100%, more elapsed time would be required to obtain them.) In this case, one might define three regions of size 250K (four regions or an average of 100% CPU demand might create contention problems) to minimize processing delays to a stream of time-critical jobs.

Thus, real systems are associated with a constraint that is a function of demand segmentation. But core fragmentation relates to only one dimension. Similar phenomena exist for CPU, tape, disk, etc.

By extending the fragmentation concept to other resource types and considering CPU in the steady state, we ignore the fact that CPU utilization for any one job, or for the workload as a whole, may vary widely from minute to minute and recognize that if normal production levels are to be met, i.e., if jobs are not to be allowed to be prolonged or to elongate because of contention for CPU cycles, even the CPU resource may be considered in terms of fixed-size, non-varying rectangles.

When fragmentation is considered for the other resource types we arrive at something that, for lack of a better term, we refer to as "Unreachable Capacity." *Unreachable Capacity* is defined as:

capacity of any one resource type that cannot be used due to a constraint or an insufficiency of any other resource type.

If, for example, we have chickens capable of producing 40 eggs per day, but have access to only 3 cartons capable of holding 12 eggs each, capacity is then balanced at 36 eggs and Unreachable Capacity is 4 eggs and 0 cartons. This example assumes that demand is of segment size 12, or that people wish to buy eggs only by the dozen, and that everyone who needs eggs also needs a carton. A logical question might be, "Why don't we gain access to one more carton and convince the chickens to lay eight more eggs?" That solution would eliminate the overhead incurred due to Unreachable Capacity.

The answer lies in the fact that capacity is demand driven. No one would rationally spend money on additional capacity just to eliminate an overhead if there were no demand to utilize the newly acquired increment. Since excess capacity that has no planned use (demand) is treated as an overhead, to acquire additional capacity with no demand would simply substitute a larger overhead for the original smaller one. Thus, if the demand for eggs is limited to 40, it's better to throw away 4 eggs and not bother speaking to the chickens about production. This phenomenon is obviously a function of the segment size of demand and each capacity type and of the degree of similarity between *n*-dimension demand space and the *n*-dimension capacity space.

A fairly straightforward procedure that can be used to quantify the magnitude of Unreachable Capacity requires gross knowledge of most segments (jobs) of the data center workload, the ability to perform basic modal analyses, and the availability of a small simulator or scheduling system. (At the expense of a small loss in accuracy, the analyst can rely on any ability he may have to draw rectangles as a substitute for the simulator. More about this later.)

We begin by graphing today's demand, as in Figure 3.13. Since our objective is to analyze where demand saturates each individual type of resource, and thereby discover where it saturates the critical resource, all (four in this illustration) major resource types are shown.

Remembering that we are attempting to characterize the effects of a data center's specific workload upon its specific capacity configuration, demand is

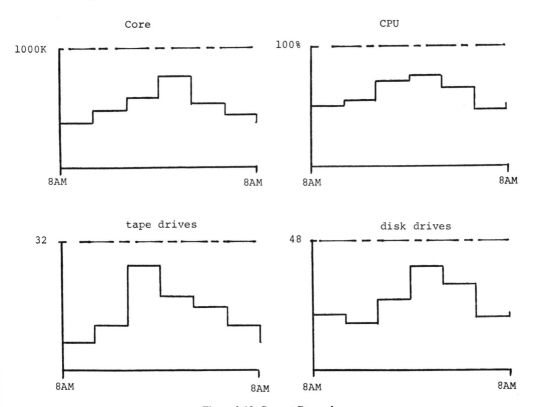

Figure 3.13. Current Demand.

divided into two classes, testing and production. Two assumptions are made. The first is that the critical resource is not already saturated. Otherwise, Unreachable Capacity for this resource (and therefore for "the computer" as a whole) obviously would be zero. The second assumption is that testing represents the embryonic stage of future production. Its current form is not characteristic of its final state, and so it cannot be used to project the characteristics of future demand.

All jobs that constitute the current production base are listed in tablular form. (Figure 3.14 lists 20 jobs, and although an actual job compendium would probably contain several hundred jobs, a sample of 20 is sufficient for purposes of illustration.) It is assumed that known future systems are included in this inventory, i.e., some application will enter the production base in the next several months and will consist of jobs 19 and 20, currently anticipated to require resources as indicated. In trying to estimate the degree of saturation of each type resource in the future, one requires some idea of what the various demand (tape, CPU, etc.) will be. Unless there is some other specific knowledge available (which should have been included in the job compendium), it can only be assumed that the overall characteristics of tomorrow's demand are the same as today's. Hence, tomorrow's equipment loading should be today's demand plus jobs representative of today's demand. A modal analysis of Figure 3.14 yields expected values of future jobs not yet in production.

For example, Figure 3.15a is a frequency histogram of main-storage requirements. We note that the range 81K–100K occurs most frequently, and we assume that future jobs of which we have no current knowledge will have main storage requirements around 81K–100K. Similarly, since jobs currently taking

Job Name	Percent CPU	Main Storage (K bytes)	Tape Drives	Disk Drives
Job 1	10	100K	3	3
Job 2	15	85K	0	0
Job 3	10	150K	1	0
Job 4	20	200K	4	1
Job 5	5	100K	0	6
Job 6	25	250K	2	0
Job 7	20	200K	3	2
Job 8	15	100K	1	4
Job 9	10	100K	3	3
Job 10	5	160K	2	10
Job 11	30	110K	6	5
Job 12	25	90K	0	1
Job 13	20	130K	0	1
Job 14	10	150K	5	3
Job 15	10	120K	2	2
Job 16	10	100K	2	3
Job 17	15	120K	3	4
Job 18	10	100K	3	2
Job 19	15	100K	1	1
Job 20	5	100K	3	1

Figure 3.14. Compendium of Jobs.

a)

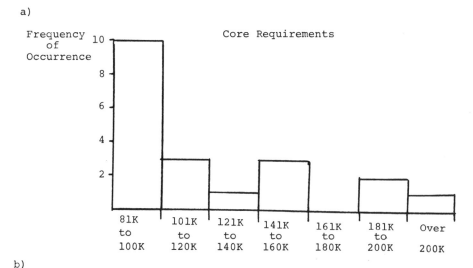

b)

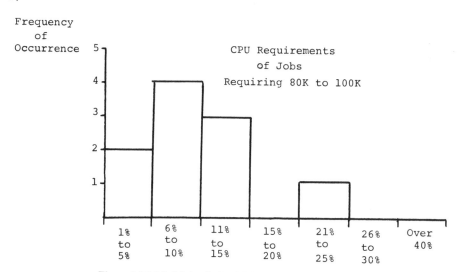

Figure 3.15. Modal Analysis of Job Resource Requirements.

81K–100K most often require 10% of the available (Relevant Capacity) CPU cycles, it is assumed that future jobs with the same storage requirements will require similar CPU allocations. Extending this process to the other major resource types, a standard job is developed and described, as in Figures 3.15 *b–d* by:

> 100K main storage
> 10% CPU
> 3 tape drives
> 3 disk drives

A number of questions arise when performing this type of analysis. Most are answered in discussions of modal analysis provided by any good statistics text.

c)

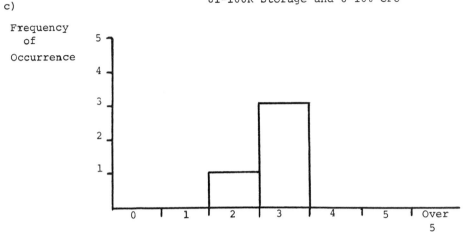

Tape Drive Requirements
for Jobs Requiring
81-100K Storage and 6-10% CPU

Frequency of Occurrence

d)

Frequency of Occurrence

Disk Drive Requirements
for Jobs Requiring
81-100K Storage, 10% CPU, and 3 Tape Drives

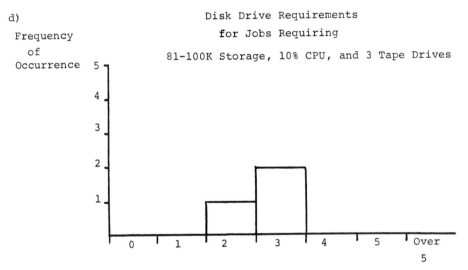

Figure 3.15. Modal Analysis of Job Resource Requirements. (*continued*)

A question pertaining to this specific application arises with respect to the order of analysis for each major resource type, i.e., does one analyze core, then CPU; the reverse; or should one start by analyzing, for example, tape drives. Unfortunately, we are dealing with something that is more an art than a science. Clearly, the analyst should begin with one of the resources he or she suspects will be identified later as the critical resource. This generally reduces the choice to main storage or CPU. Fortunately, the choice does not usually matter that much. In most instances, the results either way are not significantly different. Furthermore, the analysis is simple enough to be performed both ways and the results interpreted accordingly.

How then, does the standard job facilitate the calculation of unreachable capacity? The data center's daily operation is either driven by a scheduling system that specifies what jobs are to be run at a given time, or operators rely on their memories, running on Tuesday at 10 AM whatever they remember ran last Tuesday at 10 AM.

The scheduling-system approach to quantifying Unreachable Capacity relies on a data base that describes each job in the production base. Generally, testing or debugging is described as a long running wide band of capacity. This reflects uncertainty of the operations staff over precisely which test jobs will be submitted and the capacity each requires. The size of the band is generally determined by the average resource requirements historically required at each point during the day. Higher confidence upper bounds to testing requirements can be obtained by dealing with variances to the average. Since we are attempting to determine how much capacity can be utilized given the characteristics of a specific workload, an "infinite" number of standard jobs are added to the data base. That is, the scheduling system is instructed to keep adding standard jobs to today's schedule of demand until one or more of the major resources becomes saturated at all times. The residue, or unused portion of the remaining resources, is referred to as unreachable capacity. Where this occurs in only the noncritical resources, i.e., the critical resource becomes saturated first, unreachable capacity for the system as a whole is said to be zero.

Recalling from Chapter 2 that the computer system is characterized by the "critical resource," be it CPU, core, tape, or another resource, it should be clear that each resource type has Unreachable Capacity associated with it. Here, however, we will concentrate only on the critical resource. (It should be noted, that in the discussion of virtual systems later in this chapter Unreachable Capacity exists for the noncritical resources, tape drives, disk drives, etc., but does not exist for the CPU. For this reason, Unreachable Capacity is said not to exist for virtual systems.)

Example 3.4

Figure 3.16 describes a computer system consisting of CPU 10 units high (each unit is 10%) and 10 I/O units. Current demand is as graphed. Assuming the standard job is one unit of CPU and one of I/O, the white area adds standard jobs until either CPU or I/O is saturated. This occurs for I/O devices during each time frame, leaving CPU residuals as indicated. The white areas for both resources represent capacity that is usable but for which there is no current demand—what is commonly referred to as excess or unused capacity. The crosshatched region above excess CPU capacity is the system's Unreachable Capacity constraint. Recognizing that it averages one unit and that the CPU segment size is also one, Unreachable CPU Capacity would be calculated as one unit or 10%. Assuming CPU to be the system's critical resource, Unreachable Capacity would be said to equal 10% of capacity.

It is worth noting that the example considers a rather small number of large time intervals and large segments of capacity. Were both the intervals and segment sizes numerous and small, as in an actual case, averaging each interval's Unreachable Capacity would appear, and indeed would be, more reasonable.

Example 3.5

Assume the same demand curve as in Example 3.4 with a standard job of one CPU unit and two I/O units. Excess and Unreachable Capacity are shown in Figure 3.17.

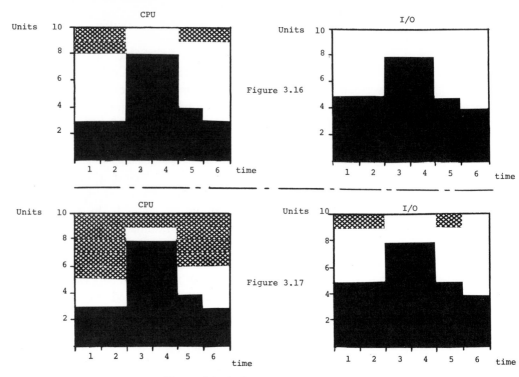

Figures 3.16–3.17. Unreachable Capacity.

While Unreachable Capacity averages 3⅓ units or one third of capacity, we see that this 33% is actually a weighted average of 10% and 45%. Relating to Unreachable Capacity as 33% would result in operational problems. (Since one would not ordinarily schedule demand into the Unreachable Capacity zone, jobs that could in fact be serviced during t_2 through t_4 would not be scheduled.) Furthermore, relating to Unreachable Capacity in this manner would result in erroneous cost analyses, as inferred in later chapters.

Obviously, demand is highly imbalanced across the interval t_1 through t_6 and, for the purposes of this type of analysis, should be segmented into two separate sets, one including t_1 through t_2 and t_5 through t_6 and the second including t_3 through t_4.

Example 3.6

Assume the same demand curve and standard job as in the preceding example but without a limit on I/O devices. We note that Unreachable Capacity is zero; as demand continues to appear, there is no constraint on I/O scheduling and the entire CPU capacity can be utilized.

Example 3.7

Recalling the demand statement given for the Headway Corporation in Example 2.4, it may be easily calculated that the standard job, if there is one in so small a job population, is:

> 15% CPU
> 1 tape
> 1 disk
> 30 minutes elapsed time

Figure 3.18 amends Figure 2.7 by anticipating how a scheduling system would simulate the placement of standard jobs on top of current Headway demand. For the sake of simplicity, we will concern ourselves only with the 9 AM to 6 PM time frame. Further, we will ignore core and deal in three dimensions instead of four.

The example is an interesting one since it describes the workload as having two distinct sets of characteristics. During the early hours, demand and the limitations of each type of capacity (tape drives, CPU, etc.) are such that Unreachable Capacity is 42%. From 5 PM–6 PM, the character changes such that Unreachable Capacity is 19%, a

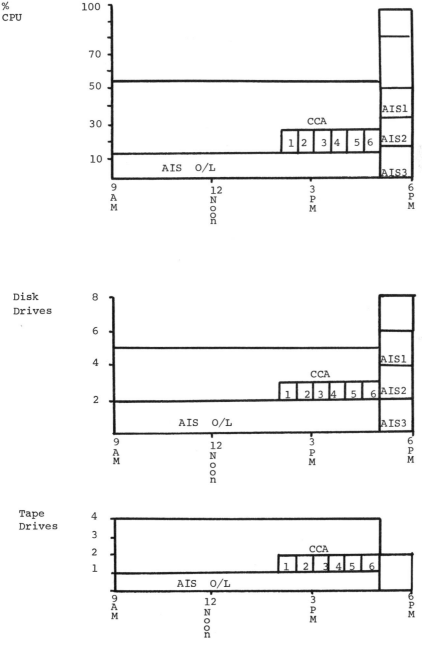

Figure 3.18. Scheduled Demand.

radical difference. Since we are concerned with maximal usable capacity, we would ordinarily concentrate on the period during which peak demand occurs. Were we to do that here, however, 19% grossly understates Unreachable Capacity and, hence, overstates the usability of capacity. It should become apparent in later chapters that this would also precipitate cost-recovery problems.

There are two alternatives. One is to average Unreachable Capacity over the entire operating cycle, from 9 AM to 6 PM. This yields a value of 39.4%, which is also misleading. The problem with averages is that they tend to be misleading for highly skewed profiles. Were the graph of Unreachable Capacity much flatter, an average would be an acceptable approximation.

But for a profile as uneven as this, it is best for capacity-planning purposes to recognize the existence of two separate and distinct demand clusters and deal with each separately. Since this approach adds another level of detail to be explained to nontechnical, senior management, it enhances communications by telling a white lie and communicating the more frequently occurring value (42%). This permits the analyst to describe the 5 AM to 6 PM penetration of demand into Unreachable Capacity as the effect of the clustering of a few anomalous members of the job population. Not only is this in fact true, but since it has the effect of reclaiming capacity otherwise lost for all eternity, the analyst also rarely has problems explaining this sort of thing to his superiors. Later, if one is looking to fully recover all costs, an average value for Unreachable Capacity would be used as input to a chargeout algorithm. (This is apparent later in Chapter 7.) As long as the analyst remains cognizant of the difference in purpose between a capacity-accounting exercise and a costing algorithm, the difference in values (most frequent value versus average value) assigned to Unreachable Capacity is manageable.

All of this yields the capacity/demand chart of Figure 3.19, where we have assumed, for the sake of example, an efficiency target of 90% (or 10% inefficiency).

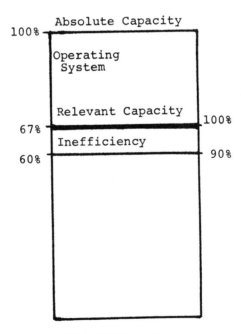

Figure 3.19. Capacity.

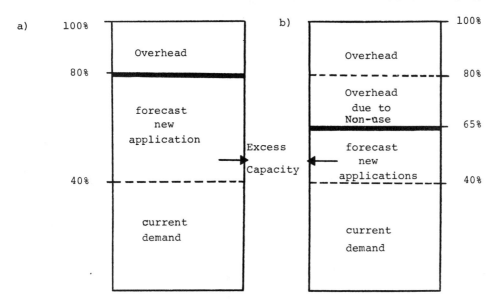

Figure 3.20. Excess Capacity as a Function of Demand.

The preceding examples make two points. One is that the constraint of Unreachable Capacity is a function of capacity- and demand-segment size, much as filling a shoe box with a child's building blocks is a function of the shape of the box and the shape and order of fit of the blocks. All four examples assumed perfect scheduling, i.e., the checkerboard problem described earlier was held to zero. This problem, if allowed to naturally remain greater than zero, would have tended to increase the values calculated for Unreachable Capacity.

A second point, often less understood, is related to the concept of excess capacity. This entity will be defined here as capacity currently unused whose use is not constrained by anything other than an absence of demand, and whose use is forecast within some reasonable timeframe.

For example, when a system is 40% utilized and its use is 20% constrained by either demand or system-related factors, it is in one of two states. One is that utilization is both theoretically and practically capable of doubling. For example, a new application is forecast in 6 months or a year that will double utilization (Figure 3.20a). The second state is that although utilization can theoretically double, there are no forecasts that it will in fact double in the next, say, 18 to 24 months. Any capacity that will go unutilized beyond the current cost-accounting period should be considered to be an overhead, not in terms of pure capacity but rather for purposes of accounting for cost. Figure 3.20b describes this for limited growth within the period. Chapters 7 and 8 explore this further, both in terms of cost-price issues and as related to dedicated-facility versus utility analyses.

Where no scheduling system exists, Unreachable Capacity can be calculated by drawing standard jobs, those rectangles of resources versus elapsed time, on top of graphs of current utilization. These graphs can be derived from any of the large number of accounting packages, software monitors, and hardware

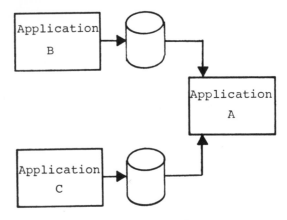

Figure 3.21. Interdependency.

monitors available on the market. With moderate care, results can be derived from this method in a fraction of the time it would take to modify a scheduling data base and to execute and reexecute the scheduling system software. Were it not for the mystifying aura surrounding numbers produced by expensive simulators produced by unknown technicians living hundreds of miles away, the results of the graphical method would be just as credible as those of the scheduling system.

A second demand-related constraint reflects the degree of interdependency among the various segments of demand. For example, application A may receive input from applications B and C as in Figure 3.21. If A's start time is required to be close to B's and C's finish time, then service to A's users depends upon events associated with B's and C's input and code stability as well as down time or other events associated with the data center during B's and C's execution. Thus, if there are problems during the processing of B or C, insuring timely completion of A can require accelerating the processing of B or C, such as by concurrent rather than single-thread execution of jobs within B, etc. This is no more than an intensified occurrence of the scheduling variances constraint and may be quantified in much the same manner. The population of applications comprising Peak Demand are examined for their resource requirements and job interdependencies and either graphical or simulation methods, similar to those already described for Unreachable Capacity, are applied. Figure 3.22 adds this factor to the capacity constraint chart.

Virtual Systems

Keeping in mind Chapter 2's Critical Resource Concept, "virtual machines," i.e., machines performing under virtual operating systems, are relieved of the constraint of Unreachable Capacity at the expense of CPU cycles. Stated in another way, the capacity-to-demand segmentation problem is relieved by breaking demand down into smaller segments, referred to as "pages" in IBM parlance and "segments" in Burroughs terminology. In addition, this resegmentation eliminates the checkerboarding problem mentioned previously. It is not that Unreachable Capacity does not exist in the virtual system, but that paging reduces Unreachable Capacity to zero for the critical (CPU) resource. And since most systems run out of CPU before encountering limitations on the number of other (I/O) devices that can be attached to the CPU, the Unreachable Capacity issue is unimportant.

As with every aspect of data processing, a cost is associated with resegmenting demand, i.e., associated with paging; the operating system consumes large amounts of CPU cycles for both the actual shuttling of pages in and out as well as for associated internal control and housekeeping.

The elimination of main storage as a significant system parameter almost universally results in CPU cycles being the critical resource. Upon first glance, the fixed size operating system representation of Figure 3.8 would seem to not apply. As discussed previously, in a virtual machine, operating-system overhead is more a function of demand: as demand grows, so do CPU cycles consumed by the operating system, as illustrated by the wedge in Figure 3.9. Because our concerns here relate more to constraints under maximal rather than minimal machine loading, we are interested in the steady-state, maximal operating system size as represented by the right side of the wedge. Hence Figure 3.8 is in fact representative of both real and virtual machines. For the sake of illustration, we will again assume operating system size (CPU cycles consumed under steady state conditions at heavy application loading) to equal about one third of Absolute Capacity.

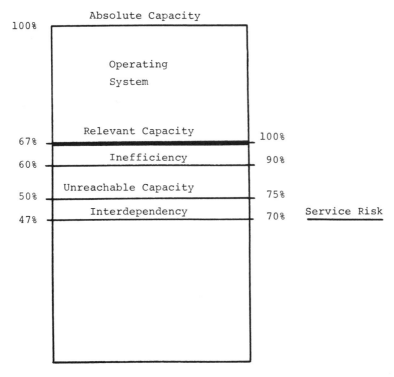

Figure 3.22. Real Capacity.

The remaining constraints on the use of capacity in virtual systems differ somewhat from those of real systems. Capacity reserved for contingencies related to inefficiency and interdependency remains the same and is shown the same size in Figure 3.23, but we recognize that the concept of Unreachable Capacity has little meaning. If, for example, 20% of the CPU is not available to a job that normally required that resource over an hour, the job will not terminate or be withheld from execution but rather, will elongate or stretch, taking the same total resource but over a longer time interval. For example, the job may receive 10% of the CPU for two hours, 15% for 80 minutes, and so on. The only real opportunity for loss of CPU capacity due to segmentation occurs with peripherals, where CPU saturation and a desire to avoid job elongation (due to queuing for CPU resources) results in conscience decisions by the data center management to not load I/O gear fully. However, since peripherals are available in small segment sizes, they are rarely constraining critical resources and, hence, Unreachable Capacity is, if anything, a trivial issue with respect to virtual systems.

Another constraint filling the void left by the absence of Unreachable Capacity is the job-elongation or job-stretch factor introduced above. While there is nothing inherently wrong with attempting to fully utilize the CPU, at some point users (particularly those of on-line systems) will voice their profound disappointment over slow response times and long batch turnaround times. Obviously, the degree of elongation (and therefore users' disappointment) is a func-

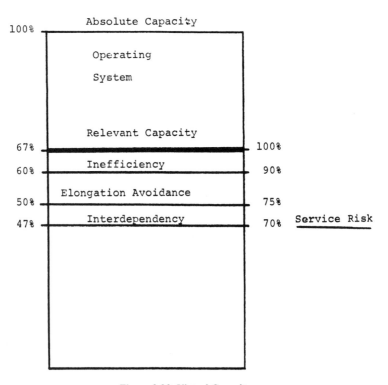

Figure 3.23. Virtual Capacity.

tion of queues to the CPU and other devices, which in turn are a direct function of the speed of various devices that comprise the computer system and are a direct function of the workload.

Job elongation can be determined using a number of methods, the simplest of which is observation. Here the analyst observes the elapsed time per unit CPU and I/O (or EXCP) for a large number of jobs executed over a wide variety of total system utilizations. The elapsed time requirement of each of a large number of jobs is examined where execution took place when the CPU averaged, for example, first 20%, then 50%, 60%, 70%, etc., for the duration of job execution. Given a sufficiently large number of observations, the tendencies of elongation factors for each utilization level begin to emerge. This method is obviously somewhat insensitive to changes in transaction volume processed by various jobs, job-code changes, and so on. However, these variables are usually identifiable at another point (external to the data center) in the corporation, and major differences in elapsed time due to these variables can usually be eliminated from the analysis. Error can be reduced still further by considering average elongation rather than the particular elongation of each individual job.

Thus, while it is sometimes a cumbersome and organizationally involved process, a rough estimate of job stretch can be obtained from this type of analysis of job-accounting data.

If the analyst is easily able to construct a benchmark sufficiently representative of each segment of the actual workload, the effort involved in the observation method can be reduced considerably. In many cases, however, preparation of a representative workload is more time consuming than the analysis it seeks to avoid.

A second method of determining average job elongation at a given utilization involves the use of queuing theory. A variety of degrees of accuracy are approachable, with the relationship of the effort required to the accuracy achieved resembling an exponential function. Remembering that our objective is to describe a service-risk point that triggers a management decision to acquire additional capacity, errors of 1% or 2% of capacity, while interesting from an academic viewpoint to some analysts, are insignificant for our present purposes. Furthermore, since the current large-scale and complex virtual operating systems provide the ability to adjust processing priorities even in midstream, if the operations staff is forced to deal with hardware loaded beyond the risk point, the staff can choose which segments of demand are to receive poorer service. Critical production can always be given resource priority at the expense of, say, minor production or testing. On average, service will remain the same, but unless there is wholesale intrusion into the risk zone, important individual application priorities and adherence to deadlines can be managed.

Job elongation is a highly complex phenomenon, involving the specifics of each of the devices that comprise the hardware, the specifics of the characteristics of job scheduling, and the specifics of the overlap of execution of each job that comprises total demand. And what makes quantifying job elongation even more complex, if not impossible, is that the procedure involves analyzing the contribution to total elongation of each job as a function of each device class, some of which are single servers, some multi-servers, some with exponential service times, others with general service times, and so on, ad infinitum. The ardent fan of queuing theory will recognize this to be a potentially huge mix of $M/M/1$, $M/M/c$, $M/G/1$, $M/G/c$.... A further refinement would be to reflect the processing priority algorithm of each device in the probability-function description.

Recognizing that life is too short to be dedicated to the evaluation of job elongation, the assumption of a single-queue, single-server environment, where demand is in packets of standard jobs, expressed as x CPU seconds and y I/Os yields results that, in the author's experience, closely agree with observation. For more detailed analyses, the reader is referred to work published by Boris Beizer.[2]

To summarize, both the observation and queuing methods have built-in inaccuracies, some due to errors in assumptions and others due to errors in observation. If one recognizes the fact that, particularly in virtual systems, the effect of continuously higher loading is continuous, not discrete or stepwise, degradation of response and service times, the service risk lines of Figure 3.22 and 3.23 are recognized to be more representative of narrow zones that should be avoided than of lines that should not be crossed.

Neither method, then, yields results of significantly greater accuracy. Generally, when the workload is mixed and consists of on-line response-oriented systems (development or testing as well as production) and CPU consumptive batch systems, the service-risk point occurs between 65% and 75% of Relevant Capacity. The precise location of the point varies with the specific model mainframe (IBM 3033, B7700, PDP 11/40, etc.), the proportion of demand that is on-line or batch, stability of job start times, and, obviously, the degree of latitude of permissible response times as well as the slack between batch job completion and successor job start times and delivery deadlines.

3.4 QUANTIFYING SERVICE RISK

The risk points developed in the preceding section reflect constraints that tend to limit response of on-line systems or batch turnaround. The points were developed in terms of maintaining a specific level of service, such as 90%, with respect to the specific size of constraints as an example for real systems, 10% for ineffectiveness, 15% for Unreachable Capacity, or for virutal systems, 15% for elongation avoidance, and so on. These constraints are all linked to that point of execution delay (real systems) or elongation avoidance (virtual systems) beyond which general output commitments or response-time commitments for on-line systems cannot be met.

What is now required is a procedure for quantifying a constraint's impact to service. If jobs are to be late as a result of a policy of loading the computer beyond a given level, how often will they be late for real systems? And for

---

[2]Boris Beizer, *Micro-Analysis of Computer System Performance.* New York: Van Nostrand Reinhold Co., 1978.

virtual systems, how much will they elongate beyond existing slack time, and, therefore, what will user's perception be of response delays?

Virtual Systems

Risk due to job elongation is a continuous function. If an observation technique from section 3.3 is used, different elongations will be associated with different utilizations; for example, none with 50% utilization, 5% with 60% utilization, 15% with 70% utilization, and so on. At some point, perhaps 15% elongation, an analysis of the typical slack between job completion and output-delivery deadlines will indicate low confidence as to whether contracted output schedules or response times can be met. Put more simply, as the slack or average difference between the time a job ends and the time output reaches the user approaches zero, the expectation of timely output delivery decreases. Hence, this process enables one to observe that confidence in service schedules decreases as capacity usage increases.

If a modeling approach is used to determine the risk point, the analyst generally proceeds by altering the background workload until the time spent in the system (in the queue plus processing) reaches that same cutoff point of slack time approaching zero.

Hence the contribution of job elongation to service risk is automatically quantified during the analysis. How inefficiency and job interdependency in turn contribute to service risk are determined for virtual systems in exactly the same manner as for real systems. These contributions are addressed next.

Real Systems

Quantitatively, the difference in the level of service that is attributable to a capacity constraint is proportional to the probability that that constraint will

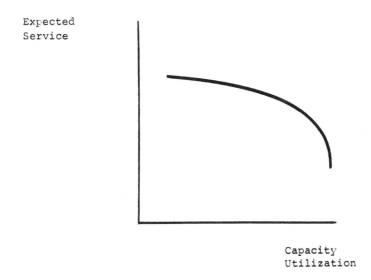

Figure 3.24. Service Degradation.

occur. For example, if one assumes that jobs are not run inordinately ahead of schedule, that output deadlines are reasonably linked to input arrival, variations of job execution from preset schedules will downgrade service roughly in accordance with the degree of scheduling variances.

Example 3.8

Assume, for the sake of example, that for some configuration 90% of all output deadlines are met 95% of the time when utilization is no more than 80% of capacity. Calculating the precise overall effect on service for the remaining 5% of the time involves observing each job that runs in the system with respect to size, variability in size, input availability variance, etc. This calculation can be accomplished only with a great deal of effort by using relatively unsophisticated techniques, should the reader be interested. In the interest of brevity, however, assume that when something unexpected occurs during the remaining 5% of the time, all deadlines are missed. This yields an expected value for service of 0.95 × 90% or 85.5%.

Assume that one system constraint consumes 10% of capacity when it occurs, and that it may be represented by the band of capacity lying between 80% and 90%. In addition, assume the constraint occurs 50% of the time. What is the effect on service?

This problem actually poses the question: What would service be if demand were permitted to grow to 90%, given the frequency and magnitude of the 10% capacity constraint? In the following explanation, we shall refer to the base demand, that which loads the system to 80% as "old" demand, and to the increase that would drive utilization to 90% as "new" demand.

As before, the solution may be obtained with varying degrees of accuracy. When calculating the marginal change to service, granularity of demand comprising the last 10% usage of capacity ("new" demand) is an important issue. If average job size for the "new" 10% is half that of the "old" 80%, then the marginal change in service would be larger than one would otherwise expect, that is, a larger number of jobs than otherwise might be expected would be subject to lateness. Moreover, the difference in granularity of the new 10% changes the average granularity of the 90% total, the new whole workload. The characteristics of demand have changed here, and we cannot be sure, without investigation, that 8/9 of this demand could be associated with 85.5% expected service, a situation that reflects the previous statement that capacity is a function of the demand it services.

For reasons of simplicity, then, it is assumed that the characteristics of demand do not change with the increase from 80 to 90% loading of the hardware.

The new expected value of service is therefore the contribution of the old:

$$(80 \div 90) \times 85.5\% + (10 \div 90) \times 50\% \ or \ 81.6\%$$

This reflects the weighted value of service at the old level (80%) plus the expectation that new demand requiring the 10% band of capacity will actually find that 10% available when it is needed.

It is important to note in the previous example that the decision knowingly to preschedule demand into the 80–90% zone would be based on two factors. The first consideration, obviously, is whether to suffer the 85.5–81.6% or 3.9% change in service. Because priorities for various applications can be rearranged either to guarantee timeliness to some or minimize lateness to others, changes in average service of less than about 10% are generally not significant. This fact is reinforced by the general inability of the user community to determine the penalty incurred when a report is not delivered according to schedule or a file not updated for an extra hour or two. Usually, these penalties can be quantified only in cases such as on-line cash management systems, on-line reservation systems, reporting requirements to regulatory agencies, etc.

The second factor relates more to perception or "bad press" among users than to actual declines in service level. If a data center is trying to maintain a reputation, that is manage the perception, of providing reliable service and of keeping its house in good order, the fact that the capacity constraint might occur 50% of the time would have great significance since the user community would receive its deliveries late on the order of half (55 percent) of the time (1 − [0.50 × 90% + 0.50 × 0%]). In an organization under pressure from its front office, even if nearly all major deliverables arrive on time, that fact can easily be overwhelmed by the "fact" that, more often than not, something, although small, often is late.

Therefore, while changes in service can be quantified numerically, the interpretation of the resultant values may not be based solely on numbers and percentages. Be that as it may, the exercises of quantifying the number of occurrences of lateness and of expressing changes in service numerically continues.

The probability of the occurrence of a constraint can be determined by sampling the percent of times the causative agents appear in the real world. For example, with regard to scheduling variances, the major constituents of Peak Demand can be examined over a relatively long period and a composite developed showing the frequency with which problems occur. Figure 3.25 illustrates this type of exercise for a 4-month interval. Figure 3.26 relates the size of each capacity constraint to the probability of its occurrence and then to its quantitative impact of service.

The implication for a real system with a low risk level at 70%, a 5% scheduling variances constraint occurring 27.6% of the time, and a 95% confidence of 90% service is that scheduling jobs into this constraint lowers the expectation of 90% service to 95% − 27.6%, or 67.4%. In other words, 90% output timeli-

	Percent of Times		
	Application A	Application B	Application C
May	18	32	41
June	0	20	70
July	0	5	36
August	9	59	41
Four Month Averages	6.8%	29.0%	47.0%

Total Four Month Average = 27.6%

Figure 3.25. Input Problems or Lateness that Resulted in Scheduling Variances.

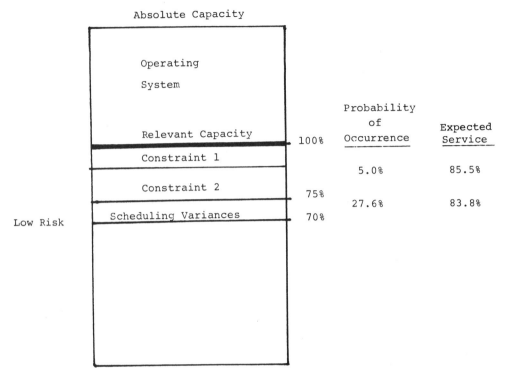

Figure 3.26. Effects of Constraints upon Service.

ness can only be expected about two-thirds of the time. Or, expected service can be approximated to drop from a lower bound of

$$0.95 \times 90\%, \text{ or } 85.5\%$$

to

$$(70\% - 75\%) \times 85.5\% + (0.95 - 0.276) \times 90\% \times (5\% \div 75\%)$$
$$= 79.8\% + 4.0\%, \text{ or } 83.8\%.$$

This equation describes the lowering of service expectations as a joint function of the probability that a group of constraints will occur and of the amount of demand that would have been placed into the capacity that has been lost to those constraints.

For environments with multiple constraints, the above process is expanded accordingly. Again, previous statements regarding uniform granularity and increased accuracy of estimate available through the use of enhanced modeling or simulation techniques continue to apply to cases of this type.

3.5 FORECASTING CAPACITY REQUIREMENTS

Since capacity is a mirror image of the computer demand that the data center faces, this section is also about forecasting demand. There are three methods that can be used to complete the forecast, each offering a degree of accuracy commensurate with the available data. The first method may be called, for lack of a better term, the "Finger-in-the-Air Method." (Some critics are prone to use harsher terms.) Here the analyst knows virtually nothing about the plans of users, either in terms of increased transaction volume or new or enhanced applications. In addition, little information regarding equipment-usage trends in the data center is available except that last year there were x peripherals and this year there are y, or that "Last year the CPU was light, but this year it's real heavy." And sometimes gross numbers may accompany perceptions such as "light" and "real heavy." When working according to this method, the analyst picks numbers out of the air to represent his perception of equipment usage in the coming fiscal year. When asked to support such projections, the rationale usually includes mention of a gut feeling about the way the shop operates. Many data centers rely on this method, so there must be something inherently good about it.

The second available forecasting technique is called the "Time-Series Method." Here the analyst admits that, for any of several possible reasons, he or she has little if any knowledge of user plans. (The key word here is "admits.") The only assumption possible is that, unless there have recently been major organizational changes, the development and marketing groups will continue to do in the future as they have done in the past. That is, demand (or capacity requirements) appear to be a function of time. Using data from one or more years, a trend line of growth rates is prepared and extended into the future (Figure 3.27).

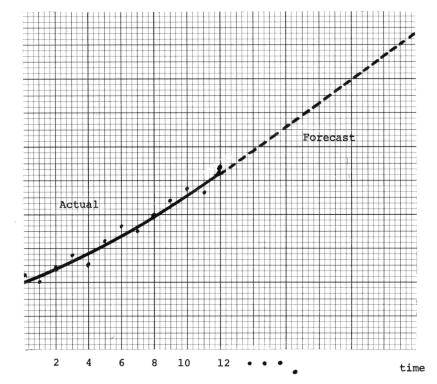

Figure 3.27. Time-Series Demand Forecast.

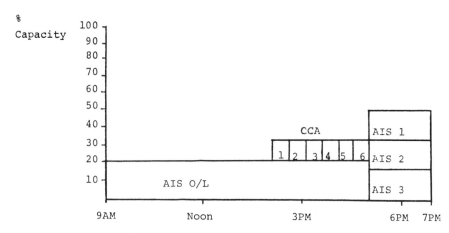

Figure 3.28. Forecast Increases to Demand.

Using a reporting interval of one month, change in average demand from each period to the next is calculated as a percent of the first period. We note that around month 20, the growth rate suddenly increased sharply. In this example, 6 to 12 months before the change in growth rate, the company underwent an organizational change. Programming staffs were taken from a centralized development group and distributed in order to become more responsive to the individual marketing and operating groups they served. The move achieved its objective of facilitating rapid change and, at the same time, had a significant, although unforeseen, capacity implication.

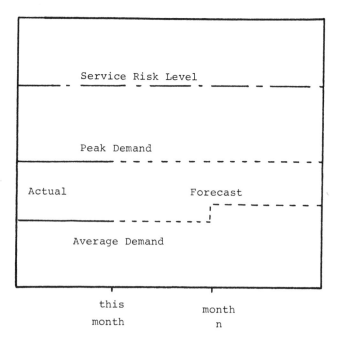

Figure 3.29. Capacity/Demand Forecast.

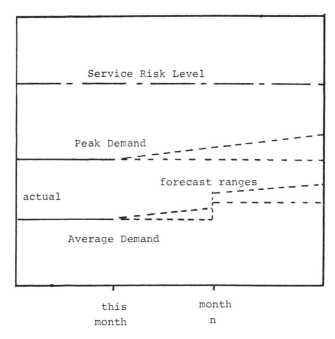

Figure 3.30. Capacity/Demand Forecast under Uncertainty.

The third forecasting technique is referred to as the "Inventory Method." Found only in corporations with well-run, highly coordinated development, marketing, and data processing operations organizations, this method is the least frequently used of demand forecasting techniques. It involves establishing a current base line for capacity, i.e., establishing current profiles of utilization, both in total and for each application that comprises demand. Over a 24-hour daily operating cycle, this takes the form of the "skyline" in Figures 2.7 and 3.18. The capacity-planning analyst receives information on anticipated increases in transaction volume from marketing groups. Either through consultation with the appropriate systems manager or by means of regression techniques, the capacity implications of these increases are determined and the skyline altered accordingly. In Figure 3.28, this activity accounts for the virtual extension of resource consumption for the on-line portion of AIS and the horizontal extension of the batch portion. New applications are described by the systems managers and added to the skylines. In Figure 3.29, the skyline is converted into a graph that describes the timing of these changes and their effect on peak and average demand.

A reasonable approach to forecasting capacity usage would be to rely on the Inventory Method but to temper it with trend data from the Time-Series Method. This combination recognizes the uncertainty associated with the incomplete data received from the marketing and development areas; not all anticipations of volume or new applications are always known at the time of the forecast; delays in implementation of new applications may be encountered, etc. This transforms Figure 3.29 into Figure 3.30.

3.6 SUMMARY

Concluding our discussion of capacity, we note that capacity is a reflection of the demand it services. Since applications require computer operators to allocate specific resources, and remembering that each month we pay hardware vendors not for EXCPs used, multiprogramming levels attained, millions of bytes moved, etc., but rather for devices that get allocated, either in total (tape drives, printers, etc.) or in part (CPUs, etc.), the Allocation Method of defining and quantifying demand and capacity is selected for consideration throughout the remainder of the text.

To facilitate the discussion of constraints on capacity in the broad sense (ignoring for the moment issues of system fine tuning) and to understand the relationship of those constraints to service risk, the Critical Resource Concept enables the discussion of capacity to focus on one resource rather than the dozens of separate parts that comprise the computer as a whole. This resource is generally the resource whose size and demand for use most limits the utilization of the computer complex. In the absence of these constraints, the critical resource may be the resource that is by far the most economically significant. Furthermore, since communicating with senior, nontechnical managers can be difficult for the data processing professional, the Critical Resource Concept assists by confining discussions to one or a highly limited number of entities, thereby eliminating the need for an open-ended discussion that the nontechnical manager might not fully comprehend and which the DPer could not effectively present.

There are three generic types of constraints on computer capacity: (1) those, like the operating system or job elongation, that are a function of the nature of the specific type of capacity being used; (2) those that are a function of the way the capacity is managed, i.e., inefficiency constraints; and (3) those that are a function of demand, including segmentation and interdependency. Each constraint presents a unique set of problems, and each can be quantified using a variety of techniques.

Service is loosely defined here as the ability to provide timely delivery of batch job outputs and to provide specified response times for on-line jobs. Given levels of service are linked to given levels of availability of capacity, and, conversely, to given limits on losses due to inefficiency. The limit on the service level any size capacity can provide is referred to as the "risk level" or "risk point." The area lying above the risk point is known as the "risk zone," an area of capacity utilization beyond the equipment's capability to provide consistently adequate service.

Finally, forecasting future capacity requirements, given a good method of accounting for demand and capacity, is simple in organizations where the marketing, systems development, and production-planning processes are well managed and coordinated.

4
PERFORMANCE/EFFICIENCY

Extending the scope of the text beyond the immediate hardware/soft-ware environment, Chapter 4 discusses the effect of the overall opera-tion of the data center upon constraints in the manual staging and destaging components of the workflow. This topic is followed by a brief description of standard computer measurement, i.e., the application of hardware and software monitors, and consideration of reliability stud-ies as a means of optimizing the availability of computer systems and of improving the efficiency of the hardware/software environment.

4.1 INTRODUCTION

Typically, in a data processing environment, performance refers to two factors: efficiency and effectiveness. Efficiency is the relationship of standard resource consumption to actual consumption. An example of, say, 90% efficiency is the case where for every 100 units of resources consumed, 90 units represent useful productive output and the remainder represent reruns or capacity wasted due to other reasons. The other gauge of performance is effectiveness, the value or worth of a particular factor or objective. Effectiveness can also have several extended meanings, including the ability to provide a particular level of service and response time. Thus, effectiveness can pertain to such considerations as whether a system can provide the user with a 5-second response time. (The scope of this discussion does not delve into another aspect of the concept of effectiveness: whether there is any intrinsic value to a 5-second response as com-pared to, for example, response times of 10 seconds or 3 seconds.)

It is important to remember that one of the major problems in a data center, or, for that matter, in any other organization, is communications. Very few technical or procedural difficulties remain completely undiscovered but they often are either not well articulated or are not communicated to the correct organizational nodes. Poor communication usually results from operations staff who see but do not understand, or who understand but do not venture beyond what they perceive as the limitations of their job description.

The previous two chapters have centered mainly on the analysis of demand for computer equipment and the quantification of that equipment. But data cen-ter performance, as compared to just computer performance, extends beyond the hardware/software complex to the other, more manually oriented work areas. Hence, it is appropriate to enlarge the scope of this chapter to include these other factors. Because data center performance relates to the performance of people, a brief discussion is also offered on the behavioral implications of some organizational alternatives of structuring efficiency improvement studies.

4.2   ORGANIZATIONAL CONSIDERATIONS

Organizationally, there are decisions that must be made regarding how to structure a study of efficiency. Any analysis of less than perfect performance, including the study of causes of inefficient or wasteful usage of capacity, has great potential for evoking negative, defensive reactions in the people who are being evaluated. The real issue here is one of "ownership" of the results of the study, that is, whether the operations staff will have problems accepting the results, whether they will understand those results, and whether the length of time that they are likely to continue to use any improvements suggested by the study will be meaningful. (Throughout the following discussion, the terms *line* and *site* are used interchangeably to refer to operations staff members. The term *staff* refers to members of support organizations, industrial engineers, etc.)

There are three ways to structure studies of efficiency. The most obvious is where the staff analysts are totally responsible for organizing and implementing the analysis. Although this removes the operations staff from the questionable position of having to audit itself, it creates other problems: defensiveness, characterized by lack of cooperation, delays, etc.; lack of understanding or ownership of conclusions drawn, characterized by an overly critical review of the results and failure to implement recommendations; and, if new procedures are imposed from above and not understood, the tendency to implement them for only relatively short durations. All these reactions can be countered, given sufficient analysts and, more importantly, enough patience. A final problem with this approach is that while it eliminates biases on the part of line personnel, it introduces potential biases among staff personnel, potentially more damaging since staff analysts tend to be less cognizant of details of the production requirements of various sectors of demand than their line counterparts.

A second study structure is based on the concept of "Physician, heal thyself." Here, the design and implementation of data gathering and analysis are assigned to the line itself, i.e., to the operations staff. The risks here are the usual risks of self-audit: lack of motivation to criticize one's own performance and the lack of introduction of fresh ideas into the production process. These negative aspects tend to diminish the positive effects of ownership and of implementation of the recommended improvements for long periods of time.

The third organizational alternative involves joint line and staff participation. This approach requires the staff area to maintain functional jurisdiction over the study and allows the line to implement data gathering and supervise analysis of the data by the staff. This also permits the staff to establish unbiased data-gathering and analysis techniques. By allowing the line the choice of approving these techniques or substituting others (for staff approval) and by allowing the line to control the data (subject to staff audit), it also provides the framework for ownership of the final results by the line. This positive effect is reinforced by allowing the line to partake in the actual analysis of the data. In effect, the joint-participation approach allows the site to avoid an incursion by half-crazed staff since it has the ability to control, within limits, the staff's actions. At the same time, the staff's audit function helps assure an unbiased effort. A disadvantage of this process, however, is that the selling process, the process of getting the line to understand and accept the study structure, takes somewhat more time than if either group acted alone.

Obviously, nothing guarantees cooperation, and there are some cases where additional leverage is required. One useful technique for securing genuine involvement of the line is to link sources of inefficiency to increased utilization, increased utilization to increased capacity requirements, and increased capacity to increased unit production costs. Then, if one can manage to link individual manager's annual performance appraisals (and raises) to their ability to lower production costs, managers will have the incentive to participate in almost any performance-improvement study. A quantitative approach that is an alternative to linking raises to lower production costs, is to get management to examine the value to the corporation in the coming year of any manager who, for whatever reason, cannot provide improvements to the production process. Either approach is generally sufficient to convert even the most recalcitrant operations manager into an ardent fan of evaluating line operations using systematic methods.

4.3 EFFICIENCY CONSTRAINTS

As applied to data processing, there is an overlap of terms when one discusses performance and efficiency. In the trade, performance usually relates to the application of hardware and software monitors to identify resource wastage by analysing the operation of hardware, operating systems, and application software. This carries the connotation of searching for capacity loading imbalances and unoptimized code in addition to investigating various types of failures. Efficiency, here, is used to describe the complement of the loss of capacity, either due to waste of rerunning jobs or due to equipment and other failures. While there is obviously an overlap since both terms are concerned with resource wastage, what is generally referred to when one discusses standard computer performance techniques is technically very distinct from the industrial engineering approach used to address inefficiency. In order to keep these two points of view separate, the discussion defers consideration of so-called computer performance techniques to later in this chapter.

In addition to considerations of hardware and software failure, the subject of efficiency also deals with manual functions. These include work-methods analysis (the evaluation of procedures used by workers in various functions) as well as the determination of how much labor is required to complete a given activity and the relationship between this standard and the actual manpower consumed. While Chapter 5 takes up some aspects of the subject, this discussion will consider methods of articulating and quantifying problems caused by hardware and software trouble as well as by manual procedures, the effect of such problems upon computer utilization and some methods for reducing their occurrence.

In the previous chapter, inefficiency was described as capacity lost due to reruns, computer down time, and so on. The first item, reruns, can be a function of machine failure, data error, or program error, but it can also result from operator error, job-setup error, and other factors. The condition that the analyst must face is not one of determining whether these causative agents exist, since every operator or user is of necessity aware of them, but rather of determining the extent to which each cause exists and the extent to which the problem of reruns is indeed a result of various causes. Stated less gently, common beliefs about the causes of certain types of operational problems often are less than fully correct; they may be based on opinions of members of the site, not on an assessment based on unbiased sifting of data. An example might be that "most reruns are caused by users delivering incorrect or defective input."

While this is not meant to imply that problems identified by experience and word-of-mouth do not exist, such pseudo analysis is often misleading and focusing on misleading issues is an ineffective way of eliminating problems. The result of such efforts can be a data center that shows a lot of "analytical" action and may actually believe it is effectively addressing problems whereas users and management perceive little or no substantive improvement. Such efforts often concentrate on specific instances of problems, where each problem is "different" than all others rather than concentrating on generic classes of problems.

Figure 4.1 provides an example of gathering raw data without establishing common causes. This case shows the results of a two-step approach that can be employed. The first column gives the code describing the general type of error that occurred, a specific type of system error, a control language (JCL) error, or a user generated error code. The second and third columns identify the job and job step where the abnormal termination occurred. Column four provides the date on which the error occurred while columns five and six furnish the job's start and end times. Since this information is automatically recorded by the computer's job-accounting package, it can be assumed to be an unbiased relatively complete set of job-failure data. The second step of data presentation in Figure 4.1 shows descriptive data added by the troubleshooting technicians. Column seven provides the initials of the technician who analysed each problem, and column eight is the technician's short description of the causative agent. This discussion assumes that as the job-accounting mechanism senses and records instances of job failure, it automatically records the resources consumed and, therefore, wasted, i.e., the contribution to inefficiency.

It should be noted that the data thus collected relate only to production jobs; abnormal termination is considered a normal characteristic of development jobs and not an indication of capacity losses—it does not indicate constraints on efficiency. (As an aside, Figure 4.2 describes the same kind of data-gathering technique applied to nonmanual, equipment failures.)

With a thorough, unbiased mechanism for gathering the data established, the discussion now turns to organizing the raw data so that rather than have each

Code	Name	Step	Date			Type	Description
JCL	CLIDLY01	STEP4	790530	0000	0015	AT	INCORRECT RESTART PROCEDURE -> CONTINUE TO PROCE
JCL	TOOSPRUP	STEP5	790629	0005	0007	AT	RESTART STEP NOT FOUND -> CORRECT AND RESUBMIT ST
JCL	IPDDJOB1		790726	0045	0055	FM	OVERRIDE INCORRECT -> CORRECT/RESTART STEP5
JCL	PCAPC009	AL	790801	0105	0110	FM	OVERRIDE INCORRECT -> CORRECT AND RESTART STEP5
S213	TOOSACUP	CB03	790626	0120	0120	FM	RESTART STEP NOT FOUND -> CORRECT AND RESTART CHKPT#3
JCL	CLASCBTR	STEP11	790106	0130	0145	TG	DSN NOT VOLSER TO PACK CHANGED IN PREVIOUS STEP ->
S222	BAROFM00	STEP7	790501	0140	0150	FM	OVERRIDE INCORRECT -> CORRECT & RESTART STEP11
JCL	RELAFD00		790530	0140	0150	TG	UNCORRECT RESTART -> CORRECT AND RESTART STEP7
JCL	MCROCUDD		790408	0200	0205	TG	WRONG RESTART STEP -> RESTART AT EDIT1
JCL	TOOSACUP	WS	790731	0200	0205	FM	OVERRIDE INCORRECT -> CORRECT AND RESUBMIT
JCL	TTHSDL2A	STEP9	790502	0210	0215	AT	KEYPUNCH ERROR -> CORRECT & RESUBMIT
JCL	EFTSRIPS	STEP1	790106	0230	0245	FM	ERROR IN OVERRIDE -> RERUN
U0502	MIS4RSTR	STEP3	790509	0230	0235	FM	INSUFF PRIMARY SPACE ALLOCATION TO RESTORE DSN ->
JCL	VTASAS60	CLRCTLG	790425	0315	0315	AT	DSN NOT FOUND -> RESTART AT SORT10 STEP
JCL	TBCSACTD	STEP8025	790726	0330	0330	AT	RESTART INCORRECT -> CORRECT/RESUBMIT
U0016	CLASCBTR		790106	0330	0335	TG	INCORRECT OVERRIDE -> RERUN
JCL	ISASIACC	STP05	790405	0335	0335	TG	INCORRECT OVERRIDE -> CORRECT & RESUBMIT RESTART
JCL	RELAFD01	STEP10	790619	0335	0335	AT	INCORRECT RESTART -> CORRECT/RESUBMIT
JCL	ISASDLY1		790317	0340	0400	TG	DSN NOT FOUND OVERRIDE ERROR -> CORRECT & RESTART
JCL	SAVGDLY1	STEP5	790503	0340	0345	TG	DUP NAME ON VOL -> SCR & RESTART STEP5
JCL	RESIGENR	STEP4	790405	0345	0345	AT	KEYPUNCH ERROR -> CORRECT & RESUBMIT
S222	CFPPUPD2		790502	0345	0345	AT	RESTART CARD LEFT OUT OF DECK -> INSERT & RESUBMI
JCL	LINEFM01	FM114	790405	0350	0350	AT	RESTART STEP NOT FOUND -> CORRECT & RESUBMIT
JCL	ISASDLY1	STP11	790201	0440	0445	FM	DSN NOT FOUND -> CORRECT RESTART ISASTP11
S213	CLOSDLY1	DLY1C	790327	0545	0550	TG	DSN NOT FOUND -> RESUBMIT RESTART
U0502	MIS4RSTR		790601	0600	0645	AT	DSNAME NOT ON DISK OR DATA SET HAS NO EXTENTS ->
S222	TCGLFD04	STEP13	790511	0630	0645	FM	CALLING FOR WRONG I/P TAPE -> UNCATLG RUN TCGLRST

Figure 4.1. Raw Problem Data.

Figure 4.2. Raw Problem Data.

S001	1	MRFSJOB5	STEP2	790128	P	0315	0325	FM	EQC ON DISK PACK -> RESTART STEP2
S001	1	MRFSJOB5	STEP3	790513	P	0200	0210	FM	S001 ON 124 -> RESTART STEP3
S001	1	MRFSJOB5	STEP3	790527	P	0200	0205	TG	S001 ON TEMP D/S 196 VS3215 -> RESTART STEP2 AS P
S001	1	MSGCC002		790131	P	1555	1600	BM	S001-4 ON VS3214 -> ATTEMPT RERUN
S001	1	MSGCC002		790206	P	0155	0159	TG	001 ON SORTFILE VS6816 -> RERUN
S001	1	MSGFC138		790404	P	0155	0215	TG	INT REQ 271 -> RERUN
S001	1	MSGXXXX	EXT	790725	P	2210	2215	FL	DCK,TSGCOUNT O.K. -> RERUN JOB
S001	1	MTOLJPST	EP1	790619	P	0700	0700	AT	EQC ON O/P -> RERUN
S001	1	NARSDUPB	COUNT	790620	P	2145	2150	PP	INCORRECT LENGTH -> RERUN JOB
S001	1	NYCDREG1	STEP1	790508	P	1735	1745	JA	INT-REQ. -> RERUN
S001	1	NYCDREG1	ST1	790628	P	2315	2325	FL	INCORRECT LENGTH -> RERUN USING ANOTHER DRIVE
S001	1	NYCDREG1	ST1	790715	P	2300	0240	TG	S001-4 ON I/P TSGCOUNT NG (NOTHING ON I/P TAPE) -
S001	1	NYCDREG1	ST1	790717	P	2300	2305	FL	INCORRECT LENGTH - 1ST REC. -> RERUN
S001	1	NYCDREG1	ST1	790718	P	0145	0150	FM	I/O ERROR ON I/P -> RERUN
S001	1	OSBIEM01	IEMSTP10	790126	P	1650	1655	FL	EQC 3A0 -> RESTART AT STEP USING DIFF DRIVE
S001	1	PACTPT02	STEP1	790501	P	1905	1910	PP	CMD ON 214 -> RERUN
S001	1	PACTPT02	STEP1	790502	P	0050	0100	FM	I/O ERROR TSGCOUNT OK -> RERUN
S001	1	PACTPT02	STEP3	790428	P	0220	0225	TG	INT/REQ I/O ERROR ON O/P -> RERUN
S001	1	PACTPT02	STEP4	790215	P	1330	1335	EF	DCK ON 394 - O/P -> RERUN
S001	1	PACTPT26	S7	790126	P	2115	2120	FL	DCK 41A -> RERUN USING DIFF DRIVE
S001	1	PAC2UPDT	S7	790405	P	1040	1050	BM	001-4 ON STORN1(6BB) -> ATTEMPT RERUN ON ANOTHER
S001	1	PAC2UPDT		790126	P	1905	1910	FL	HIT ON PASSED D/S -> RERUN
S001	1	PCAPC009		790303	P	1545	1550	EF	S001- O/P LOST- (TREAT AS EOJ) -> RUN PCAPC000- T
S001	1	PCAPC009	902	790405	P	0350	0355	TG	CMD ON CHKPT TAPE -> RESUBMIT CHKPT1 RESTART
S001	1	PCAPC009	902	790509	P	0345	0345	AT	NON-ACCEPTABLE ERROR ON PCAN01 13D -> CHKPT 7 RES
S001	1	PCAPC009	902	790721	P	0445	0445	AT	001-4 ON I/P -> RESTART AT CHECKPT 1
S001	1	PCAPC009	902	790725	P	0545	0550	AT	S001-4 ON 2/P -> CHECKPOINT 1 RESTART
S001	1	PCPCA009	STEP1	790718	P	2040	2050	JA	I/O ERROR ON I/P TAPE -> CHKPT #1 RESTART

68

problem addressed in isolation, the analyst can determine whether common causes or patterns of occurrences can be identified.

As stated previously, some information is generally available about most problem occurrences, but the information may not be clearly articulated or it may represent only partial data. Unless there is some evidence to the contrary, a good approach is to assume nothing and begin by mapping problem occurrences by time or by job occurrence, as suggested in Figures 4.3a and 4.3b. This eliminates some of the chances for personal bias and misinterpretation of word-of-mouth data in diagnosing why some problems occur. Figure 4.4 is a day-of-month frequency analysis of data like that in Figure 4.1. The example suggests a relationship between problem occurrence and the beginning (business days 1 and 2) and end (days 17 through 23) of the month. If this were a histogram of hardware failures, it would suggest a relationship between device failure and periods of intense equipment utilization, an obvious conclusion.

Another highly useful method of organizing the data is to develop a frequency histogram by time of day, i.e., a histogram similar to Figure 4.4 but where the horizontal axis represents each hour of the 24-hour daily operating cycle. Figure 4.5 presents a hypothetical example in which each data point represents the cumulative number of problems of a given type that occurred for each time period (hour, etc.) during the entire month. Reacting only to operations staff and user reports of "many" tape problems, the example assumes the analyst has mapped these problems against time. Taking the examples of Figures 4.4 and 4.5 together indicates some relationship between mid-second shift processing and tape-drive usage. Whatever methods are chosen, with the data well organized, the process of analysis, of separating perceived causes of problem occurrence from acutal causes, can begin. The theme, here, is to place ownership for problem solutions within the line. Hence, the analysis that separates perceived causes of problems from actual causes should be performed by an analyst from the line, with support from the staff area.

Any state of inefficiency is most likely a function of several types of problems. For example, if it were determined that 15% of all jobs were rerun, not all

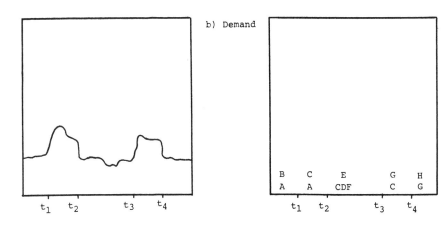

Figure 4.3. Analysis of Problem Occurrence.

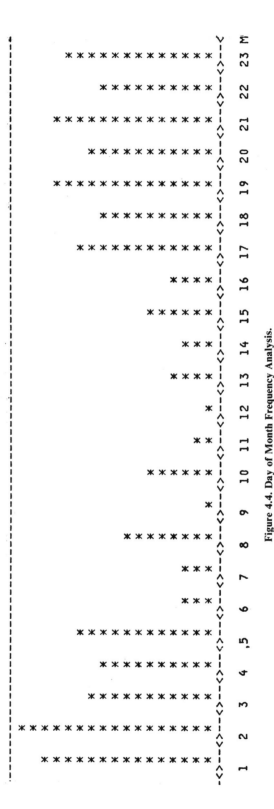

Figure 4.4. Day of Month Frequency Analysis.

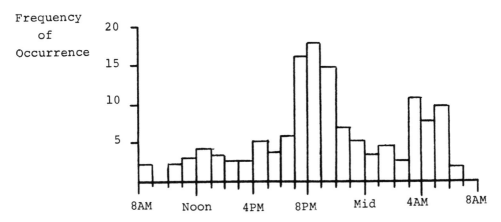

Figure 4.5. Time of Day Frequency Analysis.

reruns would be due solely to tape problems, not all solely to operator error, etc. Figure 4.6 attempts to portray multicausality by showing several problem categories, p_i, that the line analyst has hypothesized exist. The term "hypothesized" is used since the analyst has taken a great deal of data and made an educated guess that specific occurrences could be grouped into each p_i, resulting in the definition of p_i and in its quantification. But there is no proof that p_i really characterizes the grouping of individual problem occurrences and, more importantly, there is no certainty that proposed actions to reduce p_i are appropriate or will work.

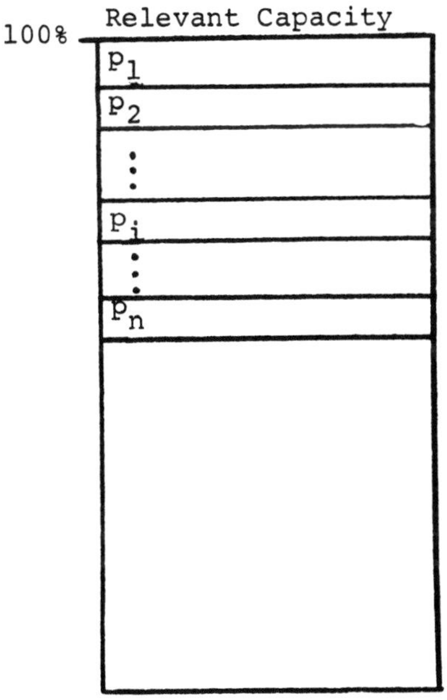

Figure 4.6. Hypothesized Causes of Inefficiency.

Under the functional jurisdiction of the staff analyst, the line analyst formally constructs a series of actions he believes will reduce each p_i. Since there will always be some job and equipment failures, and therefore capacity losses under even the best conditions, the ultimate objective is to reduce the total inefficiency to an acceptable level. The term "acceptable level" is, admittedly, somewhat arbitrary, it being difficult to determine how low one can bring the numbers and effects of problems. Some line managers would have one believe their current level of efficiency, is commendable even if it is, say, at 75%. And some theoreticians would contend anything much below 100% is unacceptable. Practically, it is hard to conceive of a situation where at least 90% is not attainable.

The correct objective, i.e., the target efficiency level, is a function of the entire environment—hardware, operating software, applications, and manual work areas. In practice, the objective is determined by examining the hypothetical causative agents for each problem type; determining the degree to which each cause can be controlled, i.e., by setting objectives for limiting the occurrence of each problem; and summing the residual degree of uncontrollability for each constraint. This sum is the complement of the targeted efficiency objective. It is described by Figure 4.7, whose left side is identical to Figure 4.6. The right side indicates the decrease over time of capacity lost to each constraint, p_i, and, hence, the increase in efficiency from the initial value, E_o, to the objective E_f. This chart can be used either as a planning tool to describe the time frame during which each p_i will shrink to its objective or as a reporting mechanism to describe actual progress in meeting the objectives.

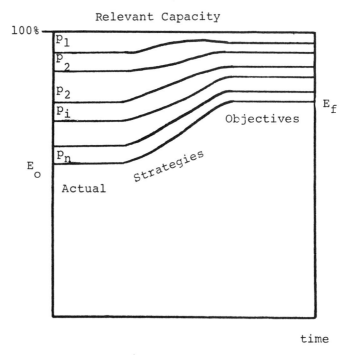

Figure 4.7. Efficiency Improvement Strategies.

In order to prove that each p_i is a valid indicator of a class of problems and, more importantly, that each remedial action is benefitting the shop to the degree anticipated, failure data for each problem type are collected for a significant period of time, usually equal to the period that was used to collect data to identify the problem in the first place. Since at least 20 to 30 data points are desirable, both from a statistical viewpoint and to span a full operating cycle, one month's data are generally required. These data are then mapped against the original data to see whether the remedial actions agree with the projections of Figure 4.7.

Example 4.1

In analysing its operation, XYZ has found that half of its reruns are associated with tape problems. Its current effectiveness was measured over the period of a month by an analyst from the operations staff. After selecting what were thought to be appropriate categories, the measurement was as follows:

EFFICIENCY CONSTRAINT	PERCENT RELEVANT CAPACITY LOST
Equipment failure	4
Job failure due to:	
Operating System	2
Application Code	2
User Input Error	4
Tape Problem	6
Operator Error	5
Output Lost	1
Total	24

Figure 4.8. XYZ Efficiency Constraints.

With efficiency currently measured at 76%, the situation obviously requires further audit. Rather than focus on each item, the example observes a portion of the analysis, that of three categories: user, input error, tape problem, and operator error.

The operations staff's immediate reaction is that these three categories reflect the fact that during the last half of the first shift, the entire second shift, and the first half of the third shift, they require more setup clerks, more tape drives, and more operators, both for the tape drives and to handle the large number of messages at the master (CPU) consoles. Together with the staff analyst, the line analyst constructs Figures 4.9 $a-c$, a time-of-day frequency analysis of the three categories being examined. These refine what many people may believe but do not articulate: the problems peak during the second shift. From this conclusion, further requirements are sought. Figures 4.10$a-$ c provide more detailed breakdowns for those occurrences that comprised the peak (second shift) of Figure 4.9. The tape-problem category is the simplest to investigate and is considered first.

From Figure 4.10a, suppose the analyst deduces there are two generic types of tape problems: those related to tape quality (creases and oxide spots) and those related to tolerances on the read/write heads of various tape drives. The objective is to seek actions

a) Frequency
of
Tape Problems

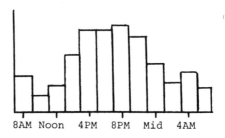

b) Frequency
of
User Input
Errors

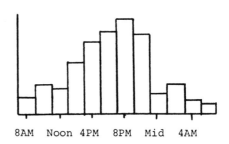

c) Frequency
of
Operator
Errors

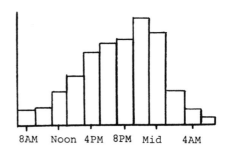

Figure 4.9. Time of Day Problem Frequency Analysis.

that will significantly reduce the occurrence of the problems and, hence, the loss of capacity.

The first tape problem, defective tapes, can be addressed by launching an intensive tape-certification program. While simple, this requires careful management; old or uncalibrated tape certifiers sometimes tend to destroy the tapes they certify. Another preventative action that can be taken requires knowledge of the use of the physical tapes. If, for example, it is known that tape data sets are small, one can multiply the expected value of the number of records per data set by the expected value of the record length. When the product is multiplied by the tape density, the length of physical tape most often used can be determined. Since most errors would occur in this often-used physical length of tape, a procedure of cutting off that amount of tape, the initial 25 or 50 feet after every 20 or 30 or so uses, would reduce the occurrence of tape errors without significantly affecting the overall tape length. This is similar in theory to the

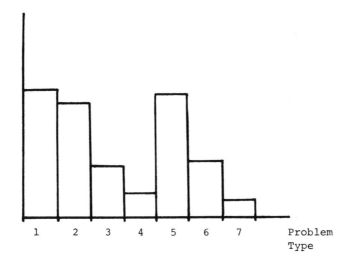

Legend:

    1. Crease on tape
    2. Spot on tape
    3. Non-standard label
    4. Non-standard EOF
    5. Unreadable tape
    6. Hardware malfunction
    7. Other

Figure 4.10 (a). Tape Problems.

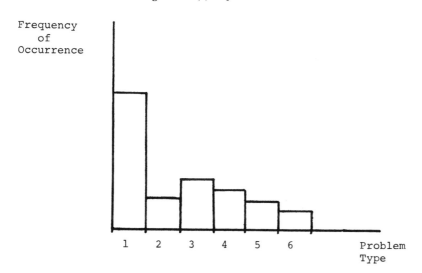

Legend:

    1. Incorrect tape serial number
    2. Missing tape
    3. Wrong tape
    4. Incorrect cards
    5. Missing cards
    6. Other

Figure 4.10 (b). User Input Error.

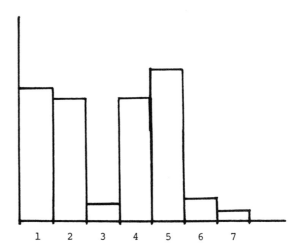

Legend:

1. Incorrect tape mounted
2. Job control statement error
3. Cards read incorrectly
4. Incorrect response to console message
5. Job run in incorrect sequence
6. Output incorrectly routed
7. Other

Figure 4.10 (c). Operator Error.

classic lightbulb replacement problem—a balance is sought between throwing away good tape and saving computer capacity that would otherwise be lost.

The second type of tape problem, head tolerances, can result in tapes that are unreadable due to read heads being somewhat askew from the tracks of information on the tape. Recognizing that this is caused by varying calibrations of read/write heads from one tape drive to another, either within one data center or from feeder data center to receiver data center, the analyst embarks on an effort to get all the maintenance engineers to conform to the same standards and similar maintenance schedules.

Knowing the size of the problem (6% and n occurrences) and the nature of the remedial actions, the analyst estimates the degree to which those actions will eliminate problem occurrences. Assume, for the sake of example, the objective is to reduce capacity lost due to tape problems to 1% within three months. A project-tracking mechanism is then established to measure the effectiveness of the actions taken. This can be represented in the form of a graph, as in Figures 4.9 and 4.10, or in tabular form.

The causes of the remaining two (non-tape) problem categories, user input errors and operator errors, being more procedural than physical, are not as easy to diagnose. Time-of-day frequency analyses, similar to that in Figure 4.9 are prepared for each subcategory shown in Figures 4.10*b* and 4.10*c*. Without actually drawing them here, assume that, as may happen, the number of occurrences for each individual subcategory is too small to provide a good statistical picture of what is happening, and that the analyst gleans little additional information from them. He then develops a frequency analysis linking problem occurrence to applications (Figure 4.11). A pattern develops indicating that 30% of the applications are involved with the majority of problems. As often happens in these cases, the analyst discovers that these are the least-documented applications. Their catalogues are not adequately described for the operations staff, nor are their job-control specifications, predecessor-feeder relationships, descriptions of actions to be taken in response to application-generated messages to the operator, user personnel to be contacted in case of problems, etc. And a rash of control problems, characterized by the subcategories of Figure 4.10*b* and 4.10*c* result. Remedial action here involves forcing the user to complete adequate production documentation. As before, the analyst selects an objective, charts or otherwise documents planned improvements across time, and records actual progress toward attaining the goal.

The major difference between the category of tape problems and the categories of user input errors and operator errors, in terms of actions required and probability of success, is that the latter two involve commitments from outside the data center. Hence, organizational pressures may have to be applied to insure adequate attention to the issues.

In addition to insuring the commitment of both line and staff management, it is important that the process of analyzing data be well structured, using for-

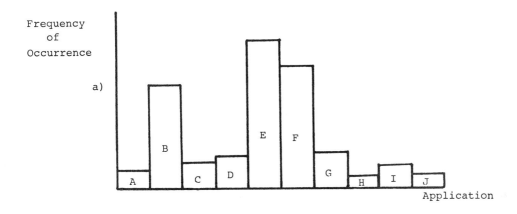

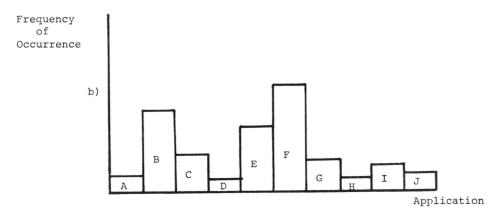

Figure 4.11 (a). User Input Error. (b) Operator Error.

mal data gathering techniques, documenting perceived causes of constraints, charting plans to implement remedial actions, and providing feedback to judge the effectiveness of those actions. Otherwise, it is remarkably easy for efficiency audits to founder, to change direction, to fail to implement changes completely.

4.4 COMPUTER PERFORMANCE

The terms "computer performance measurement," "computer performance evaluation," and all the other names by which the assessment of the efficiency of hardware and software (both operating systems and application code) are known, refer to the search for constraints within the black box commonly referred to as "the computer." There are literally dozens of types of constraints that can exist, and the details of the techniques used to identify the existence and causes of each are a function of the many types of specific hardware, operating systems, and coding techniques that can be used. The art of measuring computer performance is sufficiently broad and technical that several good texts are devoted to the subject.

Types of Constraints

The types of contraints that are grouped under the umbrella of computer performance may be divided into four main categories: (1) the analysis of hardware imbalances or bottlenecks; (2) the analysis of operating systems; (3) the analysis of hardware and software failures; and (4) the analysis of application-coding inefficiences.

Hardware imbalances, as the name implies, refers to suboptimal distribution of utilization across various devices. This can take several forms.

Example 4.2

Figure 4.12 represents a system where two sets of devices, such as banks of disk drives, are connected to one of another type of device, such as a CPU. Assume, as a first case, two-thirds of all I/O requests are sent along channel 1 to disk bank 1 and the remaining third is serviced by channel 2 and bank 2.

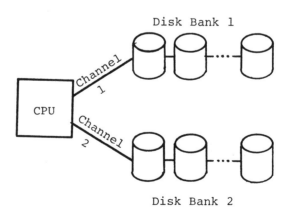

Figure 4.12. Multi-Device Configuration.

What is the average service time per I/O?

The total expected service time for any I/O operation, t_s, equals the sum of the time spent in the queue plus the time being processed by the device, disk bank 1 or 2. Assuming exponential arrivals,

$$t_s = [\rho^2 + \lambda^2 \sigma_\mu^2]/[2\lambda(1-\rho)] + 1/\mu$$

where

$$\rho = \lambda/\mu$$
$$\mu = \text{service rate}$$
$$\lambda = \text{arrival rate}$$

For

$$\lambda_1 = 32, \lambda_2 = 16,$$
$$\mu_1 = 40, \mu_2 = 40,$$

and

$$\sigma_\mu = 1/\mu$$

then

$$t_{s1} = [0.8^2 + (32^2 \times 0.025^2)]/[2 \times 32 \times 0.2] + \tfrac{1}{4}$$
$$= 0.125000$$

Similarly,

$$t_{s2} = 0.041667$$

Recognizing that performance here deals with the average time required to service an I/O request,

$$t_{avg} = (2t_{s1} + t_{s2})/3$$
$$= 0.097222$$

Balancing the load across the two I/O facilities as a second case,

$$\lambda_1 = \lambda_2 = 24$$

and

$$\rho_1 = \rho_2 = 0.6$$

it can be calculated that

$$t_{avg} = t_{s1} = t_{s2} = 0.0625$$

a decrease of 35.6% from case 1.

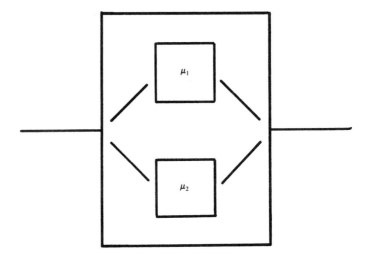

Figure 4.13. Unequal Service Times.

If I/O servicing were to account for half the elapsed time of a transaction, the example indicates that response time can be cut by 35.6% ÷ 2, or nearly 18%, merely by balancing I/O activity. Obviously, here, the game plan is to improve overall response time at the expense of users accessing device 2. There are often reasons, however, why such a tradeoff might not be acceptable, such as when operating-system modules reside on device 2 and batch-application data sets reside on device 1.

A second type of hardware imbalance occurs frequently when devices of different speeds are employed. This is diagrammed in Figure 4.13, where a facility has two devices: one with service rate μ_1 equal to half μ_2, the service rate of the second device.

Example 4.3

Assuming one is able to direct activity to one device or the other, how should the data center allocate demand between the two devices?

At first glance, one would assume the best strategy would be to assign exactly twice as much work to device 2 whose service rate is exactly twice as fast as that of device 1. Stated mathematically, and assuming

$$\mu_1 = 40, \text{ and } \lambda_1 = 30,$$

then

$$\mu_2 = 80$$
$$\lambda_2 = 30$$
$$\rho_1 = 30/40 = 0.750$$
$$\rho_2 = 30/80 = 0.375$$
$$\sigma_{\mu 1} = 0.025, \text{ and}$$
$$\sigma_{\mu 2} = 0.0125,$$

where $\sigma = 1/\mu$.

For device 1,

$$t_{s1} = [0.75^2 + (30^2 \times 0.025^2)/[2 \times 30 \times (0.25)] + 0.025$$
$$= 0.100000$$

For device 2,

$$t_{s2} = [0.375^2 + (30^2 \times 0.0125^2)]/[2 \times 30 \times (1-0.375)] + 0.0125$$
$$= 0.020000$$

Hence,

$$t_{avg} = 0.060000$$

Remembering that this exercise seeks to minimize overall average data-set service time (throughput), t_{avg}, if the faster device (number 2) is overloaded so that, for example,

$$\lambda_1 = 20 \text{ and } \lambda_2 = 40$$

then

$$\rho_1 = 0.50 \text{ and } \rho_2 = 0.50$$

and

$$t_{s1} = 0.050000$$
$$t_{s2} = 0.025000$$
$$t_{avg} = 0.033333$$

a decrease of 44.4%. The degree to which the analyst continues this type of analysis is a function of the degradation of throughput times deemed acceptable for those items serviced by the faster device.

A third type of hardware imbalance or constraint typically encountered is the "bottleneck." This can take two forms as indicated by Figures 4.14a and 4.14b. One describes the state where two devices of different service rates are linked serially. The faster device is thereby degraded to the speed of the slower device unless some alternative is developed. In the past, this type of condition led to the creation of I/O buffering so that fast CPUs could commence processing data while the slower I/O devices and channels continued fetching additional data. Another development to deal with this type of constraint was the introduction of spooled printing, so that the fast CPU did not have to wait for the slower line printer to finish before the next series of calculations were performed.

Figure 4.14b describes a variation of bottlenecking commonly found that affects I/O operations. It usually occurs as a controller attached to several I/O drives. The controller service time is small compared to that of any one I/O

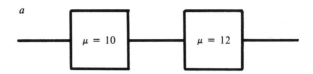

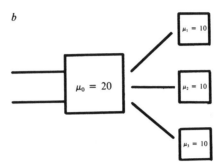

Figure 4.14. Unequal Service Times.

device, but the number of drives usually attached to one controller can result in the formation of queues, either at the controller waiting to get to a drive, or at the drive waiting to get through the controller and back to the CPU. This occurs where controllers are capable of handling only one operation at a time. This problem can be evaluated with the same basic queuing theory used in Examples 4.2 and 4.3, the difference being the complexity of the network diagram required to describe all the joint probabilities reflecting multiple accesses to the same device, simultaneous requests to access different devices requiring the dedication of the controller, and so on. (As is customary with this type of text, this is left as an exercise for the reader).

A variation of loading imbalances is suboptimal positioning of data sets. This can occur as an extension of Example 4.2, where too many of the data sets that are being accessed reside on the same I/O drive. Since the drive is capable of processing only one I/O at a time, I/O requests queue up while other drives remain unaccessed. Another type of occurrence is where the data sets are correctly put on the same I/O drive, but are physically located in such a manner as to require considerable movement of the read head. The increased head movement delays the acquisition of the data, which in turn delays the completion of processing, adds to the length of queues of I/Os waiting to be serviced, etc.

The constraints associated with operating systems include those of the selection of operating system parameters—has the systems programmer selected the correct modules to match individual job requirements, the correct performance parameters to optimally assign machine resources given the characteristics of the workload, and so on? The constraints also include that of residency; that is, given a limited amount of main storage to house the operating system, do the most frequently used modules reside there or must they be retrieved from I/O devices, disks, or drums each time they are requested? This type of consideration generally includes trade-off analyses between the cost of incrementing main storage (if technologically feasible) and the perceived value of improved response time for on-line jobs or earlier termination for batch jobs. In extreme cases, when the activity of these nonresident modules is quite large and CPU usage is approaching saturation, that is, the service-risk point, these studies consider the quantity of CPU cycles recaptured (by reducing operating system overhead) and their value in delaying acquisition of the next segment of CPU capacity.

The analysis of hardware and software failures is self-explanatory, involving quantifying the effect on service of intermittently eliminating resource availability from on-line jobs and quantifying the capacity lost each time hardware fails or batch jobs must be rerun.

"Application-coding inefficiencies" refer to constraints on response times of on-line jobs and capacity wasted due to less-than-optimal coding techniques arising from programmer-generated (as opposed to operating-system) code. One such case was given in Example 2.1, where CPU time was shown to decrease as the programmer regrouped the data into larger blocks. Other examples of coding inefficiencies include redundant indexing, not matching the selection of machine instructions to the specific logic requirements of programs, and so on.

Measurement Tools

There are a variety of tools available to address the foregoing problems. The ability to use some of them is a function of the specific hardware/software environment being considered. Some merely gather data, while others provide diagnostic aids. Most are classified either as software monitors or hardware monitors. A third class of tool, simulators, do not measure or provide data but allow the analyst to estimate the result of certain changes that may be contemplated for the hardware/software environment.

Software monitors are programs that reside in the computer and observe activity (Figure 4.15). Under the control of part of the operating system, the software monitor is able to see which modules of the remainder of the operating system are used and how frequently. Since this remainder has all the tables indicating the state (busy or idle) of all the I/O devices, it is also able to develop statistics on I/O utilization and contention.

Another aspect of software monitors is their ability to observe applications. This is done in two ways. Some software monitors are used for job accounting purposes. Since the monitor has access to most information to which the operating system has access, it is able to link device usage to job names. Hence, it is in the unique position to report on equipment utilization and error (and other job-termination) codes as a function of specific job names. Obviously, with the addition of some sorting functions and a pricing structure, software monitors become the foundation for many computer chargeout packages. Other software

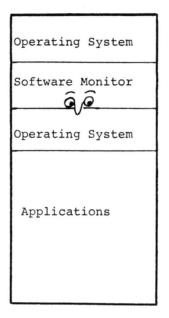

Figure 4.15. Software Monitor Operation.

monitors are used to analyze the efficiency of the code. This takes the form of developing histograms of usage for each section of code. Figure 4.16 gives an example in which a job's code is broken into 10 segments. Here the monitor tells the analyst that 50% of the CPU cycles consumed by this job are consumed between addresses 300 and 400. The analyst infers that if any savings are to be realized, they are most likely to be found in the address space.

While seemingly ideal, software monitors have several limitations or drawbacks to their use. The first is that since they are programs, there is a certain amount of machine overhead associated with their use. Generally, it is no more than 1%–5% of the available CPU cycles, unless special, short-duration, inten-

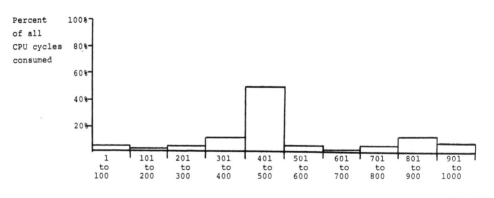

Figure 4.16. Frequency Histogram of CPU Usage.

sive measurements are being taken. The problem arises when the data center finds three or four monitors, each having specific strengths that it believes it cannot do without. One may be a job-accounting package, another an on-line monitor to provide operators with instant pictures of utilization, a third an on-line scheduler, etc. It is not difficult to run CPU overhead up to 20%. Thus, there should be a great deal of self-discipline associated with software monitor usage if they are not to affect applications response time and elapsed time. A second limitation is that software monitors are machine and operating-system dependent; for example, one developed specifically for use on IBM equipment cannot be used with Burroughs devices. Moreover, one that is developed for IBM's MVS will not necessarily function with IBM's DOS/VS, and so on. Since software monitors reside under the control of an operating system, and since the operating system controls one computer, a third limitation is the inability to simultaneously analyze the activities of two or more interacting computers. Since the software monitor only links events to the internal clock of its own host, it cannot always be used effectively in computer networks, where each computer maintains its own internal clock. Finally, software monitors are usually designed to cover a wide variety of measurements. Hence, they are flexible to the extent that what is desired is possible under the framework of the software monitors' existing code. Any measurement requirement outside that framework cannot be satisfied.

"Hardware monitors" are devices that attach directly to the computer's circuitry and measure activity by sensing voltage changes, much in the same manner a TV repairman diagnoses problems with a voltmeter. The key to this activity is the ability to procure from the computer manufacturer a list of points within the circuitry where, for example, an increase in voltage signifies use of the CPU, a decrease indicates access to a tape drive, etc. Figure 4.17 is a schematic of a typical commercial hardware monitor, with a series of perhaps over 100 probes to sense voltage changes in various circuits, hardwired Boolean logic to provide combinatorial counting of signals, a tape or disk drive to record data for posterity and future analysis, and, often, a minicomputer to provide control over the operation of the monitor and, in some cases, reduction of the collected data.

The major advantages of hardware monitors stem from the fact that they reside external to the devices they measure; that is, they do not require software that resides within the host CPU. (Exceptions to this include options offered by some monitor vendors to perform additional measurements. But here we are actually referring to a breed of hybrid hardware/software monitors, where many of the constraints previously associated with software monitors apply.) Other advantages of hardware monitors include the ability to measure various devices without having to consume host CPU cycles and high flexibility in terms of being able to satisfy the analyst's measurement objectives. Although the number of things that can be measured is limited only by the host computer manufacturer's ability and willingness to provide the necessary points to which probes should be connected, because every measurement relies on specific points in the circuitry, each measurement, or change in measurement, requires reat-

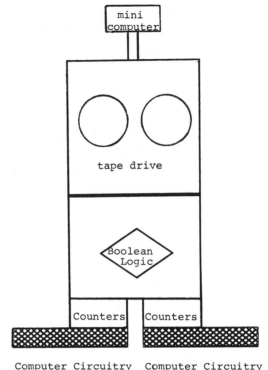

Figure 4.17. Hardware Monitor Schematic.

tachment of some number of probes. So, while there is tremendous flexibility in choosing factors to measure, doing so results in the expense of some additional manpower. Other limitations include the physical number of probes and counters available with the monitor(s) used and signal amplification problems as distances between the monitor and the device being monitored grow large (usually at about 200 feet).

A word of caution. Since hardware monitors are electronically active devices, and the equipment to which they are attached is also electronically active, proper grounding of the monitor becomes an issue of concern. Grounding is a funny thing. It can be done improperly and never cause problems under most conditions. Or it can be done correctly but, if there are intermittent failures in the electronics of some part of the host or physical plant that supports the host (power generators, water pumps, etc.), some night the reader might see his computer turn to carbon. Or, he might see his performance analyst turn to carbon. While this type of event rarely happens (admittedly, statistics are not much of a consolation), careful attention to grounding conditions in the entire shop, including the complex wiring under the floor as well as auxiliary equipment, and careful attention to the interrelationship of grounds for the monitor and all equipment to which it is attached (i.e., is everything on a common ground or are there potential differences), can make the probability of such an incident lower than that of being struck by lightning.

Summary of Tools

Every measurement device has some type of bias or limitation in the manner in which it collects data, either due to limitations inherent in sampling techniques or in its ability to gain access to data. When applied properly, the difference between data obtained by hardware monitors and that obtained by software monitors is usually no more than 5%, not enough to suggest a different conclusion or change a decision. Hence, the decision to use one or the other is a function of flexibility requirements, the specific brand of computers requiring study, etc. The overriding requirement is that of a technically competent analyst whose feet touch the ground, a professional who understands the usefulness of addressing only those problems that directly and currently affect capacity and/or service and who is able to put aside issues that relate only to the joys of measurement. It is sometimes difficult to find an analyst who recognizes that there is an economic benefit to releasing capacity constraints, especially CPU capacity constraints, only in those few instances where actual new acquisitions would have occurred or where leasing arrangements permit the removal of existing equipment without substantial penalty.

4.5 RELIABILITY

As an adjunct to the failure-mode analyses described in the previous section, reliability studies are concerned with the minimization of failure rates, either by the segmentation of hardware into smaller, unconnected dedicated systems or by the introduction of additional, redundant hardware.

The segmentation approach, of which Figure 4.18 is a typical example, generally buys additional reliability at the cost of increased hardware expenses. The left-hand portion describes a two-machine computer center where each machine has a capacity of three and a failure rate of 0.02, that is, each machine considered by itself is inoperable 2% of the time. A failure rate of 2% can represent a mean time between failure (MTF) of 98 hours and a mean time to repair (MTR) of 2 hours, a MTF of 50 hours and a MTR of 1, etc. While these alternative failure and repair rates have different implications for the stability

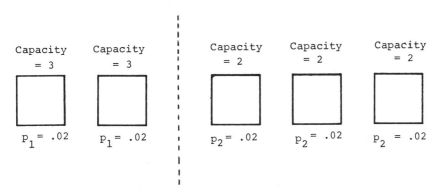

Figure 4.18. Capacity/Reliability Alternatives.

STATE NUMBER	MACHINE OPERABLE	PROBABILITY OF STATE	CAPACITY AVAILABLE
1	1, 2	0.96040	6
2	1, ~2	0.01960	3
3	~1, 2	0.01960	3
4	~1, ~2	0.00040	0

Figure 4.19. Table of Capacity Availability.

of the operation, they do not affect this discussion. The probability of failure on the left can be written as

$$p(\sim 1) = 0.02$$
$$p(\sim 2) = 0.02$$

where $p(1)$ is the probability machine 1 is operable, $p(\sim 2)$ is the probability machine 2 is down, etc. Figure 4.19 expands the list of failure states to consider the full range of possibilities.

From this figure, it is observed that 0.0392 or 3.92% of the time the data center will be operating at half capacity and 0.04% of the time it will be shut down. Resegmenting capacity to three smaller machines, each with a capacity of 2 and each with the same 2% probability of failure gives the range of capacity availabilities shown in Figure 4.20.

Thus segmentation reduces the probability of having the full set of capacity available since the more devices one has, the greater the probability that some will fail. Offsetting this is the fact that failures are not as devastating as in the dual-machine environment—the site is virtually never completely shut down and only about 0.12% of the time, in this example, do hardware problems result in less than two-thirds of the capacity being available. The cost of the increase is the difference in expense between n small machines and m large ones (where $n > m$), the increased requirement for supportive hardware (disks for operating system residence, channels, etc.) and increased staff required to support the additional machines.

STATE NUMBER	MACHINES OPERABLE	PROBABILITY OF OCCURRENCE	CAPACITY AVAILABLE
1	1, 2, 3	0.94119	6
2	1, 2, ~3	0.01921	4
3	1, ~2, 3	0.01921	4
4	1, ~2, ~3	0.00039	2
5	~1, 2, 3	0.01921	4
6	~1, 2, ~3	0.00039	2
7	~1, ~2, 3	0.00039	2
8	~1, ~2, ~3	0.00001	0

Figure 4.20. Table of Capacity Availability.

The other approach to increasing reliability is the redundant equipment approach. Here, computer systems receive increased equipment that is meant to take over in the event of a failure. For example, Figure 4.21a is our hypothetical computer, with a box containing CPU and channel, a box containing a disk controller, and a bank of disks. Ignoring the probability that a disk drive may fail, the probability that the system will fail is the compound probability that the CPU and/or the controller will fail. From Figure 4.19, the failure rate is seen to be 3.92%, but there are two methods of improving it. One way is to install a second controller, as an alternate path with access to the disk bank, as in Figure 4.21b. Since the probability that both controllers will be down concurrently is approximately 0.0004, the probability the system is down is:

$$0.98 \times 0.0004$$
$$+0.02 \times 0.0004$$
$$+0.02 \times 0.9996$$

or 2.04%. In large, complex systems, where multiple banks of disks (to use this example) are accessible or shared by multiple controllers or CPUs, this method is hard to manage well, i.e., it is difficult to spread I/O accesses optimally across I/O devices during different times of the day. This is the classic device conten-

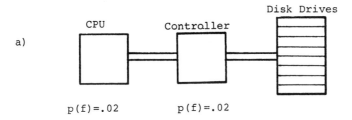

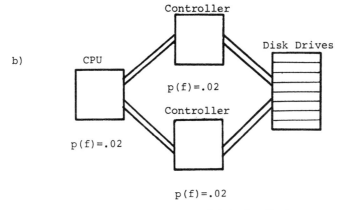

Figure 4.21. Reliability Increases through Redundant Equipment.

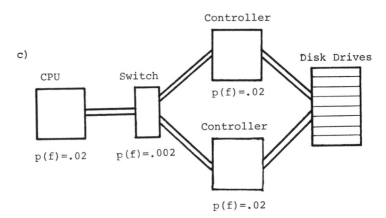

Figure 4.21. (*continued*)

tion problem. Hence, the analyst must be careful when using this method of increasing reliability to avoid adding the potential cost of degraded performance to the expense of the additional equipment.

The second method, shown in Figure 4.21c, avoids the contention problem by using one controller as a prime device and relying on a switch to cut over to the

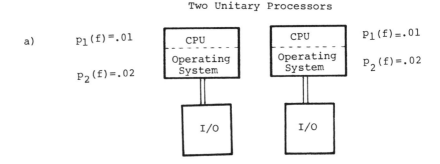

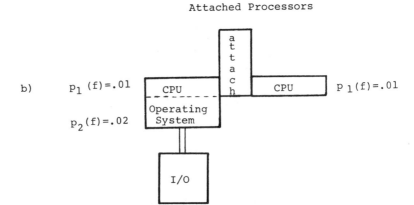

Figure 4.22. Capacity/Reliability Alternatives.

c)

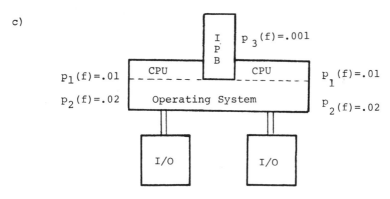

Figure 4.22 (*Continued*)

second controller in the event of failure of the first. This approach is not as good as it would at first seem to be since the switch, another piece of hardware, also can fail. Assuming, for the sake of example, its failure rate is 0.2%, the joint probability that neither the CPU nor the switch will fail is:

$$(0.98 \times 0.998) = 0.978$$

Since the probability that both controllers will be down at the same time is 0.0004, the probability the entire system is down (the joint probability of CPU/ switch failure and failure of both controllers) is:

$$1 - 0.978 \times 0.9996$$

or 2.24%. Hence, while the addition of the switch limits the contention problem the tradeoff is a somewhat smaller gain in reliability.

A variation of the added equipment approach to optimizing reliability may be seen in the manner in which some data centers attempt to back-up their CPUs. Figure 4.22 shows three alternatives of maintaining a given level of capacity, say 2, and of addressing the issue of reliability. The first, part a, is two single (unitary) processors, each with its own addressable I/O. Assuming failure rates of 1% for each CPU and 2% for each operating system, Figure 4.23 describes the probability of one unitary system being available, recognizing that the system is totally unavailable if either the CPU or the operating system fails. "O" indicates operable; "F" indicates failure mode.

Squaring these probabilities provides the joint probability that either one or

CPU	OS	PROBABILITY OF OCCURRENCE	CAPACITY AVAILABLE
O	O	0.97020	1
O	F	0.01980	0
F	O	0.00980	0
F	F	0.00020	0

Figure 4.23. Table of System Availability.

SYSTEM 1	SYSTEM 2	PROBABILITY OF OCCURRENCE	CAPACITY AVAILABLE
O	O	0.94129	2
O	F	0.02891	1
F	O	0.02891	1
F	F	0.00089	0

Figure 4.24. Table of Capacity Availability Two Unitary Processors.

both of the two unitary systems will be operable. An alternative to this two-step calculation would be a table 16 rows long (the number of combinations equals 2^n). Whenever one deals with duplicate sets of capacity, as in this case, the analyst has this type of short cut available.

Figure 4.22b describes the second capacity/reliability alternative, the so-called attached processor or AP: one computer system with one set of addressable I/O gear and two CPUs. Each CPU operates concurrently with the other and has access to all I/O devices and memory. Generally, the second CPU results in something less than doubling of the available CPU cycles. But, as an example of the most optimistic case, assume the attached processor system provides the same capacity as Figure 4.22a's two unitary processor system and that all failure rates are the same. Figure 4.25 represents part of the failure event matrix.

The multiprocessor (MP) system of Figure 4.22c is actually two separate computer systems melded into one by joining the CPUs. The joining is usually accomplished via hardware, the actual device sometimes called an inter-processor bus (IPB). Once enabled, IPB permits each CPU to access all the memory and I/O devices of the other. The two systems become a single one that can be again split back into two in the event the IPB fails or if some special processing requirement materializes. The attraction of the MP to most is that the full set of I/O gear and all the data sets it houses are usable even if one CPU fails. What many forget to consider is whether the surviving CPU can provide sufficient CPU cycles to service those devices and the programs that access them in addition to servicing its own workload. Hence, the use of the MP's reliability implies degraded servicing of demand on the remaining CPU. This can be managed so that critical on-line applications will not suffer degraded response or critical batch jobs will not excessively elongate. This aside, some data centers

CPU$_1$	CPU$_2$	OS	PROBABILITY OF OCCURRENCE	CAPACITY AVAILABLE
O	O	O	0.96050	2
O	F	O	0.00970	1
F	O	O	0.00970	1
O	O	F	0.01960	0

Figure 4.25. Table of Capacity Availability—Attached Processor.

| CAPACITY | PROBABILITY OF ALTERNATIVE | | |
AVAILABLE	UNITARY PROCESSORS	AP	MP
2	94.13	96.05	96.05
1	5.78	1.94	1.94
0	0.09	2.01	2.01

Figure 4.26. Comparison of Reliability Alternatives.

treat the MP feature as just an automated clerk that shifts jobs from a failing CPU to a healthy one and automatically throws switches to make data available to those jobs.

In terms of reliability, the major difference between the MP and two unitary processors is the additional piece of hardware (the IPB) and one large operating system for both CPUs rather than one small one for each. Figure 4.26 compares the reliability of the three alternatives, two unitary systems, an AP, and an MP. The MP figures assume the same failure rates for the CPUs and operating system and a 0.001 rate for the IPB and were calculated using a process identical to that of Figures 4.23 through 4.25.

Obviously, these results are dependent on the characteristics of the specific hardware and operating system software used. If, as is sometimes the case, operating-system software for MP systems is more complex than that for unitary and AP systems, its higher failure rate will reduce overall reliability advantages.[1] For example, it can be shown that increasing the probability of failure of the MP operating system to 2.5% results in:

| CAPACITY | PROBABILITY OF |
AVAILABLE	OCCURRENCE
2	95.56
1	1.93
0	2.51

Hence, the analyst must do a good deal of research to determine what other installations have experienced with similar hardware and software configurations before he or she can reasonably predict reliability differences between alternative capacity scenarios.

The final method of addressing reliability included in this discussion relates to optimizing the reliability of being able to access data spread across several devices. Figure 4.27 describes a data set that, for performance reasons, is spread across three disk drives. Assuming that the failure rate for a disk drive is 0.005, the probability of job failure resulting from the inability to access data on a disk drive that has failed can be calculated to be $1 - 0.98507$ or 1.49%. Alternatively, if the data were reallocated into two drives, the probability of failure would be 1.00%, i.e., reliability can be increased by reducing the level of redun-

[1]M. Lieberman, "To Multiprocess or Not to Multiprocess," presented at the Computer Performance Evaluation Users Group (CPEUG), 14th meeting, 1978.

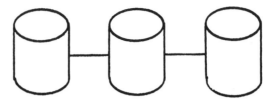

Figure 4.27. Data Access Reliability.

dant equipment. The cost of the reliability improvement is increased contention at each disk drive. The measurement techniques described earlier in this chapter can be used to determine whether the level of increased contention has any significance in terms of the performance of the applications that access the data.

4.6   SUMMARY

Concluding the discussion on the efficiency of data center operations, we see that constraints on efficiency, that is, the factors of production leading to loss or waste of capacity, are generically similar to those of any other production facility—some are caused by factors inherent in the equipment or technology employed, some are a function of the manner in which that technology is operated, and others are related to manual methods. Actions taken to reduce the frequency of occurrence and the effect of these constraints, or even simply their identification and quantification, are sometimes made more difficult by organizational sensitivities, if the line or operations personnel are too defensive to criticize its own performance and reluctant to accept fully a performance audit by outside staff. In such cases, a delicate balance of involvement by both line and staff in efficiency audits is required if the line is to retain significant ownership of potential improvement recommendations.

Once organizational issues are settled, a variety of industrial engineering techniques are available to help articulate the causes of capacity losses, quantify their effect, and measure the progress of remedial actions. A variety of hardware and software tools are available to address more technically oriented computer problems, such as suboptimal distribution of loading across devices, inefficiencies in operating system installation, and application-code inefficiencies. While these tools primarily gather data, other tools, including simulators, models, and queuing theory, are available for those analysts who are too intelligent or too inexperienced to use normal intuitive solutions. Finally, basic reliability studies are valuable for projecting gains in efficiency as a function of increased (or sometimes decreased) equipment costs, as well as for projecting the loss in throughput or response time that sometimes accompany reliability changes.

5
STAFFING

This chapter describes a method of addressing problems associated with data center staffing that melds traditional industrial engineering techniques with data processing's unique requirements. The scope of this methodology extends to defining and quantifying demand in all sectors of the data center floor; segmenting the data center into a finite member of discrete workstations (using the traditional definition of workstation); selecting appropriate standard-setting techniques; and establishing manpower requirements and line-balancing opportunities at various confidence levels. The methodology centers about the development of production standards, widely used in other industries, for labor expended in the data processing operation.[1]

5.1 INTRODUCTION

Traditionally, those involved with evaluating data processing operations have been almost exclusively concerned with internal computer performance—operating system and application efficiency, hardware contention, and so on. There has also been some concern with production constraints in the more traditional industrial engineering sense as described in Chapters 3 and 4—segmenting capacity, matching job assembly/disassembly to computer capacity, and providing operations feedback controls for use in early detection of work-handling problems.

But the deepening trend of ever-decreasing hardware cost of computing lessens the payback of traditional computer performance improvement efforts. The trend towards distribution of computing resources reinforces the declining value of these efforts by reducing capacity-segment size and limiting the utility of unused computer capacity.

The element that increases in significance with each of these trends is the continually increasing cost of labor. For corporations that choose the large-scale utility, the proportion of costs attributable to labor is increasing. While some technological advances, (such as tape file conversion to mass storage devices and automated JCL/job schedules), limit this increase, the trend in large-scale job shops remains one of an increasing proportion of costs attributable to the human side of operations. In corporations that choose to dedicate smaller seg-

---

[1]M. Strauss, "Developing Standards for Staffing DP Centers," presented at the Computer Measurement Group (CMG) IX Conference, San Francisco, Calif., 1978

ments of capacity, the effect is to create redundant support-oriented functions at each computer site, resulting in a lack of control over the level of corporate DP staff.

The procedure developed in this chapter relates tasks associated with processing jobs to manpower requirements. The results can be applied against manual demand or workload to provide maps of staff requirements for each task. Finally, the maps for each task can be compared to each other to determine whether line-balancing opportunities exist.

5.2 DEMAND AND WORKSTATIONS

When examined in its most basic form, the data center is no different than other production lines. Figure 5.1 illustrates this fact: material is subjected to some process that results in output. The actual format is, for the moment, unimportant. That which makes data processing unique (in terms of the application of work measurement techniques) is the variability within individual segments of demand. Understanding this concept requires a successful structure or format for relating to demand and the ability to distinguish demand from utilization.

The formatting or definition of demand is relatively simple; demand should be structured according to those resources that must be specifically scheduled or reserved for the production function as described in Chapter 2. Within the data center, two classes of demand exist: manual and automated. Automated demand relates to the requirement for the allocation of computer resources, CPU, tape drives, etc.; this has been addressed in earlier chapters. Manual demand relates to tasks required in preparation for, or supportive of, automated (in particular computer) processing.

It is easily understood that within manual demand are several subclasses of demand (Figure 5.2): some relating to job setup; some with the actual computer processing of the job, or the job stream; some to job take down, or disassembly; and still others that are primarily supportive in nature. (Here, the term "job" is used in the typical data processing sense of the word.)

As in all other production centers, work in the data center is divided into direct and indirect labor. Direct labor is involved in the actual processing or building of the desired end product. Examples of this type of work are mounting tapes, assembling job control cards, bursting finished printed output, and so on.

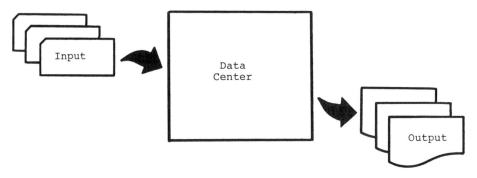

Figure 5.1. Functional Flow Diagram.

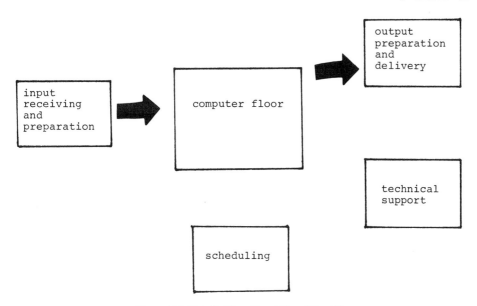

Figure 5.2. Detailed Functional Flow Diagram.

Indirect labor is supportive of the production line and entails work such as logging input, scheduling production, delivering finished output, and attending to system problems. Indirect labor often occurs in small (one- or two-person) segments. In these cases, there is usually little payback to the effort invested in developing production standards. Other cases, such as those involved with technical support, are difficult to measure accurately due to several factors, including the lack of a definition of what task success (completion) criteria are and the strategic (as opposed to tactical) nature of certain tasks. For example, technical (system) troubleshooters are retained to service what are highly variable and, it is hoped, random events. The rest of their available time is applied to what is basically housekeeping. Thus, although it may be technically feasible to develop a "troubleshooting" standard, such a standard would have little utility, i.e., little effect on staffing or performance evaluation decisions.

In no case, however, should more than a small segment—10% to 15%—of a work force be classified as unmeasurable. Often, when an analyst sees an exception to this rule of thumb, the cause is usually incorrect segmentation of manual demand into its various subclasses. On some occasions, the analyst performing the standards study is overwhelmed by the variability that occurs within each task. (Such variability is discussed at length in Section 5.4.)

Once the simple task of identifying and separating subclasses of demand, hereafter referred to as "tasks," is completed, the organizational structure of the study may be easily set. Each task is associated with a geographic area on the data center floor. These areas are referred to as "workstations." Some workstations, such as the master console, are simple and consist of only one type of activity: while many different types of messages at the console must be responded to and several logs manually updated, no other type of activity is required. Furthermore, the operators remain in one place. The workstation *is* the console.

Other workstations are, of course, somewhat more complex. The responsibilities of the tape operator, in addition to mounting and dismounting reels of tape, include walking to tape racks, in some cases walking to a tape library, and cleaning read/write heads. Furthermore, a workstation can encompass more than one physical location, although in this case, the bulk of the tape operator's activities centers about one locale. Finally, depending on the quantity of manpower expended on each of the various subtasks and the objectives of the standards study, the analyst has the option of separating the standard into components as deemed appropriate. (Figure 5.3 translates the demand components identified in Figure 5.2 into workstations.)

5.3   STANDARD-SETTING TECHNIQUES

A "standard," for the purposes of this exercise, is a reference point against which other points, events, or requirements may be judged. For example, 70°F may be used as a standard to determine whether today's temperature is warm or cold. However, the concepts of warm or cold, like efficient and inefficient, are qualitative, relative terms. If, for example, one is trying to store ice cream, 40°F, while cold compared to the standard, may cause certain marketing problems. In a similar manner, production standards, if arbitrarily set too low, will

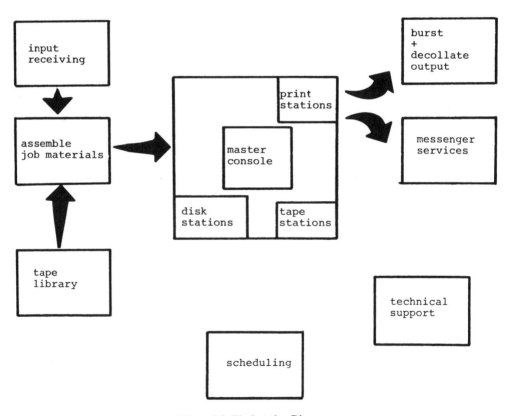

Figure 5.3. Workstation Diagram.

cause production problems and, if set too high, will encourage overstaffing and raise production costs. Usually, data processing staffing standards, if they exist at all in an organization, are developed using the "gut-feeling" technique.

The analyst performing the standards study, however, has several more scientific, unbiased techniques available. These include linear programming models, basic motion studies (MTM), standard data, stopwatch analyses, work sampling, and studies based on historical data. The analyst's choice of methods should be a function of the conditions and objectives of the standards study as well as the ease of implementation.

In setting a time standard for any task, the intention is to determine the amount of time that should be required for an average worker to complete that task. Thus, if one were to study tape operators, the intent would be to determine the time required for an average operator to complete the given task. Note that neither the best nor worst operator speeds is addressed, only the average.

Linear Programming

This technique is the simplest, in terms of implementation, of all the techniques described herein for application to workstations with highly variable task components. The effect of large degrees of variability will become apparent during the discussions of MTM and standard data that follow.

Linear programming concerns itself with the optimal allocation of scarce resources among a set of often competing demands. Mathematically, it is expressed in the form:

$$Z = \Sigma C_i X_i \qquad (5.1)$$

subject to a set of restrictions of the form:

$$A_{ij} X_i \leq B_i \qquad (5.2)$$

Several restrictions apply to these relationships for which the reader can refer to any good text on basic operations research or on linear programming. It is sufficient here to state that our purpose will be to minimize the total time required at a workstation, Z, to complete the required task(s).

The implementation of this technique, the "simplex method," involves examining the work performed at each workstation to identify a small number (usually three to seven) of items characteristic of and hopefully highly correlated to, the work or output of that station. For example, at the tape workstation, one would probably choose the number of tapes mounted, the number of trips to the tape library, the number of tapes cleaned, etc. Elapsed job time could also be used if that variable were correlated to overall activity at the tape station. (Note that this discussion refers to all tape drives taken together as one workstation.) These variables become the A_{ij} in equation 5.2. The X_i are the time requirements that we are attempting to calculate for each variable. The B_i are the total productive time spent in the workstation being evaluated. This value is obtained by summing the time in residence at the workstation by all workers and subtracting time spent on breaks and idle time.

(It should be noted that "idle time" is defined as a period in which no work was performed or assigned. This would include periods when no work was either in or queued to the workstation. Time an operator spent cleaning read/write heads while waiting for a tape mount to be issued would not be included in idle time but rather would be included as productive time, B_i. In this manner, overheads to any data center function would automatically be included in the standard being developed.)

Thus, at the end of a day, an inequality can be written of the form $A_{i1}X_i \leq B_1$. The reason this relationship is an inequality is that the time spent, B_1, on all tasks, X_i, is an actual, not standard value. It has not yet been subjected to any type of validation or minimization and, hence, could contain some "slack time." Since the relationship is reflective of the average of a group of workers, not just the fastest, there is, by definition, no chance that B_i is less than the sum of all $A_{i1}X_i$.

"Slack time" reflects potential added time spent performing a task due to worker inefficiencies such as slow speed, errors requiring rework, etc. For example, if the period being sampled was concurrent with the annual corporate New Year's Eve celebration, one might suspect that some manpower ostensibly expended on mounting tapes was not being fully productive in the industrial engineering sense.

For this reason, one would not take a workstation with m variables and collect m days of data to produce a set of m simultaneous equations in m unknowns. Rather, n data samples $(n > m)$ are collected, creating n inequalities in m unknowns. These inequalities are converted to equations by the simplex methods through the introduction of slack variables, X_{m+1} to X_n. Again, this process is well defined in several available texts.

The next issue to be addressed is that of quantifying the objective function to be minimized, $Z = \Sigma C_i X_i$. Careful thought of the process yields the concept that we are attempting to determine the unit manpower required for a representative mix of activity within the workstation. This leads to the conclusion that, given that all variables are of equal weight or importance, each C_i should represent the average or expected value of the corresponding A_{ij}. While this represents a slight bending of the rules for the simplex method, the error thereby introduced into this type of application is small. In fact, given the granularity of staffing, the error is usually insignificant. Without this shortcut the analyst must revert to techniques that are described later—methods-time measurement (MTM) and others. After examining those passages, the reader will agree that the small error introduced by the linear programming method is preferable to the alternatives.

If, instead of observing equal volumes or weights as above, the volume of the variables is of the ratio of, say, 50:2:1, or if one determines one variable is generically much more significant than the others, other statistical approaches may be desirable. This could be the case if setup clerks had as their only task pulling job operating instruction sheets from a file and passing them to a key-punch section. Here, if it were determined that the significant factor was number of jobs handled, the objective function would be developed by using this variable as the prime variable, rather than the number of job sheets pulled and/or number of cards punched.

It should be noted that while each X_i represents the unit time associated with each individual variable, it is Z, the time required to produce a normal mix of work, that is the significant output of this process. This vector may be unitized for subsequent demand/manpower loading analyses (discussed in Section 5.4).

The only remaining task required to complete the discussion of the application of the simplex method is to determine the number of data points required to provide a sufficient degree of statistical confidence in the final standard. Remembering that the variables represent only the significant production results or indices, one should understand that the productive time, B_i, reflects time spent on all activities within the workstation and that the objective function, Z, represents the amount of time that should be required for all activities on a typical or standard day. Hence, there is imperfect correlation between the standard produced and the daily mix of variables.

If the standard developed by the foregoing process is applied to each data point (i.e., each day's data), this imperfect correlation will result in varying degrees of recovery. An example is given in Figure 5.4.

Here, it is assumed that analysis has yielded the given solution of X_i and that the matrix A_{ij}, B_i represents data collected from actual observations. Applying X_i to the matrix yields, in the case of data point 1, a manpower requirement of 81 $[(3 \times 3) + (8 \times 4) + (8 \times 5)]$ against an actual manpower expenditure of 110. This yields a "recovery" of 81 ÷ 110, or 74%. Continuing this process for the remaining nine data points yields a mean of 88.8 and a variance of 14.0. Assuming these recoveries to be normally distributed, a t test is performed to determine the confidence that the standard is in error by no more than some percentage. In the example shown, t is the t-statistic for 90% confidence and k is the acceptable error, in this case 0.1 or 10%. As is evident, this example indicates that at this point in the process, a minimum of just over 12 data points are needed for the desired confidence. For 95% confidence and no more than 5% error, the required number of data points would be approximately 20, and so on. In the real world, one generally insures that the number of such data points would represent a minimum of a full operating cycle. Thus, if the data point represented a full day's production and the businesses the applications processed in the data center had a 22-day operating cycle, a minimum of 22 data points should be included in the analysis.

MTM AND STANDARD DATA

MTM

MTM, or methods-time measurement, is a standard-setting technique requiring the analyst to define each task in terms of basic motions: grasps, reaches, key strokes, eye movements, etc. This method is by far the most difficult and time-let $X_1 = 3$ $X_2 = 4$ $X_3 = 5$

Objective
Function $5.9X_1$ + $8.1X_2$ + $7.3X_3$ =   86.6

Time Period	A_{i1}	A_{i2}	A_{i3}	B_i	Percent Recovery
1	3	8	8	110	74
2	4	5	7	81	83
3	5	9	10	96	105
4	6	8	7	102	83
5	8	6	6	97	80
6	8	11	5	94	99
7	4	7	9	104	82
8	6	10	6	101	87
9	8	5	8	109	77
10	7	13	7	88	118

$$\mu = 88.8$$

$$\sigma = 14.0$$

$$N = \left(\frac{\sigma\,t}{k\,\mu} \right)^2 = \left(\frac{1.40 \times 2.228}{.1 \times 88.8} \right)^2 = \text{12.3 samples required}$$

Figure 5.4. Testing for Statistical Confidence.

consuming to implement and requires the use of highly experienced work-method analysts; it also has the potential of being the most accurate. Some MTM units are given in Figure 5.5.

Typically, the analyst visits every workstation and develops an in-depth knowledge of each task and subtask in all their variations. For example, a study of a setup area would include an examination of the work required to prepare all jobs for execution. If part of that function was to prepare tape labels, the analyst would break that function down to a reach of some number of inches for the blank form(s), a grasp, a retrieve, and a release. This process would be repeated for the required pen or marker. The number of charaters on the label and the eye movements required by the worker to follow what he was writing would be multiplied by the standard times for writing a character, eye movements, etc., and added to the times for the preceding activities. If the label had

Standard Data

CODE	CFC-ON-01	
TYPE	CLERICAL — FASTEN AND/OR UNFASTEN	
DATE APRIL 1963		**PAGE** 1 OF 1
PREPARED BY V.A.		**APPROVED BY** R.D.R.

TITLE CLIP (PAPER) — PUT ON

STARTS WITH CLIP IN HAND   **ENDS WITH** MATERIAL FASTENED

INCLUDES SEE ELEMENT ANALYSIS   **LIMITATIONS**

M T M ELEMENT ANALYSIS

DESCRIPTION — L.M.	freq.	CONVENTION	TMU	CONVENTION	freq.	DESCRIPTION — R.M.
HOLD PAPER			15.2	M 12 C		CLIP TO PAPER
			—	G 2		BETTER CONTROL
			16.2	P 2 SE		ALIGN
			10.6	AP 2		OPEN
			5.6	G 2		BETTER CONTROL
			2.5	M 1 A		CLIP ON
			2.0	RL 1		
			52.1			
ROUNDED TO			52.0			

Figure 5.5. Example of MTM and Standard Data.

to be attached to a control sheet, the time needed to obtain the control sheet and attach the label would similarly be calculated and added to the total. If 10 other activities had to also be performed for the setup, they too would be similarly defined and calculated. All this measurement would be a very exacting, time-consuming process.

The difficult part of developing a standard in this manner occurs if there are any variations in the defined task. For example, if a tape label had 10 fields but any of the last three were not necessarily filled out, this subtask would have eight variations, one for each permutation. Each task would correspondingly have a slightly different time requirement. If, for all jobs that had these requirements, the number of labels varied between one and seven, there would be 56 possibilities and 56 different standards required. Developing standards for console operators, whose jobs are even more varied, would be proportionally more exhaustive.

Next, the methods analyst would take the requirements of these subtasks and all the other subtasks in all their permutations and prepare to compile an overall standard. Two alternatives are available: the preparation of a standard for an individual job or the preparation of a weighted standard that is generic to the production process.

In the first case, the analyst examines the variability of each subtask only as a function of one job (or application); that is, he determines historically how frequently job A required one tape label, two labels, etc., and develops a weighted average of each subtask's requirement. This is done for all subtasks, thereby producing an expected value of the manpower required each time job A passes through the workstation. This type of analysis provides valuable information for environments whose workload changes quickly or is highly transient. But the effort required is enormous, and each time the user changes the application, the standard may have to be adjusted.

The second alternative, the process-oriented standard, takes the frequency-weighted, job-oriented standards and weights them according to the relative frequencies of the occurrences of each of the various jobs. Since the overall workload changes more slowly than each of its components, the process-oriented standard would have a longer useful life.

Standard Data

Standard data represent packets or compilations of MTM standards for frequently referenced subtasks. For example, if one were developing an MTM standard for a quality control clerk who performed a dozen functions, each of which concluded with carrying a package to an output window, rather than rewriting that portion of the standard for each function, the analyst would develop it once and then invoke it thereafter. This type of standard is used primarily in heavy industry where a job might require, e.g., the installation of a carburetor. Only one line rather than dozens would need be referred to by the analyst.

So, while the theoretical potential accuracy of MTM standards is high, the high degree of effort required for development and maintenance would suggest MTM's use only for relatively invariant tasks such as keypunch, key to disk, etc.

Time Ladders

Time ladders or historical data are logs that individuals keep to record the amount of time actually spent performing a task. The problem with this type of measurement is that it only relates how much time an activity did take, not how much it should take. Thus, we are left uninformed as to whether worker efficiency or speed was adequate.

Generally, if a group of workers performs several tasks, time ladders may be used if a significant percentage, say 25%, are also subject to either MTM-type or linear-programming standards. The latter two methods will provide a means of leveling or performance testing the time ladder standards. For example, if one of the tasks is given a 1.0-minute standard according to MTM and a 1.2-minute standard with the time-ladder technique, all time ladder standards for that same group of workers are adjusted or "leveled" down 0.2/1.2, or 16.7%.

The discussion of standard setting techniques complete, the chapter next discusses methods of quantifying demand.

5.4 QUANTIFICATION OF MANUAL DEMAND

The preceding sections have described the manner in which manual activity within the data center can be broken down into a finite number of tasks and in which alternative methods of developing standard execution times for each task can be devised. It now remains to develop a methodology for utilizing these standards in order to determine total staff requirements for each workstation or to substantiate the need for existing staff levels.

The discussion of the linear-programming approach to standard setting described a data-gathering approach wherein a count of the number of executions of each task (or set of variables) was maintained for a specified time interval. As we shall now see, the selection of that interval is key to the process of mapping labor requirements.

The data-recording process essentially takes a continuous stream of events—the arrival and subsequent servicing of pieces of demand—and converts that stream into a series of discrete occurrences of "packets," or accumulations of demand.

Each such packet represents the sum of events across some time interval and, as such, has the effect of smoothing demand across that interval. A count of, say, 1000 tape mounts for a day has a different character than two counts of 300 and one count of 400. Going into further detail, a daily count of 1000 has a significantly different character than, say, 23 counts of 40 and one count of 80 mounts. A standard that is prepared using the smoothed daily count will include a certain amount of slack time not characteristic of other time intervals. The application of that standard across noncorresponding time intervals will produce misleading demand maps. This is illustrated is Figure 5.6a; where the total number of setups is 1440. For the sake of the example, it is assumed a standard-setting technique has been previously selected and has produced a standard of 5 minutes. A daily demand map would indicate a staff need of 17.1 per day (1440 setups × 5 minutes per setup ÷ 420 man-minutes per work day) or 5.7 (rounded to 6) per shift. A second shift map (hours 9–16) would yield a staff requirement of 5.0 (60 × 5 ÷ 60). Similarly, first and third shift maps would indicate staff requirements of 5.8 or 6 (average of 70 setups/hour) and 4.2 or 4 (average of 50 setups/hour). And hour 4, averaging 100 mounts/hour would yield a workforce requirement of 8.3 or 8.

Thus, the obvious—the interval during which demand is quantified is, itself, a determinant of the standard. Any time interval selected will produce a standard accurate over that time period, but the finer the resolution, the more useful the standard for relating to shorter duration peak load periods. If one were to develop a daily standard, a graph of demand would be a straight line at 60. A shift standard would yield a step function for demand, 70 for first shift, 60 for second, and 50 for third. The 1-hour standard provides the demand graph shown in Figure 5.6a.

In selecting the appropriate period size, one is faced with the trade-off between ease of sampling (both for the analyst and the staff recording their

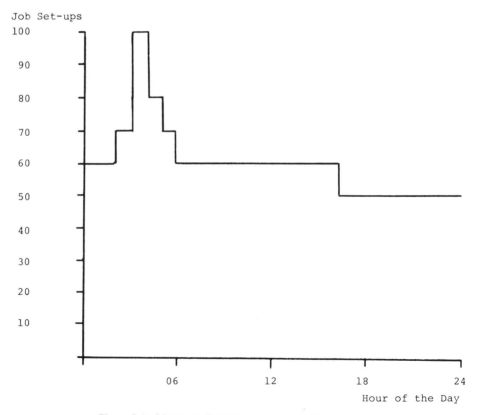

Figure 5.6a. Manpower Requirement Map at 50% Confidence.

activities) and standard sensitivity. Aiding in this decision process is the fact that the characteristics of the workstations themselves often suggest natural limitations to the degree of sensitivity. Setup stations that prepare jobs to be run for the following shift rarely can benefit by reducing the interval to less than one half or a whole shift. This is also true in cases where tasks are completed in stages over a long period. Conversely, in a tape-mounting workstation, the delay permissible in starting or completing jobs is often such that periods in the range of 30 to 60 minutes are acceptable.

This explanation of demand mapping assumes either a one-point sample or the average of a large number of samples. That is to say, the value of 100 in

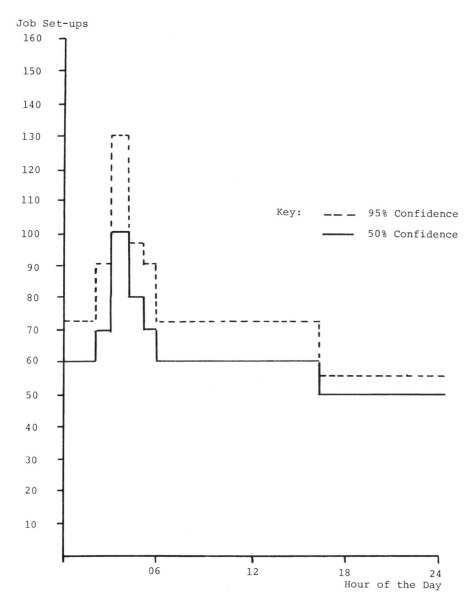

Figure 5.6b. Manpower Requirement Map at 95% Confidence.

Figure 5.6*a* for hour 4 may be an average of 20 or 30 sample periods. Recognizing that while this represents a relative peak load across a daily operating cycle, it becomes evident that a great deal of care must accompany the conversion of raw demand statistics into a meaningful demand map. Typically, the analyst will perform an analysis of the sampled population. A normally distributed sample set would be accommodated by the development of mean and variance statistics, a multimodal sample set would lend itself to standard modal analyses.

Once the type of statistical analysis has been selected and performed, one may interpret the demand chart (as in Figure 5.6*a*) with respect to confidence

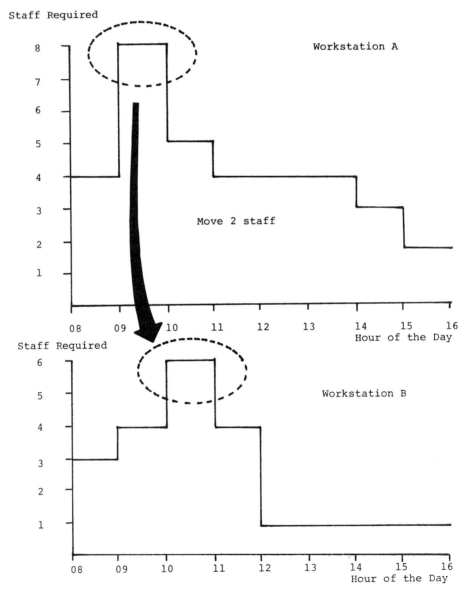

Figure 5.7. Line Balancing.

levels. For example, if the sample leading to Figure 5.6*a* was normally distributed, the values graphed would be averages for the total number of days sampled, i.e., the 100 for hour 4 would be an average of perhaps 20 samples. If associated with this average was a standard deviation of, for example, 15, while 100 would be peak demand on 50% of the days, 130 [100 + (2 × 15)] would represent a 95% confidence upper bound on peak demand; thus, one would expect to have to staff for no more than 130 setups per hour in order to handle peak demand 95% of all work days. This would have the effect in the example of raising the staff requirement from 8 to 10.8 or 11 (130 × 5 ÷ 60). The result would change Figure 5.6*a* to Figure 5.6*b*. The level of confidence selected is a somewhat arbitrary decision on the part of management that is tempered by the fit of demand to the nearest integer.

This process completes the statement of demand for a single workstation. When the process is continued for each additional workstation, a set of local charts will result depicting each area's pattern of staff requirements. This procedure often graphically illustrates the dependency of one station's peak on a preceding station. For example, tape station peaks often precede off-line printer peaks, and setup peaks precede peaks on the computer floor. The process known as "line balancing" involves identifying opportunities for lowering overall staff requirements by moving workers from one station to another as the demand for various stations alternatively crest and ebb. Figure 5.7 illustrates a simplified example of this process. Section A, peaking from 9 AM to 10 AM, requires a maximum of eight staff; section B peaks at 10 AM to 11 PM and requires a maximum of six. Yet, by reassigning staff, both stations can be covered with only 12 people. While this process is obvious, it is usually difficult to identify and implement without developing graphic illustrations.

5.5 SUMMARY

Thus we have seen that data center managers need not indulge themselves by maintaining unjustified staff levels. Data processing is only another type of production process, albeit somewhat more automated than most; and staffing in a data processing area ought and can be subject to the same basic managerial criteria as any other production process.

6
BUDGETING

The capability to adequately manage a budget and budget variances is a prerequisite to the understanding of cost/price discussion in Chapter 7 and the utility/dedicated-facility discussion of Chapter 8. This chapter, then, is intended as a brief overview of the budgeting process, focusing only on the development of expense and capital budgets, depreciation methods, and lease versus purchase analyses. The reader is referred to other appropriate sources for more details and for discussions of other related accounting topics: income and expense posting; methods of accounting for receivables and payables; handling accruals, etc.

6.1 INTRODUCTION

As we shall see in the next chapter, the issue of computer processing charges is often a very sensitive one. If one is permitted to enter the realm of prices, there is no single scheme that will not upset at least a sizable minority of data center customers. In such a case, a firm, clear structure for determining costs is required if the development of the pricing structure is to be methodical and rational. If, instead of pricing, one is limited to a purely cost-based charging structure, then, for reasons of auditability, one again requires a clear structure for determining costs of services. That structure is a good operating budget, accounting both for expenses and depreciated capital.

6.2 OPERATING BUDGETS

In setting up an operating budget, the intent is to articulate and then control the various components of production costs. The order we shall impose on grouping certain expenses into categories anticipates potential categories for charging that will be more fully discussed in the next chapter. But for our immediate purpose, it may be briefly stated that, whenever possible, the budget will be structured either by function (labor–materials assembly, labor–tape workstations, supplies–printing, etc.) or by equipment classification (equipment–CPU, equipment–printers, etc.). The practice of matching budget structure to costing formats greatly simplifies the process of reevaluating costs (or prices) for alternative configurations or demand scenarios.

Figure 6.1 briefly outlines the structure our budget is to take.

Direct
    Direct Labor
    Direct Materials
Indirect
    Variable
        Indirect Labor
        Indirect Materials
        Power
    Fixed
        Equipment Rental
        Equipment Depreciation
        Supervisory Salaries
        Insurance
        Postal and Shipping
        Communications—Telephone
        Other

Figure 6.1. Operating Budget.

Direct labor traditionally includes only manpower positioned at equipment: master console operators, tape operators, printer operators, etc. All other staff members, a sizable majority, comprise what is generally classified as indirect or supervisory labor. Direct materials classically refers to only those materials that physically comprise part of the final product, in this case printed output (paper), tapes, and disk packs.

It should be noted that the objective of most automation efforts is to reduce overall production costs even if a by-product of those efforts is a shift in direct to indirect or variable to fixed ratios. In data processing, this shift is generally pronounced. But most managers recoil at the prospect of overhead being of the same general magnitude as direct costs, of fixed costs being equal to, or greater than, variable costs. There are several pages to read before these ratios become apparent, and readers who suspect they are prone to this type of reaction ought to consult a good text on the subject or go directly to Chapter 8, hoping for the best.

We now look to budgeting for equipment, labor, and supplies in more detail, guided by the assumptions that the data center has the equipment described in Figure 6.2a and staff described in Figure 6.2b. Staff levels are for a three shift operation and are broken down more precisely later.

6.3 EQUIPMENT BUDGETS

The purposes of the equipment budget are:

1. to describe all expenditures and depreciation directly related to each equipment category;
2. to facilitate the development of unit processing costs; and
3. to set up a structure to control expenditures by measuring future variances from the budget.

Equipment Category	Vendor	Quantity	Leased/Owned
Model A CPU	A	1	Leased
Model A CPU	A	1	Leased
9 Track Tape Drives	A	16	Leased
9 Track Tape Drives	B	16	Leased
7 Track Tape Drives	B	4	Leased
3 Megabyte Add'l			
Core	B	2	Leased
4 Channel Increment	A	2	Leased
Model D Disk Drives	A	32	Leased
Model D Disk Drives	B	32	Owned
Model X Printers	B	2	Leased
Model X Printers	A	2	Owned
Card Reader/Punch	A	2	Leased
Communications			
Controllers	A	2	Leased
Modems	C	4	Leased
Terminals	A	30	Leased
Terminals	C	30	Leased
COM	D	1	Leased
Burster/Decollator	A	2	Leased

Figure 6.2a. Budgeted Equipment.

Figure 6.3 begins this process by describing how the budget analyst might begin recording expenses of each piece of equipment.

The example illustrates several items that often detract from the simplicity of the budgeting process. One is that market values fluctuate and that identical pieces of equipment can be acquired at different times at different costs. Here, the CPUs were acquired perhaps years apart, accounting for the difference of $2000 in January's rental expense. Further, changes made to existing leases, total lease renewal, extension of term, etc., can change monthly expense. This is reflected by the change of monthly expense for CPU#1 from October to November.

Using different vendors often translates to differences in monthly expense. This is the source of the difference in cost of 9-track tape drives between Vendor A and Vendor B. In addition, because some leases cover only a certain number of hours of equipment operation during a month, some equipment also requires budgeting for "additional use" charges. Examples of these charges are included

Workstation	Function	Three Shift Staff Level
CPU/Master Console	Supervisor	3
	Operator	6
Tape Pool	Supervisor	3
	Operator	7
Tape Library	Clerk	6
Print Pool	Supervisor	3
	Operator	3
Bursting & Decollating	Operator	3
COM	Operator	1
Materials Assembly	Clerk	7
Messenger Service	Clerk	6
Capacity/Performance Planning	Analyst	1
Budgeting and Costing	Analyst	2
Production Manager	Manager	3
Staff Manager	Manager	1
Data Center Management	Manager	1
Secretarial Staff	Secretary	3
	Total	59

Figure 6.2b. Budgeted Staff.

for some equipment categories. Finally, since maintenance is usually included in lease charges, some disk drives and printers here are shown to have only rental expenses, while the others show only maintenance charges.

As anyone who has had even minimal exposure to the budgeting process knows, these are but a few of the demons that lie waiting for the budget analyst.

6.4 DEPRECIATION

In a shop where some equipment is owned rather than leased, the equipment budget would not be complete without at least one depreciation entry. Depreciation is supposed to reflect the decreasing useful life of an asset. "Useful life" is usually determined by the tax analyst for tax purposes rather than by the capacity analyst for capacity-planning purposes.

There are a large number of methods of depreciating an asset. Some are supported by your local Internal Revenue Service agent. While the intent here is to describe methods of addressing equipment depreciation, software packages and monies invested in the devoelopment of applications are depreciated in much the same way as hardware. Some of the most widely used depreciation methods include the following four.

Rental Expense:

Item	Jan.	Feb.	Mar.	Apr.	May	Jun.	Jul.	Aug.	Sept.	Oct.	Nov.	Dec.	Total
CPU #1	30000	30000	30000	30000	30000	30000	30000	30000	30000	30000	27000	27000	354000
CPU #2	28000	28000	28000	28000	28000	28000	28000	28000	28000	28000	28000	28000	336000
Tape Drives -16 9trk Vendor A	9600	9600	9600	9600	9600	9600	9600	9600	9600	9600	9600	9600	115200
Tape Drives -16 9trk Vendor B	—	—	6000	6000	6000	6000	6000	6000	6000	6000	6000	6000	60000
Tape Drives - 4 7trk Vendor B	4500	4500	4500	4500	4500	4500	4500	4500	4500	4500	4500	4500	54000
Disk Drives - 32 Model D	36000	36000	36000	36000	36000	36000	36000	36000	36000	36000	36000	36000	432000
Printers - 2 Model X, Vendor B	3800	3800	3800	3800	3800	3800	3800	3800	3800	3800	3800	3800	45600
Main Storage - 2 3 meg. incr.	8000	8000	8000	8000	8000	8000	8000	8000	8000	8000	8000	8000	96000
I/O Channels - 2 4 chan. incr.	9000	9000	9000	9000	9000	9000	9000	9000	9000	9000	9000	9000	108000
Card Reader/Punch - 2	2000	2000	2000	2000	2000	2000	2000	2000	2000	2000	2000	2000	24000
Burster/Decollator - 2	500	500	500	500	500	500	500	500	500	500	500	500	6000
Communications Controllers - 2	9000	9000	9000	9000	9000	9000	9000	9000	9000	9000	9000	9000	108000
Modems - 4	500	500	500	500	500	500	500	500	500	500	500	500	6000

Figure 6.3. XYZ Corporation: 19XX Equipment Budget.

Figure 6.3. XYZ Corporation: 19XX Equipment Budget. *(continued)*

Item	Jan.	Feb.	Mar.	Apr.	May	Jun.	Jul.	Aug.	Sept.	Oct.	Nov.	Dec.	Total
Terminals - 30 Model A	3750	3750	3750	3750	3750	3750	3750	3750	3750	3750	3750	3750	45000
Terminals - 30 Model C	3000	3000	3000	3000	3000	3000	3000	3000	3000	3000	3000	3000	36000
Com System	5500	5500	5500	5500	5500	5500	5500	5500	5500	5500	5500	5500	66000
Sub-Total	153150	153150	159150	159150	159150	159150	159150	159150	159150	159150	156150	156150	1891800
Add'l. Use Expense:													
Tape Drives-16 9trk, Vendor B	—	—	625	625	625	625	625	625	625	625	625	625	6250
Tape Drives-4 7trk, Vendor B	250	250	250	250	250	250	250	250	250	250	250	250	3000
Printers - 2 Model X, Vendor B	395	395	395	395	395	395	395	395	395	395	395	395	4740
Core - 2 3 meg. incr.	835	835	835	835	835	835	835	835	835	835	835	835	10020
Sub-Total	1480	1480	2105	2105	2105	2105	2105	2105	2105	2105	2105	2105	24010
Equipment Depreciation:													
Disk Drives - 37 Model D, Vendor B	27324	27324	27324	27324	27324	27324	27324	27324	27324	27324	27324	27324	327886

115

Item	Jan.	Feb.	Mar.	Apr.	May	Jun.	Jul.	Aug.	Sept.	Oct.	Nov.	Dec.	Total
Printers - 2 Model Y, Vendor A	2976-	2976-	2976-	2976-	2976-	2976-	2976-	2976-	2976-	2976-	2976-	2979-	35715-
Sub-Total	30300-	30300-	30300-	30300-	30300-	30300-	30300-	30300-	30300-	30300-	30300-	30301-	363601
Total	184930-	184930-	191555-	191555-	191555-	191555-	191555-	191555-	191555-	191555-	188555-	188556-	2279411-

Figure 6.3. XYZ Corporation: 19XX Equipment Budget. (*continued*)

116

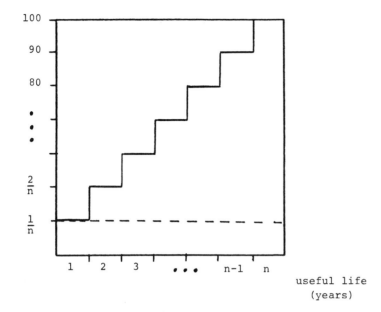

Percent
Book Value

Key:

————————— cumulative depreciation

– – – – – annual depreciation

Figure 6.4. Straight-Line Depreciation Method.

- **Straight-Line Method**
  This method divides the value of an asset into n equal parts where n (usually expressed in years) is the asset's useful life (Figure 6.4). Hence, a $113,000 asset with a useful life of 7 years and an estimated residual value of $1000 would be depreciated at the rate of $16,143 ([$113,000 − $1000] ÷ 7) per year.
  This method has the effect, obviously, of spreading depreciation tax deductions equally over n years.
- **Sum-of-the-Years-Digits Method**
  Corporations wishing to take early advantage of tax deductions or to balloon their costs early in the life of the equipment choose an accelerated depreciation method: the sum-of-the-years-digits method assumes a residual value at the end of the equimpent's life that is not depreciated. The depreciation over 7 years is calculated by multiplying the cost ($113,000) less residual value (assumed here again to be $1000) by a fraction. The denominator is constant for each period and is equal to the sum-of-the-years digits, here equal to 7 + 6 + 5 + 4 + 3 + 2 + 1 or 28. The numerator declines each period, or year, and is equal to the number of years of useful life left in the equipment. Figure 6.5 calculates how the method applies to the given example.
  Since current regulations permit the corporation to change depreciation

YEAR	COST LESS RESIDUAL VALUE	RATE	ANNUAL DEPRECIATION	ACCUMULATED DEPRECIATION AT YEAR END	BOOK VALUE AT YEAR END
1	$112,000	7/28	$28,000	$28,000	$85,000
2	112,000	6/28	24,000	52,000	61,000
3	112,000	5/28	20,000	72,000	41,000
4	112,000	4/28	16,000	88,000	25,000
5	112,000	3/28	12,000	100,000	13,000
6	112,000	2/28	8,000	108,000	5,000
7	112,000	1/28	4,000	112,000	1,000

Figure 6.5. Sum-of-the-Years-Digits Depreciation Method.

methods once, a return to the straight-line method is possible in the final year, allowing the remaining, or salvage, value to be written off.

• **Declining-Balances Method**
Another accelerated depreciation method, this technique doubles the rate used by the straight-line method but applies the rate anew each year to the remaining, as yet undepreciated residual book value. Applied to the previous 7-year example, the declining-balances method is shown in Figure 6.6.

The residual book value, or salvage value, is written off the books in the final year. In effect, the corporation returns to the straight-line method by the final year (or, if desired, earlier). The size of the residual is a function of the declared useful life of the asset. Note how the residual changes when the useful life is declared to be 5 years as in Figure 6.7.

The residual is lower and the earlier tax advantages are greater, but the duration of tax advantages is 2 years shorter.

• **Units-of-Production Method**
Another method commonly used in many industries is the "units-of-production method," which assumes that asset life is directly related to some measure of production or output volume. Two examples of units of measure that might be used are hours of operation and pages printed. The only restriction is that there be some bona fide method of establishing asset life as a direct function of the unit of measure.

As an example, if asset life were rated at 3 million units of output and

YEAR	UNDEPRECIATED BALANCE	RATE	CURRENT DEPRECIATION	CUMULATIVE DEPRECIATION	RESIDUAL BOOK VALUE
1	$113,000	0.286	$32,286	$ 32,286	$80,714
2	80,714	0.286	23,061	55,347	57,653
3	57,653	0.286	16,472	71,819	41,181
4	41,181	0.286	11,766	83,585	29,415
5	29,415	0.286	8,404	91,989	21,011
6	21,011	0.286	6,003	97,992	15,007
7	15,007	0.286	4,288	102,280	10,720

Figure 6.6. Declining-Balances Depreciation Method.

YEAR	UNDEPRECIATED BALANCE	RATE	CURRENT DEPRECIATION	CUMULATIVE DEPRECIATION	RESIDUAL BOOK VALUE
1	$113,000	0.40	$45,200	$ 45,200	$67,800
2	67,800	0.40	27,120	72,320	40,680
3	40,680	0.40	16,272	88,592	24,408
4	24,408	0.40	9,763	98,355	14,645
5	14,645	0.40	5,858	104,213	8,787

Figure 6.7. Change in Residual Value.

annual output for 7 years was as described in Figure 6.8, our $113,000 asset would be depreciated as shown below, assuming a residual of zero.

This method, then, has the effect of ballooning depreciation in the latter years, assuming a growing demand base. While this method could be of value in a revenue-producing, service bureau environment, it would be difficult to prove in any kind of audit that computing equipment had a useful life of some finite number of EXCPs, seconds of application-state CPU cycles, or units of software work.

This method, while seemingly well suited to a capacity mirror image of Chapter 2's CPU-EXCP demand-accounting method (and, perhaps, to some of the other methods), is actually quite ill suited to application against computer capacity. It would require the analyst to establish upper bounds on such items as the number of EXCPs that a given I/O drive is capable of supporting over, for example, 7 years; average 7 year multiprogramming levels as a function of disk drives, printers, etc.; the number of records that could be moved among various devices that comprise an ever changing equipment configuration; and so on. It is difficult to imagine statistics such as these being developed, much less defended, before the various regulatory agencies.

Figure 6.9 compares depreciation schedules over 7 years of the first three methods: straight-line, sum-of-the-years-digits, and declining-balances.

As stated before, these are only the most commonly used methods. The analyst is free to use whatever method he or she deems appropriate, providing the logic behind its use can be substantiated to the appropriate regulatory agen-

YEAR	UNDEPRECIATED BALANCE	PRODUCTION VOLUME	CURRENT DEPRECIATION	CUMULATIVE DEPRECIATION	RESIDUAL BOOK VALUE
1	$113,000	250K	$ 9,417	$ 9,417	$103,583
2	103,583	300K	11,300	20,717	92,283
3	92,283	375K	14,125	34,842	78,158
4	78,158	425K	16,008	50,850	62,150
5	62,150	500K	18,833	69,683	43,317
6	43,317	550K	20,717	90,400	22,600
7	22,600	600K	22,600	113,000	0

Figure 6.8. Units-of-Production Depreciation Method.

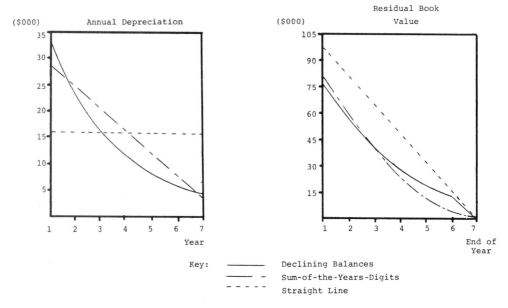

Figure 6.9. Comparison of Depreciation Methods.

cies. Often, one method is used for the firm's internal books and another for tax purposes, usually in order to gain tax leverage and perhaps to decrease the number of regulatory agencies that might have to be satisfied. But the expense of using two methods of depreciation includes the introduction of an entire second set of cost schedules and the associated ongoing internal reconciliation of both sets of books.

Figure 6.10 is the capital budget for the disks and printers described as owned in Figure 6.2a. Acquisition dates (and, hence, depreciation initiation dates) are assumed for the sake of example. Figure 6.11 is the resultant annual depreciation schedule. The total depreciation for years 19XX is presented on a monthly basis at the end of the equipment budget in Figure 6.3. Figure 6.12 summarizes the equipment budget.

The issue that naturally follows concerns the conditions that determine whether equipment should be purchased or leased.

6.5   LEASE VERSUS PURCHASE CONSIDERATIONS

Decisions of whether to lease or purchase are at the heart of the capital-budgeting process, the process of allocating funds to fixed assets, i.e., property, plant, and, for the case at hand, equipment. This process involves the evaluation of alternative investment proposals, the evaluation of associated cash flows, and the acceptance of selected proposals based on their agreement with predetermined "success" criteria. These criteria relate to specific corporate objectives of return on investment, return on assets, management of debt and liquidity ratios, etc. A wide topic with implications far beyond the management of the corporate data center, our discussion here is limited to methods of determining the relative

The table is rotated 90°. Column headers: Item ID - Serial No., Year 1, Year 2, Year 3, Year 4, 19XX (Year 5), Year 6, Year 7, Year 8, Year 9, Year 10, 11, 12, 13

Item ID – Serial No.	Year 1	Year 2	Year 3	Year 4	19XX	Year 6	Year 7	Year 8	Year 9	Year 10	11	12	13
Disk Drives Model D Vendor B Qty: 8 Ser. Nos. 1-8	584600												
Disk Drives Model D Vendor B Qty: 8 Ser. Nos. 9-16		559900											
Disk Drives Model D Vendor B Qty: 8 Ser. Nos. 17-24			590200										
Disk Drives Model D Vendor B Qty: 8 Ser. Nos. 25-32				623000									
Line Printer Model Y Vendor A Qty: 1 Ser. No. 1	115000												

Figure 6.10. XYZ Corporation: Equipment Capital Budget.

	1	2	3	4	5	6	7	8	9	10	11	12	13
Line Printer Model Y Vendor A Qty: 1 Ser. No. 2			135000—										
Total	639600—	557400—	725200—	623000—	0—	0—	0—	0—	0—	0—			

Figure 6.10. XYZ Corporation: Equipment Capital Budget. (*continued*)

Item ID – Serial No.	Year 1	Year 2	Year 3	Year 4	19XX	Year 6	Year 7	Year 8	Year 9	Year 10	Total
Disk Drives Model δ Ser. Nos. 1-8	74943 –	74943 –	74943 –	74943 –	74943 –	74943 –	74943 –	0 –	0 –	0 –	524600 –
Disk Drives Model δ Ser. Nos. 9-16	0 –	79629 –	79629 –	79629 –	79629 –	79629 –	79629 –	79626 –	0 –	0 –	557400 –
Disk Drives Model δ Ser. Nos. 17-24	0 –	0 –	84314 –	84314 –	84314 –	84314 –	84314 –	84314 –	84316 –	0 –	590300 –
Disk Drives Model δ Ser. Nos. 25-32	0 –	0 –	0 –	89000 –	89000 –	89000 –	89000 –	89000 –	89000 –	89000 –	623000 –
Sub-Total	74943 –	154572 –	238886 –	327886 –	327886 –	327886 –	327885 –	252940 –	173316 –	89000 –	2295200 –
Line Printer Model γ Ser. No. 1	16429 –	16429 –	16429 –	16429 –	16429 –	16429 –	16426 –	0 –	0 –	0 –	115000 –
Line Printer Model γ Ser. No. 2	0 –	0 –	19286 –	19286 –	19286 –	19286 –	19286 –	19286 –	19284 –	0 –	135000 –
Sub-Total	16429 –	16429 –	35715 –	35715 –	35715 –	35715 –	35712 –	19286 –	19284 –	0 –	250000 –
Total	91372 –	171001 –	274601 –	363601 –	363601 –	363601 –	363597 –	272226 –	192600 –	89000 –	2545200 –

Figure 6.11. XYZ Corporation: Annual Depreciation Schedule.

123

Rental

CPU	$690,000
9 Track Tape Drives	$175,200
7 Track Tape Drives	$ 54,000
Disk Drives	$432,000
Printers	$ 45,600
Core Incr.	$ 96,000
I/O Channels	$108,000
Card Reader/Punch	$ 24,000
Data Communications	$195,000
COM	$ 66,000
Sub-Total	$1,885,800

Add'l Use

9 Track Tape Drives	$ 6,250
7 Track Tape Drives	$ 3,000
Printers	$ 4,740
Core	$10,020
Sub-Total	$ 24,010

Depreciation

Disk Drives	$327,886
Printers	$ 35,715
Sub-Total	$ 363,601
Total	$2,273,411

Figure 6.12. XYZ Corporation 19XX Equipment Budget.

merits of equipment purchase versus equipment lease; the issues of asset, debt, and liquidity ratios are left unaddressed. It is assumed that the optimization of future cash flows is all that is at issue.

To illustrate the problem at hand, consider the previous case of the $113,000 piece of equipment. If an alternative to purchase is a 7-year lease with monthly payments of $1750, should the equipment be leased or purchased?

There are generally four methods of analysis that can be used. The reader will note that the first two are somewhat misleading and that the second two, which deal with discounted cash-flow techniques, are much preferred.

- **Payback Method**

    The payback method is based on the determination of the number of years required to recover the initial cash investment. It is calculated as the ratio

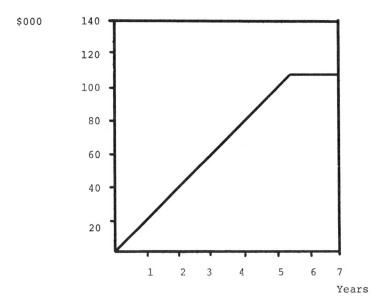

Figure 6.13. Stated Value of Investment.

of the initial fixed investment to the annual cash flows. If our alternative to a $113,000 purchase is $1750 per month on a 7-year lease, the payback period is:

$$\$113{,}000/\$1750 = 64.6 \text{ months}$$

or

5.4 years

There are problems with this method. First, it does not consider the time value of money: the method treats the last $1750 installment as equal to the first. Clearly, $1750 today has greater value than $1750 in 64 months from now. Second, this method does not consider cash flows after the payback period, as Figure 6.13 suggests. The horizontal (time) axis is considered only until the end of the payback period. So, if one $113,000 piece of equipment can be used for 84 months and another for 64.6 months, the payback method cannot identify the longer-returning investment as superior. Where the supply of capital is not unlimited, this flaw in methodology is critical.

Hence, the payback method cannot be considered adequate for determining the relative merits of lease/purchase alternatives.

- **Average Rate of Return Method**
The average rate of return method concerns the ratio of the average annual savings to average investment. In our example, if the purchase alternative is selected, net average annual savings is $21,000 (elimination of $1750 per month lease × 12) less depreciation charges. Assuming zero salvage value and 7-year straight-line depreciation, net average annual savings equals $21,000 less ($113,000 ÷ 7), or $4857 pretax and $2429 after tax. The average rate of return, then, is

$$\text{average rate of return} = \$2{,}429/\$16{,}143 = 15.1\%$$

Here again, the time value of money is not accounted for and the meaning of 15.1% is thus somewhat obscure.

- **Internal Rate of Return (IRR) Method**

This method determines the percent of annual return on an investment, given an initial cash outlay, A_o, and anticipated periodic cash inflows/outflows, A_j. In an environment where there is not an infinite amount of capital available to fund investments, the IRR method considers an investment acceptable to the corporation if its rate of return, i, is larger than that of competing investment alternatives. In simpler terms, if the corporation can choose between two investments, one with a return of 8% and the other with a return of 10%, the method recognizes that the corporation will always choose the latter, all other factors (risk, strategic objectives, etc.) being equal.

The IRR method may be expressed by the equation

$$A_o = A_1/(1 + i) + A_2/(1 + i)^2 + A_3/(1 + i)^3$$
$$+ \ldots + A_n/(1 + i)^n \quad (6.1\,a)$$

or

$$A_o = \sum_{j=1}^{n} A_j/(1 + i)^j \quad (6.1\,b)$$

where i is the discount rate (rate of interest) for a given period and n is the number of periods.

Each term,

$$A_j/(1 + i)^j$$

is merely an expression of the periodic cash flow discounted by j periods of compound interest at rate i. For example,

$$\$1000/(1 + 0.10)^2$$

represents the present value of $1000 two periods in the future at an interest rate of 10% per period, compounded at the end of each period. Thus, the above would have the value:

$$\$1000/1.21 \text{ or } \$826.45$$

For the case of multiple periodic cash flows,

$$\sum_{j=1}^{n} A_j/(1 + i)^j,$$

the calculation of A_o is exhaustive if the A_j are not all the same. Since we are dealing with purchase/lease decisions here, and since lease payments are generally uniform throughout the life of a lease, our task is much simpler. Equation 6.1 degenerates to

$$A_o = A \sum_{j=1}^{n} 1/(1 + i)^j \qquad (6.2)$$

which may be represented by

$$A_o = A \cdot (1 - [(1 + i)^{-n}]/i) \qquad (6.3)$$

where $1 - [(1 + i)^{-n}]/i$ is referred to as the discount factor.

Example 6.1

The XYZ Corporation has determined that there is sufficient future demand to justify acquisition of the $113,000 machine mentioned earlier. Funds are available to purchase the device, but there is a competing use for the funds—the firm can purchase a note guaranteeing 9.75% interest compounded annually for 7 years. Monthly payments on a seven year lease are $1750. Should XYZ purchase or lease?

Restating the problem into classic IRR exercise terminology, a change in cash flow of $1750 per month for 84 months will occur as a result of a $113,000 initial investment. Assume zero salvage value at the end of the term. Hence,

$$113,000 = 1750 \times [1 - (1 + i)^{-n}]/i$$

Solving an IRR problem is an iterative process. We guess first at $i = 10\%$ per annum. Then,

$$10\% \text{ per annum} = .7974\% \text{ per month and}$$
$$\$113,000 \stackrel{?}{=} 1750 \times [1 - 1.007974^{-84}]/0.007974$$
$$\stackrel{?}{=} 1750 \times [1 - .513158]/0.007974$$
$$or \ 1750 \times 61.053$$
$$= \$106,843, \text{ less than } \$113,000.$$

Similarly, we try 9% and 8% per annum (see Figure 6.14).
The precise value can be obtained by interpolation:

9%	$109,989
i	113,000
8%	113,288

$$(8 - i)/(8 - 9) = \$288/3299$$
$$i = 8 + \$288/3299, \text{ or } 8.09\%$$

Since purchase yields only 8.09% per annum, the decision here would be to lease the equipment and invest in the 9.75% note.

i (ANNUAL)	i (MONTHLY)	DISCOUNT FACTOR	CASH FLOW PRESENT VALUE
10%	.7974%	61.053	$106,843
9%	.7207%	62.851	109,989
8%	.6434%	64.736	113,288

Figure 6.14. Calculation of IRR.

Example 6.2

Assume the same as above but the monthly lease payout is $1850. Should the equipment be leased or purchased?

Referring to the discount factor schedule developed in the Example 6.1, we check the present value at 10%.

$$PV = \$1850 \times 61.053 = \$112,948$$

Interpolating, i, the return from investing $113,000 in the equipment is found to be:

10	$112,948
i	113,000
9	116,269

$$i = 10 - 52/3321, \text{ or } 9.98\%$$

The decision is slightly in favor of purchase.

It should be understood that other factors can significantly alter the final outcome. If, for example, the cost of funds to the corporation is 13%, the fact that 9.98% is slightly greater than 9.75% is irrelevant. This leads to the next discounted cash-flow technique, net present value.

- **Net Present Value (NPV) Method**

  Net present value is similar to IRR in that it discounts future cash flows so that immediate capital expenditures (cash outflows) can be directly compared to future cash inflows (or, in our case, the avoidance of future cash outflows in the form of lease payments). The method can be expressed as an equation of the form:

$$NPV = A_o + A_1/(1 + i) + A_2/(1 + i)^2 + A_3/(1 + i)^3 \quad (6.4a)$$
$$+ \ldots + A_n/(1 + i)^n$$

or

$$NPV = A_o + \sum_{j=1}^{n} A_j/(1 + i)^j \quad (6.4b)$$

All the terms on the right side of Equations 6.4a and 6.4b are the same as in Equations 6.1a and 6.1b. The difference between NPV and IRR is that rather than search as we did in the IRR to determine what rate of return the investment offers, the NPV tests whether i, the minimum rate of return acceptable to the corporation, results in an acceptable discounted cash flow, i.e., a discounted cash inflow with a present value large enough to offset the initial cash outflow, the capital investment A_o.

Example 6.3

Our $113,000 piece of equipment can be leased from the vendor for 4 years at $3000 per month. The minimal acceptable return to XYZ is 15%. All capital is depreciated by the declining balances method; the equipment has a useful life of 7 years. Should financing be by lease or purchase? Assume that XYZ can sell the equipment for the remaining book value at the end of the 4-year period.

The final cash inflow would result from the sale of the equipment at the end of the 4-year period. The remaining book value is calculated as:

YEAR	INITIAL BOOK VALUE	CURRENT DEPRECIATION	REMAINING BOOK VALUE
1	$113,000	$32,286	$80,714
2	80,714	23,061	57,653
3	57,653	16,472	41,181
4	41,181	11,766	29,415

Figure 6.15. Depreciation Schedule.

Then,

$$
\begin{aligned}
\text{NPV} &= -\$113,000 + 3,000 \times [1 - (1.0117149)^{-48}]/0.0117149 \\
&\quad + 29,415/(1.15)^4 \\
&= -\$113,000 + 3,000 \times .4282468/.0117149 + 29,415/1.7490063 \\
&= -\$113,000 + 3,000 \times 36.555733 + 16,818 \\
&= -\$113,000 + 109,667 + 16,818 \\
&= +\$13,485
\end{aligned}
$$

Since the discounted future cash inflows exceed the initial $113,000 cash outlay, the correct decision is purchase.

Example 6.4

The ABC Leasing Company is much more experienced in dealing in the used computer equipment market and believes it can sell the equipment discussed in the previous example for $35,000 after 4 years. Assuming it too seeks a 15% return, what is the minimum monthly payment it can offer XYZ on a 4-year lease? How does this affect XYZ's decision?

In order to obtain the solution, we set the NPV equal to zero to obtain the cutoff point and solve for A, the minimum monthly lease payment ABC can offer.

$$0 = -\$113,000 + 36.556 \, A + 35,000/(1.15)^4$$

or

$$36.556\ A = \$113,000 - 20,011$$
$$= \$92,989$$
$$A = \$2,544$$

Thus, ABC's lease would be $3,000 − $2,544, or $456 cheaper per month.

The effect on XYZ's decision can be calculated two ways. One is to reexecute the *NPV* equation, Equation 6.4. This would yield:

$$NPV = -\$113,000 + 2,544 \times 36.556 + 16,818$$
$$= -\$113,000 + 92,997 + 16,818$$
$$= -\$3,185$$

The negative sign indicates the present value of future cash inflows is less than the $113,000 purchase price. The decision has changed to lease.

The other method of calculating the effect upon the decision is merely to apply the discount factor to the difference between the two monthly lease rates and subtract the result from the original NPV:

$$\$3,000 - 2,544 = \$456$$
$$\$456 \times 36.555733 = \$16,670$$
$$\$13,485 - \$16,670 = -\$3,185$$

as before.

6.6 NET PRESENT VALUE DECISIONS UNDER UNCERTAINTY

The preceding section assumed perfect knowledge of the future. In particular, it assumed firm knowledge of the decision criterion (a minimum acceptable return of, e.g. 15% per annum) and of the longevity of the investment (such as a period of 4 years, no more, no less). Such perfect foresight rarely exists, and the effect of such assumptions can be significant. A better approach is to modify the standard results by relating to expected values. The technique is the same as that for dealing with uncertainty in any other decision model. Figures 6.16 and 6.17 illustrate how this is accomplished.

Some process is subject to external influences that can affect its final outcome or payoff. Let these influences, which need not be mutually exclusive, be termed A and B. The result is a set of outcomes, one for each of four states:

EVENT STATE	DESCRIPTION
1	Neither A nor B
2	A but not B
3	B but not A
4	Both A and B

For the sake of example, assume the probability of existence of each state and the associated outcome (payoff) to be:

EVENT STATE	PROBABILITY OF OCCURRENCE	OUTCOME	EXPECTED VALUE
1	60%	10	6.0
2	10%	11	1.1
3	20%	3	0.6
4	10%	7	0.7
	100%		8.4

Figure 6.16. Expected Outcome.

Hence, even though event state 1 is significantly more probable than any other state, a decision based solely on the outcome of state 1 would be grossly misleading.

Example 6.5

Assume the same $1850 monthly lease payment as in Example 6.2. Also assume a 50% chance that the time value of funds will be 9.5% annually (0.759% monthly) for the

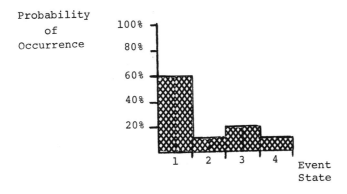

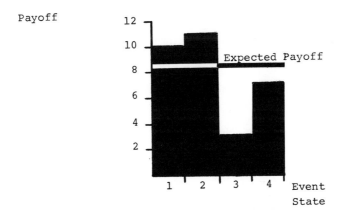

Figure 6.17. Determinaton of Expected Payoff.

entire 7 years and a 50% chance it will increase to 11.0% for the last 6 years. Is the decision to purchase or lease?

The problem here is to calculate

$$NPV = A\left[\sum_{n=1}^{12} 1/(1 + 0.00759)^n + \sum_{n=13}^{84} 1/(1 + 0.00873)^n\right]$$

To overcome the difficulty of calulating this exhaustively, we recognize

$$\sum_{n=13}^{84} 1/(1 + i)^n = \sum_{n=1}^{84} 1/(1 + i)^n - \sum_{n=1}^{12} 1/(1 + i)^n$$

Since 1.11 annualized equals 1.00873 monthly,

$$\sum_{n=1}^{12} 1/(1 + 0.00873)^{12} = [1 - (1 + 0.00873)^{-12}]/0.00873$$

$$\text{or } 11.346$$

and,

$$\sum_{n=1}^{84} 1/(1 + 0.00873)^{84} = [1 - (1 + 0.00873)^{-84}]/0.00873$$

$$\text{or } 59.354$$

Therefore,

$$\sum_{n=13}^{84} 1/(1 + 0.00873)^n = 59.354 - 11.346$$

$$= 48.008$$

$$\sum_{n=1}^{12} 1/(1.00759)^n = 11.428$$

So, for the case where i increases to 11.0%,

$$NPV = A_o + A \times \text{net discount factor}$$
$$= -\$113,000 + A \times (11.428 - 48.008)$$
$$= -\$3,004$$

which is a lease indicator. For $i = 9.5\%$ for the full 84 months, the discount factor is 61.943 and,

$$NPV = -\$113,000 + \$1,850 \times 61.943$$
$$= +\$1,595$$

which by itself is a purchase indicator. Finally, the expected value of the NPV is:

$$NPV_e = 0.5 \times (-\$3,044) + 0.5 \times (+\$1,595)$$
$$= -\$725$$

The net decision is slightly in favor of purchase.

Example 6.6

Assume that our $113,000 piece of equipment is to support a particular application, and that XYZ plans to replace the application with another in 4 years to accommodate a forecast change in the marketplace. The equipment will be obsolete in the changed marketplace, hence the 4-year lease in Example 6.4. XYZ has failed to recognize there is a 20% chance the anticipated market change will be delayed 1 year and a 10% chance it will be delayed 2 years. For simplicity, assume monthly lease payments can continue unchanged after the initial 4 years. Did XYZ make the correct decision in example 6.4?

If XYZ can still sell the equipment for the remaining book value, this is recalculated as:

YEAR	INITIAL BOOK VALUE	CURRENT DEPRECIATION	REMAINING BOOK VALUE
5	$29,415	$8,404	$21,011
6	21,011	6,603	15,008

Figure 6.18. Depreciation Schedule.

The NPV for year 5 is then calculated as:

$$NPV_{60} = -\$113,000 + 2,544\,[1 - (1.0117149)^{-60}]/0.0117149$$
$$+ 21,011/(1.15)^{60}$$
$$= -\$113,000 + 109,194 + 10,446$$
$$= +\$6,640$$

Similarly for 6 years,

$$NPV_{72} = +\$16,763$$

The expected value of the NPV is then:

$$NPV_e = 0.7 \times (-3,185) + 0.2(+6,440) + 0.1(+16,763)$$
$$= +\$774$$

Thus, XYZ's original decision to lease was incorrect.

The uncertainty surrounding the variables upon which purchase/lease decisions are based are generally somewhat more complex than in the preceding case, reflecting factors such as investment tax credit applicability, future tax positions resulting from either market conditions or other corporate write-offs, interest rate volatility, and the effects of future economic cycles. But these factors must be addressed for the capital budgeting process to be adequate. Fortunately for the data processing manager, the corporate controller generally addresses these issues, and the resulting policies are dictated to all other corporate departments.

With the purchase/lease decisions made and the resulting depreciation schedule established (Figure 6.11 and the latter part of Figure 6.3), we return to complete the expense budgeting process.

6.7   LABOR BUDGETS

The labor budget categorizes the entire workforce according to the equipment category, for direct labor, or the staff function, for indirect and supervisory functions. As with the equipment budget, the labor budget has the purposes of describing expenses, facilitating the development of unit processing costs, and setting up a structure to control variances from budget. Figure 6.19 provides an example of a labor expense budget based on the staff described by Figure 6.2*b*. In order to simplify matters, all supervisory personnel are listed at about $17K, all operators at about $14K, clerks at about $11K, staff analysts at about $20K, and secretaries at about $10K. Nine percent raises are scattered throughout. Benefits, at 30%, are lumped at the bottom for the sake of simplicity.

6.8   SUPPLY BUDGETS

Figure 6.20 describes the final component of our operating budget, the portion that describes supplies and other miscellaneous items. These include postage and shipping, telephone expenses, insurance, local transportation, business trips, staff-related education, etc.

6.9   OPERATING BUDGETS SUMMARIZED

Figure 6.21 presents the operating budget as a simple four-line summary of its three major components: equipment, labor, and supplies. As with each of the components, we note the bottom line can vary from month to month. It will become apparent in the next chapter that this factor presents problems when attempting to charge-out 100% of all expenses on a monthly basis, as many DPers are wont to do. If the reader considers expense accruals, lags at month end from invoice receipt to check issuance, advantages of prepayment of certain expenses, and payment arrangements such as quarterly-in-arrears, it becomes clear that linking monthly expense recovery to the corporation's books can be misleading. Therefore, as one considers the various components of the operating budget, it is important to maintain the distinction between this, a bookkeeping function, and the related cost-accounting implications. In other words, the budget, and even its variance tracking mechanisms, exists to guide, not to describe rigid "laws" of expense, income, and, therefore, cost.

   Figure 6.22 restates the budget according to the structure set forth in Figure 6.1. We note how direct costs account for only 14.6% of the total budget, 16.1% if one considers expense only (i.e., if depreciation is not considered). And variable costs, the sum of direct plus variable indirect, account for under 25% of the total. Since these ratios are markedly different from those of the more commonplace, i.e., more labor- and materials-intensive production lines, there is often a great deal of initial reluctance on the part of senior and budget man-

Figure 6.19. XYZ Corporation: 19XX Labor Budget.

Item	Jan.	Feb.	Mar.	Apr.	May	Jun.	Jul.	Aug.	Sept.	Oct.	Nov.	Dec.	Total
Consoles													
operators	7000	7100	7100	7300	7300	7300	7400	7500	7500	7500	7500	7600	88100
supervisors	4250	4250	4380	4380	4380	4380	4380	4380	4650	4650	4650	4650	53380
Tape Drives													
operators	5800	6100	8550	8550	8550	8550	8550	8550	8550	8550	8550	8550	97700
Supervisors	4380	4380	4380	4380	4380	4570	4570	4510	4650	4650	4650	4650	54230
Tape Library													
clerks	5520	5520	5520	5660	5660	5820	5820	5820	6000	6200	6200	6200	69280
Printers													
operators	3500	3600	3700	3800	3800	3800	3800	3800	3800	3800	3800	3800	45000
supervisors	4250	4250	4250	4250	4500	4500	4650	4650	4650	4650	4650	4650	53900
Bursting/Decoiliating operators	3500	3500	3700	3700	3700	3700	3700	3700	3700	3700	3700	3800	44100
Com operator	1150	1270	1270	1270	1270	1270	1270	1270	1270	1270	1270	1270	15120
Materials Assembly clerks	6400	6820	6600	6700	6800	6900	7000	7000	7000	7000	7000	7000	81900
Messenger Services clerks	5500	5500	5500	5660	5660	5820	5820	5820	6000	6000	6000	6000	69280
Capacity/Performance Planning analyst	1650	1650	1650	1650	1650	1800	1800	1800	1800	1800	1800	1800	20850

	1	2	3	4	5	6	7	8	9	10	11	12	13
Software Maint. & Development analysts	8300-	8460-	8620-	8780-	9050-	9100-	9100-	9100-	9100-	9100-	9100-	9100-	106910-
Budgeting & Costing analysts	3330-	3330-	3330-	3480-	3480-	3480-	3630-	3650-	3630-	3630-	3630-	3630-	43210-
Production Manager	2520-	2750-	2750-	2750-	2750-	2750-	2750-	2750-	2750-	2750-	2750-	2750-	32750-
Staff Services Manager	2520-	2750-	2750-	2750-	2750-	2750-	2750-	2750-	2750-	2750-	2750-	2750-	32750-
secretary	850-	915-	915-	915-	915-	915-	915-	915-	915-	915-	915-	915-	10915-
Data Center Mgt. Manager	3300-	3300-	3300-	3300-	3300-	3300-	3300-	3300-	3300-	3300-	3300-	3300-	39300-
secretaries (3)	2520-	2750-	2750-	2750-	2750-	2750-	2750-	2750-	2750-	2750-	2750-	2750-	32750-
Sub-Total	75860-	71855-	80895-	81495-	82645-	83395-	83395-	83995-	84765-	84765-	84765-	84965-	989725-
Benefits @ 20%	23758-	23358-	24268-	24577-	24724-	25019-	25168-	25199-	25430-	25430-	25430-	25489-	296916-
Total	98618-	101311-	105163-	106502-	107439-	108414-	109063-	109194-	110195-	110195-	110195-	110454-	1286643-

Figure 6.19. XYZ Corporation: 19XX Labor Budget. *(continued)*

Item	Jan.	Feb.	Mar.	Apr.	May	Jun.	Jul.	Aug.	Sept.	Oct.	Nov.	Dec.	Total
Printer Flatpack	10000	10000	10000	10000	10000	10000	10000	10000	10000	10000	10000	10000	120000
Printer Special forms	5000	5000	5000	5000	5000	5000	5000	5000	5000	5000	5000	5000	60000
Printer Ribbons	50	50	50	50	50	50	50	50	50	50	50	50	600
Tape Drives Tapes	200	200	200	200	200	200	200	200	200	200	200	200	2400
Tape Drives Cleaning Agents	25	25	25	25	25	25	25	25	25	25	25	25	300
COM Film Developer	2000	2000	2000	2000	2000	2000	2000	2000	2000	2000	2000	2000	24000
Computer Ops. Power	800	800	800	800	800	800	800	800	800	800	800	800	9600
Insurance	2000	0	0	2000	0	0	2000	0	0	2000	0	0	8000
Telephone	300	300	300	300	300	300	300	300	300	300	300	300	3600
Postal Fees	150	100	100	150	100	100	150	100	100	150	100	100	1400
Travel	750	0	0	750	0	0	750	0	0	750	0	0	3000
Entertainment	100	100	100	100	100	100	100	100	100	100	100	100	1200
Recruiting	0	0	2500	0	0	0	0	0	0	0	0	0	2500
Premises	2000	2000	2000	2000	2000	2000	2000	2000	2000	2000	2000	2000	24000
Education	1000	0	0	0	0	0	1000	0	0	0	0	0	2000
Other	250	250	250	250	250	250	250	250	250	250	250	250	3000
Staff Services Mgt. Telephone	300	300	300	300	300	300	300	300	300	300	300	300	3600
Postal Fees	50	50	50	50	50	50	50	50	50	50	50	50	600
Travel	1000	0	0	1000	0	0	1000	0	0	1000	0	0	4000

Figure 6.20. XYZ Corporation: 19XX Supply Budget.

	1	2	3	4	5	6	7	8	9	10	11	12	13
Entertainment	100	100	100	100	100	100	100	100	100	100	100	100	1200
Premises	600	600	600	600	600	600	600	600	600	600	600	600	7200
Education	600	0	0	600	0	0	600	0	0	600	0	0	3600
Other	100	100	100	100	100	100	100	100	100	100	100	100	1200
Data Center Mgt.													
Telephone	150	150	150	150	150	150	150	150	150	150	150	150	1800
Postal Fees	25	25	25	25	25	25	25	25	25	25	25	25	300
Travel	1000	0	0	1000	0	0	1000	0	0	1000	0	0	4000
Entertainment	150	150	150	150	150	150	150	150	150	100	150	150	1800
Premises	100	100	100	0	100	100	100	100	100	100	100	100	200
Education	1000	0	0	0	0	0	1000	0	0	0	0	0	2200
Other	200	200	200	200	200	200	200	200	200	200	200	200	2400
Total	30000	23600	25100	28800	23600	22600	30000	22600	22600	28000	22600	22600	279300

Figure 6.20. XYZ Corporation: 19XX Supply Budget. *(continued)*

138

Item	Jan.	Feb.	Mar.	Apr.	May	Jun.	Jul.	Aug.	Sept.	Oct.	Nov.	Dec.	Total
Equipment	184430-	184430-	191055-	191055-	191055-	191055-	191055-	191055-	191055-	191055-	188055-	188056-	2279411
Labor	98618-	101211-	105163	106502-	107439-	108414-	109063	109194-	110195-	110195-	110195-	110951-	1286643
Supplies	28000-	22600-	23100-	26000-	22600-	22600-	28000-	20600-	22600-	26000-	22600-	20600-	299320
Total	311048-	306041-	319318-	323557-	319094-	322069-	328118-	320849-	323850-	327250-	318850-	319710-	3865354

Figure 6.21. XYZ Corporation: 19XX Budget Summary.

Direct Costs			
Direct Labor			
Console operators	88100		
Tape operators	97200		
Printer operators	45000		
Bursting/Decollating operators	44100		
COM operator	15120		
Benefits	86857		
Sub-Total		376377	
Direct Materials			
Printer Abtpack	120000		
Printer special forms	60000		
Printer ribbons	600		
Tapes	2400		
COM film & developer	24000		
Sub-Total		207000	
Total Direct Costs			583377
Indirect Costs			
Variable			
Indirect Labor.			
Materials Assembly	81900		
Messenger Services	69280		
Tape Library	69280		
Benefits	66139		

Figure 6.22. XYZ Corporation: 19XX Operating Budget.

Figure 6.22. XYZ Corporation: 19XX Operating Budget. (*continued*)

Indirect Materials		
Power	300 –	
Equipment –	9600 –	
Add'l. Use	24010 –	
Sub-Total		320209 –
Fixed		
Equipment Rental	189,800 –	
Equipment Depreciation	363601 –	
Supervisory Salaries	161,310 –	
Staff Services	169910 –	
Production Mgt.	33750 –	
Staff Mgt.	43665 –	
Work Center Mgt.	72250 –	
Benefits	143922 –	
Insurance	8000 –	
Premises	32400 –	
Postal Fees	2300 –	
Telephone	9000 –	
Travel	1000 –	
Entertainment	4300 –	
Recruitment	2500 –	
Education	6400 –	
Other	6600 –	
Sub-Total		296468 –
Total Indirect Costs		328,977 –
Grand Total		3865354 –

agement to accept them as "good" or as indicating a well-controlled operation. This is unfortunate and generally due to a lack of familiarity of the effect of automation (especially computer) projects.

6.10 SUMMARY

We see, then, that the purpose of the operating budget, in addition to the usual objectives of establishing expense plans and variance controls, is to establish a framework from which one can determine costs of each of the services offered by the data center. This framework is used for any of three reasons: (1) only as a source for passing on costs as charges to users; (2) as a basis for developing a service pricing scheme; or (3) as a mechanism to facilitate demonstrating to management how data center expenses are translated into services specific users receive.

While the bookkeeping portion of expense budgeting is simple, those items associated with capital budgeting are not. One must:

1. Choose between straight-line and accelerated depreciation;
2. Decide whether to establish a second set of books for tax purposes and constantly reconcile with the original set established for expense control; and
3. Perform complex purchase/lease decisions to determine whether newly acquired capacity should be expensed or depreciated.

We next consider chargeout methods for allocating expense and depreciation costs to specific users according to the services they receive.

7
CHARGEOUT—COSTS VERSUS PRICES

Chapter 7 examines the differences between costing and pricing, both in terms of definition and of meeting objectives related to user behavior and perception. While the mechanics of chargeout rate development are provided with respect to accounting techniques, structuring and implementing chargeout software is considered a systems issue and is not within the scope of this text.

7.1 INTRODUCTION

At the very least, computer chargeout, or "chargeback," as it is sometimes called, should accomplish three objectives:

- Allocate portions of the budget to specific segments of demand according to some preset strategy;
- Enable stricter control over the expense budget as a function of demand and, therefore, enhanced ability to manage expenses down; and
- Facilitate better communications with senior management.

The first two points will become more apparent with the remainder of this chapter. The final point, communications, is probably strategically as important. Since the costs of data processing, its implementation and operation, are often the least understood portion of the overall production cycle to senior, nontechnical managers, there is usually a good deal of frustration associated with their attempts to manage the data processing corner of the corporation. They do not always understand the technology involved nor can they communicate in the semitechnical jargon they hear from their data processing subordinates. They do, however, understand budgets, and they do understand the translation of budgets into cost/price strategies. And the ability to match the structure of data processing demand and budget accounting to that of the rest of the corporation does much to bridge the communications gap that traditionally exists between data processing and senior management.

Hence, good demand/budget-accounting systems and good chargeback systems have organizational as well as economic benefits.

7.2 COSTS VERSUS PRICES

Most data processing charging schemes merely separate total expense into a finite number of segments and then divide by an estimate of future activity,

EXCPs, I/O work, connect hours, etc. Since these activity measures do not necessarily relate to demand (as we saw in Chapter 2), the segmentation of total expense does not necessarily relate logically to capacity. As an example, consider a service bureau's changing structure of CPU seconds, connect time, and tape mounts. All the data communications gear is usually lumped under connect time and the I/O costs (tape drives, disk drives, and printed output) are lumped somewhere else, most likely under the CPU. In such a case, the job that takes two tape drives for 10 minutes is probably treated in the same manner as the one that takes five drives for 1 hour. And if both jobs utilize exactly the same amount of CPU time, they are probably charged identically, even though they obviously require different amounts of resources. The same would be true for the chargeout structure where I/Os are counted. If two jobs used the identical amount of CPU time and passed the identical number of I/Os, even though they may require vastly different allocation of peripherals resources, they again are probably charged identically.

This leads to the pivotal point in chargeback—the difference between costing and pricing and the circumstances under which each should be used. Webster defines cost and price as the following:

Cost: the amount . . . paid for something.
Price: the terms for which something is done; the cost at which something is obtained.

That there is a principle difference between these terms is probably the least understood, yet most important, aspect of computer chargeout. Costs are, by definition, the expenses suffered by the data center in obtaining the equipment, labor, supplies, etc., required to service demand. Prices are whatever revenue structure the data center believes is acceptable to its user community. They need not relate directly to either the budget or demand. Note that there is nothing inherently superior about chargeout as a function of cost or about chargeout as a function of price. What matters is that both corporate management and the data center agree on a preset strategy. For example, if the strategy is to provide services within the corporation as efficiently as possible, the data center will want to adopt a structure that matches elements of demand to specific segments of the operating budget. If, on the other hand, the corporation's strategy is to compete effectively in the data processing services market, it is required that the structure of the chargeback system should match the user community's perception of what a fair and equitable charge should be while providing the required profit margin.

But regardless of what the circumstances are, all such strategies require a projection of future corporate demand (or market penetration) as well as of the resulting investments in equipment, supplies, etc. Restated, it is dangerous for the data center to construct a pricing scheme without first understanding its cost structure, a lesson too many service bureaus have learned the hard way. To facilitate this understanding, the price equals cost chargeback structure is considered first. The issue to be addressed is how one combines corporate knowledge of periodic (most often annual) expenses and of demand to develop a cost structure.

7.3   COST CHARGEBACK—DEFINITION

Fundamental to the construction of a cost chargeback system is the determination of exactly what comprises a cost. As stated previously, most data processing "costing" systems merely separate total expenses into a finite number of segments and then divide by total activity—CPU seconds, EXCPs, I/O work units, etc. The inconsistencies of this approach can best be illustrated with an example.

Example 7.1

Harold is a computer cost analyst for the XYZ Corporation. Everywhere Harold has gone he has seen jobs charged according to the number of CPU seconds and I/Os consumed. Last year, a new system was implemented and, as forecast by the systems manager, it consumes 1000 CPU seconds per day and 20,000 disk I/Os. Using XYZ's charging algorithm of 5¢ per CPU second and 0.2¢ per disk I/O, Harold informed the corporation that the estimated monthly charge of operating the new system would be $1100 for CPU and $880 for disk, or $23,760 per year. The corporation decided the system just met their minimal return on investment criteria. Did Harold create a cost or a price?

Actually, Harold created a disaster. The new system provides on-line, but infrequent, access to a large data base. The systems manager, constantly aware of management's romance with instant access to corporate financial data, is the person responsible for XYZ's purchase of that last bank of disk drives in Figure 6.11 that is resulting in annual depreciation expenses of $89,000. The quoted expense of $23,760 associated with ongoing operation of the system was grossly understated and management had no means of making a rational cost/benefit development decision. Harold is now unemployed.

Unfortunately, the example is not as exaggerated as it seems when taken into the context of being just another application implemented in a medium-scale computer utility. It highlights an important fact:

> If cost is the amount of expense the data center incurs as a result of acquiring equipment from a vendor, the unit of cost is determined by what the vendor sells.

For example, if XYZ paid a vendor $623,000 for a huge bucket of disk EXCPs, its cost then would have been so many cents for each consumable EXCP. And, in fact, everything from the vendor's brochure to his standard lease or purchase agreement would state everything in terms of EXCPs. And everyone in the data center would fondly remember the day when they received delivery of their first bucket of a trillion EXCPs only to find it leaked and left a trail of little EXCPs all the way back to the factory.

But, obviously, XYZ did not buy EXCPs, they bought disk drives. And, as Chapters 2 and 3 stated, no job uses EXCPs, it only executes EXCPs as it uses allocated disk space. So the unit of cost is disk space allocated. In fact, since all hardware is allocated (which, by the way, is the reason the units-of-production depreciation method of Chapter 6 fails for computer equipment), the units of cost are expressed in terms of allocation. There is one exception to this rule in practice—namely, if there is no simple method of measuring allocation of a device. This is somewhat true for the case of CPU charges where the direct measure from most job-accounting systems is CPU minutes or seconds. However, since the measure of allocation would be the percent CPU allocated multiplied by the job elapsed time or

$$(CPU\ seconds/job\ elapsed\ time) \times job\ elapsed\ time$$

the case is trivial. A second case exists for some printers, when elapsed time for printing is not always captured. But since paper costs often are a significant portion of total printing costs, entities such as lines of print or page counts often provide a good approximation of expenses due to printing.

In general, though, it is possible to identify budgeted expenses of processing, i.e., to identify the true cost of computer processing, for approximately 75% of the total operating budget. At that rate, even if one made a 40% error on a job's use of the remaining cost/production factors, the total error in job cost calculations would not exceed 10%. And since several jobs of any one user probably have somewhat compensating errors, the total error to that user is often small. Be that as it may, there are methods for improving even this level of error, specifically, unbundling staff support costs from other computer processing charges. More about this later.

7.4 DEVELOPMENT OF BUNDLED COST ACCOUNTS

The actual development of unit costs presupposes the identification of categories to be measured, the existence of an operating budget for some fiscal period, and a reasonably accurate forecast of demand for that fiscal period. The first example dealt with here is that of "bundled costs," i.e., when support or ancillary services are lumped with the core computer processing services. A more accurate approach, unbundled costs, will be addressed next after the basic costing process is understood.

The categories, or indices, to be measured for chargeout purposes are identical to those included in the definition of demand. If they were not, chargeout categories would not be the same as the capacity categories that earlier chapters have defined as being identical to demand indices. For the operating budget developed in Chapter 6, these indices will be taken to be: CPU seconds, tape drive allocation, disk drive allocation, and pages of print.

In order to develop unit costs for each of these four prime indices, it is necessary to regroup equipment, supplies, and staff. Expenses for items other than these four, such as channels or controllers, will be folded into the prime indices. This is in agreement with the manner in which capacity and demand are treated by the Allocation Method described earlier. The problem facing the cost analyst is how to distribute these other costs accurately. The reader should be aware that, as with any cost-accounting exercise for any other industrial setting, there are a certain number of value judgments that will have to be made that will have some effect (although minor) on the final outcome. The small degree of the effect should become apparent as the exercise proceeds.

Figure 7.1 represents a first cut at determining the annual cost for CPU.

The reduction of the CPU equipment account by an amount equal to the additional I/O channels assumes the basic CPUs are equipped with 4-channel boxes and the increment described in Figure 6.3 brings the total number of channels to 8 per CPU. These costs are being removed from the CPU account and will be redistributed to the three I/O accounts, tape, disk, and printer, to reflect the fact that the function of channels is to transport data to and from I/O devices. One might object by citing the fact that, were it not for channels, the CPU would have nothing with which to compute, and, therefore, a portion of the channel cost should, indeed, be allocated to the CPU account. A retort would be that the data the CPU acts on is physically stored in main storage, or other I/O buffers, and then accessed by the CPU. The arguments go on forever in much the same manner two accountants might discuss any other time and materials issue. What is important, however, is that whichever cost allocation assumption is used should be rational and supportable, be consistent with generally accepted accounting practices, and be consistent with other assumptions made in other parts of the accounting process.

The size of the reduction, $108,000 is also a value judgment. The effect of bundling upon vendor charges, of including the price of the first four channels in the price of the CPU, is unknown. The assumption that this contribution was the full $108,000 value of the additional channels is probably not correct, yet probably not less correct than other assumptions. The selection of a value is at the cost analyst's discretion.

The reader will note that, unlike channels, main-storage costs have been added to the CPU account. Here it has been recognized that no job can make use of the CPU without utilizing main storage. In a virtual environment, that is, when the computer uses a virtual operating system, it is sometimes difficult to measure the precise amount of real storage utilized by any one job. Figure 7.1 reflects this by folding main storage costs into the CPU account. In doing

EQUIPMENT TYPE		ANNUAL EXPENSE
CPU	$690,000	
Less two 4-channel blocks	(108,000)	
Subtotal		$582,000
Additional core-lease	$ 96,000	
Additional core-add'l use	10,020	
Subtotal		106,020
Total		$688,020

Figure 7.1. CPU Account (Partial).

so, the assumption is made that usage of real main storage is roughly proportional to CPU usage, i.e., "big" jobs using large amounts of CPU cycles are apt to use much more main storage than "little" jobs using little CPU. In practice, this is often the case. If it were not, one of two states would exist. The first would be that all jobs require nearly the same amount of real main storage, in which case the computer in effect would be operating as a real, not virtual system. Main storage would then probably become one of the key measures or indices and would be cost accounted on an equal basis as CPU. The second state would be that small CPU consumers require significantly more main storage than large jobs using large amounts of CPU. Generally, this is either an irrational assumption or an indication that the sector of demand comprising large jobs coincidently is the sector that results in a great deal of paging. But paging is a performance issue, and as indicated in earlier chapters, the distinction must be maintained between capacity/demand issues, including chargeout, and performance issues.

Allocating labor and other expenses is a somewhat less straightforward process. While some of these expenses are obviously directly related to one index or another, others are not. For example, although 100% of the console operator's salary certainly should be allocated to the CPU, it is unclear what proportion of the production manager's salary should be allocated to the CPU. The distribution of other expenses such as postal fees, insurance, etc. is even less straightforward. The best course of action, given this type of problem, is to proceed as far as possible with each chargeout index and then consider the remaining items.

Concluding the first cut at developing the CPU account, obvious contributions due to labor (including benefits) and supplies are added to equipment.

Equipment	$688,020	
Labor		
Console operators	114,530	
Supervisors		
	69,394	
Supplies	—	
Total		$871,944

Figure 7.2. CPU Account (Partial).

Figure 7.3 describes the equipment contribution to the 9-Track Tape Drive Account.

Note that the 7-track tape drives that generally have specialized uses, have been omitted and will be handled separately. Accordingly, of the six channels assumed dedicated to servicing tapes, 32/36 or 5.3 are allocated to 9-track drives. Labor and supplies have been calculated in a similar manner. Figures 7.4 and 7.5 are the corresponding partial accounts for disk drives and printers.

Here again, channel allocations are assumed for the sake of example. The

	ANNUAL EXPENSE
EQUIPMENT	
Tape Drives—Rental	$175,200
Tape Drives—Add'l Use	6,250
I/O Channels (5.3)	71,550
Subtotal	$253,000
LABOR	
Operators	112,320
Supervisors	62,435
Subtotal	174,755
SUPPLIES	
Tapes	2,133
Cleaning Agents	267
Subtotal	2,400
Total	$430,155

Figure 7.3. 9-Track Tape Drive Account (Partial).

	ANNUAL EXPENSE
EQUIPMENT	
Disk Drives—Leased	$432,000
Disk Drives—Depreciated	327,886
I/O Channels (8)	108,000
Subtotal	$867,886
LABOR	
—	—
SUPPLIES	
—	—
Total	$867,886

Figure. 7.4. Disk Drive Account (Partial).

	ANNUAL EXPENSE
EQUIPMENT	
Printers—Lease	$ 45,600
Printers—Depreciation	35,715
Printers—Add'l Use	4,740
I/O Channels (2)	27,000
Subtotal	$113,055
LABOR	
Operators	58,500
Supervisors	70,070
Subtotal	128,570
SUPPLIES	
Flatrack	120,000
Ribbons	600
Subtotal	120,600
Total	$362,225

Figure 7.5. Printer Account (Partial).

	ANNUAL EXPENSE	
EQUIPMENT		
Tape Drives—Rental	$54,000	
Tape Drives—Add'l Use	3,000	
I/O Channels (0.7)	9,450	
Subtotal		$66,450
LABOR		
Operators	14,040	
Supervisors	7,804	
Subtotal		21,844
SUPPLIES		
Tapes	267	
Cleaning Agents	33	
Subtotal		300
Total		$88,594

Figure 7.6. 7-Track Tape Drive Account (Partial).

reader will note that the sum of the preceding accounts falls far short of including all equipment, labor, and supplies. Thus, we now need to determine how to handle the remainder. This is consonant with the Allocation Demand-Accounting Method's definition of capacity and demand, where a group of perhaps dozens of variables is managed by keying on the critical four or five and treating the others as supportive items. We are in the process, then, of determining how to distribute or allocate the cost of these support items to the key production (chargeout) indices.

Considering equipment first, we note the unaddressed equipment includes the group of four 7-track tape drives, the COM facility, all 60 terminals, the communications (controllers and modems) gear, and card reader/punch. Figure 7.6 provides the 7-track tape drive partial account.

The COM facility is recognized as providing services markedly different from those of the other computing equipment. Hence, it should be charged out as a separate facility under the same general management as the computer facility. Its partial account is given in Figure 7.7.

The communications gear clearly is for the support of the 60 terminals. Therefore, wherever terminal costs are booked, a proportional allocation of communications costs will be booked. The terminals are employed by the data center's clients, or users, as job-entry devices, inquiry devices, etc., as well as by the data center operations staff and software maintenance staff. For the purpose of example, we assume that the user community employs 50 of these devices

	ANNUAL EXPENSE
Equipment	$ 66,000
Labor	15,120
Supplies	24,000
Total	$105,120

Figure 7.7. COM Account (Partial).

and the data center 10. Clearly, the user's 50 have no connection to any item in the supply budget or labor budget. Their total account is then:

EQUIPMENT	% COST ALLOCATED	ANNUAL EXPENSE	
20 Model A	100%	$30,000	
Modem Allocation	33%	2,000	
Controller Allocation	33%	36,000	
	Total Model A		$68,000
30 Model B	100%	$36,000	
Modem Allocation	50%	3,000	
Controller Allocation	50%	54,000	
	Total Model B		$93,000

Figure 7.8. User Terminal Account (Tootal).

Since these devices are dedicated to specific users, the chargeout for each individual device is not a rate based on usage, as will be the case for the four prime chargeout indices, but rather a surcharge equal to the total expense divided by the number of devices. For example, the charge for one Model B terminal is calculated as $93,000 ÷ 30, or $258 per month.

How, then, are the remaining terminal costs handled? Of the 10 Model A terminals remaining, assume the operations staff uses one at each master console, one in the tape pool, and one in the printer pool. These clearly should be posted to the CPU, tape, and printer accounts. The allocation of the cost of the remaining six, $20,400, assumed used by the software maintenance and other staff components is somewhat judgmental. While their use is in support of the data center, there is usually no indication, in practice, of the distribution of the staff areas' efforts with respect to each of the four major indices. Hence, there is usually no information relevant to distributing the terminal costs. Two options available are simply to divide the $20,400 expense into four equal parts or divide them according to the bottom line of the partial accounts, i.e., in the proportion of 871.9 : 518.8 : 867.9 : 362.2, or 33.3% to CPU, 19.8% to tape, 33.1% to disk, and 13.8% to printer. For both options, the tape contribution can be split between 9-track and 7-track drives. Employing the first option yields the following increments to each chargeout index:

ACCOUNT	NO. DRIVES DIRECT	COST FOR DIRECT TERMINALS	ALLOCATION FOR STAFF TERMINALS	TOTAL TERMINAL EXPENSE
CPU	2	$ 6,800	$ 5,100	$11,900
Tape—9-Track	0.89	3,026	4,539	7,565
Tape—7-Track	0.11	374	561	935
Disk	—	—	5,100	5,100
Printer	1	3,400	5,100	8,500
Staff	6	20,400	—	—
		$34,000	$20,400	$34,000

Figure 7.9. Terminal Contributions.

It is difficult to determine precisely how each index, CPU, tape, disk, or printer, benefits from the last remaining piece of equipment, the card reader/punch. Its use is generally to input source decks for new jobs, facilitating changes to existing jobs, and for facilitating various changes to operating systems. In the absence of any other knowledge, it is distributed equally to all four prime chargeout indices. In practice, an analysis of its specific uses might provide a more accurate method of distributing its costs but its contribution is far too small to warrant much attention. These items now complete, the remaining labor and supply expenses are addressed.

The allocation of the residual labor expense varies according to item. Tape library and bursting/decollating expenses are, respectively, allocated 100% to the tape accounts and printer account. Since most of the staff areas—capacity/performance planning, software maintenance, and management—would have little, if anything, to do with the COM facility, they are allocated equally to the CPU, tape, disk, and printer accounts. Assuming materials assembly costs are unrelated to COM usage, they, too, are allocated equally to these four categories in the absence of any other specific knowledge. Again, equal dispersion of these costs is a matter of judgment and other methods, if supportable, are acceptable. The allocation of the staff management function is increased by a proportion of the data center management expense. The proportion is determined by the data manager's estimate of the division of his time between production and staff services. The example assumes this to be 50%.

The remaining labor categories—production management, the residual data center management, budgeting, and messenger services—also clearly relate to the COM facility in addition to all of the above. This confuses matters somewhat since the COM area, as described in terms of staff by Figure 6.2b and by the budget, is so small. In order to determine ("rationalize" might be a more honest term) an allocation factor, we note two alternatives. One is that there are eight organizational components in the production division. This would suggest an allocation factor of about one-eighth, or 12%. If instead, we noted there are five general chargeout categories—CPU, tapes, disk, printer, and COM—and that COM was much smaller than the other categories, both in size and in criticality to the production process, it would seem appropriate that COM receive a smaller allocation than the other four. If it received half, the allocation would be 11%. With these estimates in close proximity, the example arbitrarily chooses 11%.

Of the remaining supplies, none can be accurately allocated directly to device or chargeout category. Paralleling earlier allocation judgments, the example distributes supply expenses associated with computer operations (production) and data center management in the same manner as labor. Data center management supplies are split 50% to staff and the rest allocated accordingly to the other five classes. Since the staff area would have little, if anything to do with the COM facility, its supply expenses are allocated equally to the CPU, tape, disk, and printer accounts, as were its labor expenses. Figure 7.10 summarizes the distribution of these equipment, labor, and supply expenses chargeout category.

Item	CPU Account	Tape Accounts	Disk Account	Printer Account	COM Account	Re-Alloc. to Staff Svcs.
Tape Library labor		100 %				
Bursting/Decollating labor				100 %		
Materials Assembly labor	25 %	25 %	25 %	25 %		
Messenger Services labor	22½%	22½%	22½%	22½%	11 %	
Capacity/Perf. Planning labor	25 %	25 %	25 %	25 %		
Software Maint & Dev. - labor	25 %	25 %	25 %	25 %		
Budgeting & Costing labor	22½%	22½%	22½%	22½%	11 %	
Production Mgt. labor	22½%	22½%	22½%	22½%	11 %	
Computer Operations supplies	22½%	22½%	22½%	22½%	11 %	
Staff Svcs. Mgt. labor	25 %	25 %	25 %	25 %		
supplies	25 %	25 %	25 %	25 %		
Data Center Mgt. labor	11.8%	11.8%	11.8%	11.8%	54.8%	50 %
supplies	11.8%	11.8%	11.8%	11.8%	52.8%	50 %

Figure 7.10(a). Distribution of Labor and Supply Items.

Figure 7.10(b). Distribution of Labor and Supply Items.

Item	CPU Account	Tape Account	Disk Account	Printer Account	Com Account
Tape Library labor		90064 —			
Bursting/Decollating labor				57330 —	
Materials Assembly labor	26617 —	26618 —	26617 —	26618 —	
Messenger Services labor	20039 —	20039 —	20039 —	20040 —	9901 —
Capacity/Perf. Planning labor	6716 —	6716 —	6716 —	6777 —	
Software Maint. & Dev. – labor	34946 —	34946 —	34946 —	34945 —	
Budgeting & Costing labor	12209 —	12209 —	12209 —	12209 —	6036 —
Production Mgt. labor	9473 —	9473 —	9473 —	9473 —	4683 —
Computer Operations Supplies	18972 —	18972 —	18972 —	18971 —	6413 —
Staff Svcs. Mgt. labor	14191 —	14191 —	14191 —	14192 —	
Supplies	5050 —	5050 —	5050 —	5050 —	
Data Center Mgt. Alloc. Direct	10420 —	10420 —	10420 —	10421 —	5752 —
Alloc. via Staff	11206 —	11206 —	11208 —	11208 —	

154

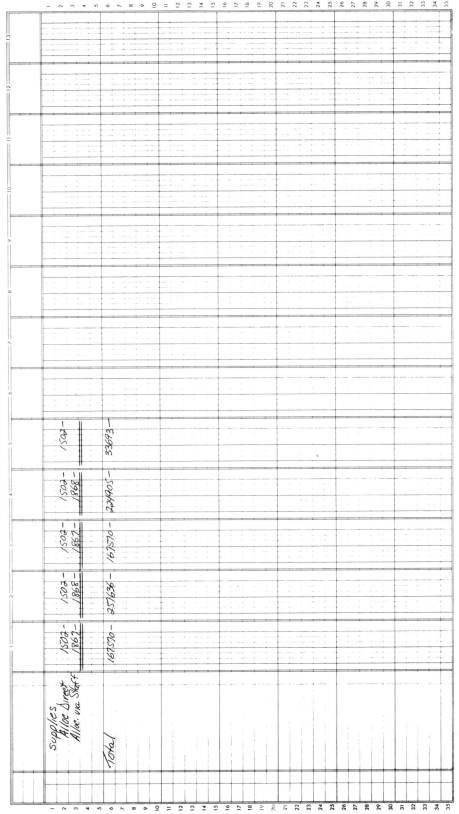

Figure 7.10(b). Distribution of Labor and Supply Items. (*continued*)

	1	2	3	4	5
Supplies					
Alloc. Direct	1503 –	1503 –	1503 –	1503 –	1503 –
Alloc. via Staff	1862 –	1868 –	1867 –	1868 –	
Total	167570 –	235636 –	161570 –	234905 –	33673 –

Figure 7.11 shows the final CPU account, i.e., the total annual expense to be associated later with CPU demand.

An example of an I/O account, 9-track tape drives is provided in Figure 7.12.

The reader may develop the remaining accounts as an example or refer to Appendix C. Figure 7.13 provides total expenses for all accounts. When added to the remaining, separately chargeable items,

Terminals—Model A	$68,000
Terminals—Model B	93,000
Special Forms	60,000

these accounts indeed prove to the full $3,865,354 annual budget. Prior to matching demand to the numbers in Figure 7.13 and developing actual charge-

	ANNUAL EXPENSE	
EQUIPMENT		
CPU	$582,000	
Add'l Core—Lease	96,000	
Add'l Core—Add'l Use	10,020	
Card Reader/Punch Allocation	6,000	
Terminals and Data Comm.—Direct	6,800	
Terminals and Data Comm.—Allocated	5,100	
Subtotal		$705,920
LABOR		
Console Operators	114,530	
Supervisors	69,394	
Materials Assembly	26,617	
Messenger Services	20,039	
Capacity/Performance Planning	6,776	
Software Maintenance and Development	34,746	
Budgeting and Costing	12,209	
Production Management	9,473	
Staff Services Management	14,191	
Data Center Management		
Direct	10,420	
Staff Contribution	11,708	
Subtotal		330,103
SUPPLIES		
Direct	—	
Computer Operations	12,972	
Staff Services Management	5,050	
Data Center Management		
Direct	1,502	
Staff Contribution	1,687	
Subtotal		21,211
Total		$1,057,234

Figure 7.11. CPU Account (Final-Bundled).

	ANNUAL EXPENSE	
EQUIPMENT		
Tape Drives—Rental	$175,200	
Tape Drives—Add'l Use	6,250	
Card Reader/Punch Allocation	5,333	
I/O Channels (5.3)	71,550	
Terminals and Data Comm.—Direct	3,026	
Terminals and Data Comm.—Allocated	4,539	
Subtotal		$265,898
LABOR		
Operators	112,320	
Supervisors	62,435	
Tape Library	80,057	
Materials Assembly	23,660	
Messenger Services	17,812	
Capacity/Performance Planning	6,023	
Software Maintenance and Development	30,885	
Budgeting and Costing	10,852	
Production Management	8,420	
Staff Services Management	12,614	
Data Center Management		
Direct	9,262	
Staff Contribution	10,407	
Subtotal		384,747
SUPPLIES		
Tapes	2,133	
Cleaning Agents	267	
Computer Operations	9,729	
Staff Services Management	3,788	
Data Center Management		
Direct	1,127	
Staff Contribution	1,500	
Subtotal		18,544
Total		$699,189

Figure 7.12. 9-Track Tape Drive Account (Final-Bundled).

INDEX	ANNUAL EXPENSE
CPU	$1,057,234
9-Track Tape Drives	669,189
7-Track Tape Drives	121,516
Disk Drives	1,046,376
Printers	607,450
COM	142,589
Total	$3,644,354

Figure 7.13. Chargeout Index Totals.

out rates, it is important to understand the significance of selecting the correct fiscal period for these calculations.

7.5   SIGNIFICANCE OF THE FISCAL PERIOD

The preceding is no more than regrouping the annual operating budget to reflect the basic structure of demand and capacity. How, then, does all this relate to the way in which demand and capacity were quantified in Chapters 2 and 3?

Figure 7.14 repeats earlier pictorializations of capacity/demand and adds the dimension of cost. For simplicity's sake, assume the periodic expense associated with capacity is $100. The leftmost column describes the processing cost as a function of different levels of capacity usage. The task here is to select that unit cost corresponding to expected usage during the fiscal period. I.e., if the $100 represents the operating budget for a full year, the process seeks to select a unit cost that is invariant for one year and that represents average usage or demand during that year. If, for some reason the corporate fiscal calendar was based on a 2-year or other interval, one would instead select a unit cost representative of average usage for 2 years, and so on.

Note how Figure 7.14 assigns costs to each capacity constraint. At 100%

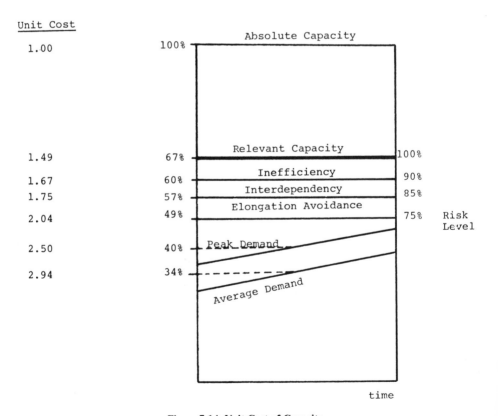

Figure 7.14. Unit Cost of Capacity.

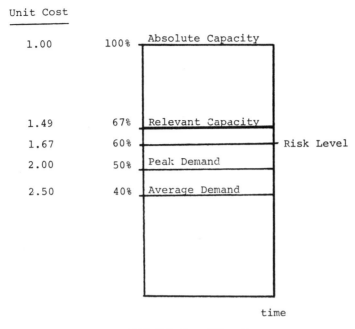

Figure 7.15. Unit Cost of Capacity.

Absolute Capacity, the $100 translates to $1.00 for each 1% of capacity. The operating system, which consumes one-third of capacity, reduces available capacity to 67% of Absolute Capacity and, hence, increases costs to $1.49 (i.e., $1.00/0.67) for usage of each percent of Relevant Capacity. In this manner, one can calculate the payback during a fiscal period of efforts to reduce capacity constraints, as described in Chapter 4. One can also calculate the effect upon unit cost of alternative service levels that could be offered during the fiscal period as a function of alternative elongation factors. For example, given the constraints in Figure 7.14 that lower usable capacity to 57% of Absolute Capacity, suppose one determined through analysis that increasing capacity held in reserve to avoid job elongation from 10% to 15% of Relevant Capacity would result in a 10% increase to output timeliness. Clearly, the cost of the service increase would be 5% of Relevant Capacity and would bring the risk level down to 47% of Absolute Capacity. The resulting change to unit processing cost during the fiscal period would be:

$$(2.13 - 2.04)/2.04, \text{ or } 4.4\%$$

This describes how unit costs are increased as decisions are made, whether consciously or not, to limit the degree to which any set of capacity is utilized. The unit cost that one would use for chargeout purposes is referred to as the "average unit cost," and reflects the average usage of capacity during the entire fiscal period. Thus, if Figure 7.15 reflected capacity usage for every month in a 1-year fiscal period, unit cost would be $2.50. In Figure 7.14, where demand increases during the fiscal period, the average unit cost is determined by taking the average of Average Demand during the entire period and relating it to cost. In the example, demand rises from 47% of Relevant Capacity, on average to 55%. This growth rate is continuous but may be approximated by an exponential rate of 1.44% per month compounded monthly. The average is 51.02%, or 34.18% of Absolute Capacity. Hence, average unit cost is $2.926 for the entire period.

Note how this approach places greater emphasis on accounting principles than it does on the mechanics of chargeback. For example, in the first month of the year, demand will average 31.49% of Absolute Capacity. At $2.926 per percent, the chargeout or recovery rate is only $92.14 per annum. Similarly, the last month of the year will see 36.85% Average Demand for a recovery rate, or $107.82 per annum. But on average throughout the accounting period, the rate will be $100. (Because we are dealing with an exponential function, the mean of the 12 monthly demand levels is slightly askew from the average of just the first and last months. A brief calculation by the reader will prove the error to be exactly the same as the error by which $92.14 and $107.82 do not average to $100.) The process of overrecovering in some months and underrecovering in others is referred to as variable recovery.

Variable monthly recoveries, i.e., a condition of charging out something other than precisely 100% of monthly expense, are particularly distasteful to many in data processing. While it would be possible to alter the chargeout mechanism to allow periodic rates that would provide full recovery each and every month, to do so would create three alternative problems. First, planned unit costs are a function of a unified statement of anticipated demand directly related to the operating budget. The fiscal period associated with the operating budget is almost universally 1 year, so defining an artificial "expense period" of one month is somewhat of a departure from standard cost accounting. A move to 12 monthly chargeout rates, then, would actually be a move to 12 separate price structures whose design is to emulate the cost structure (chargeout indices) and, at the same time, to recover fully, i.e., to provide a zero profit margin. Since there are no overwhelming economic, financial, or accounting implications associated with the period of 1 month as a reporting interval, there are no overwhelming reasons to force full recovery on a monthly basis.

Second, if one were to force the adoption of monthly rates, one would divide monthly demand by monthly expense. If the objective is mainly to fully recover monthly expenses, one can justifiably raise the question as to whether expense should be treated on a cash or accrual basis.

The cash basis of accounting is the method that would attempt to reflect actual cash outflows in the chargeout rates. However, this method is subject to variations in payment methods, such as prepayment, payment quarterly-in-arrears. This in turn would cause variations in chargeout. For example, if in Figure 7.11, CPU and core were billed quarterly-in-arrears, then for 2 months out of each quarter, 65% of the expense would be deferred and the CPU rate would be about 30% of what it would be on a straight-line or average basis. These costs would catch up in the third month and balloon the costs up to about 230% of what they would be otherwise. Although not usually so pronounced, this type of change would be commonplace with the printer account where paper and other forms are often prepaid months in advance. Delays between billing dates, receipt of bills from vendors, and dispensing payments further complicates use of the cash basis since even the data center has no idea what expenses passed entirely through the corporate payment mechanism until well after the reporting period has ended. Hence, there could be large delays between computer usage and the issuance of bills to users.

If, on the other hand, expenses are handled on an accrual basis, there is little difference between each monthly accrual and one-twelfth of the annual budget. (An exception would be the case of an enormous, general increase in capacity during one month that signifies either the acquisition of equipment dedicated to a specific set of uses, and therefore is separately chargeable, or signifies a response to a general increase in volume, in which case cost-per-unit demand would not change radically.) If there, indeed, is little difference between each monthly accrual and one-twelfth of the annual budget, then there is little reason to adopt monthly chargeout rates based on accruals. The only effect would be to chargeout excess capacity differently. Because excess capacity exists primarily where capacity segment size is large, only the CPU account is affected. But since the CPU account usually represents no more than one-third of the total expense, if the CPU were highly unutilized, the amount of expense that would be charged out differently under this scheme would be small. For example, if usage were forecast to be only two-thirds of the risk level, the magnitude of the change would be only 0.33×0.33, or 11% in the worst month. On average across the entire year, there would be no net change. Thus, in terms of the accounting, either by cash or accrual, there is no significant advantage to adopting chargeout rates that vary month to month.

The third problem associated with adjusting chargeout rates monthly is that doing so creates a good deal of uncertainty in the user community. At a given level of computer demand, or of transaction volume, charges from the data center would be neither predictable nor repeatable. This type of policy would be severely restrictive to the marketing areas who could no longer predict incremental costs of increased market penetration, planned changes to customer services, etc. At the same time, users attempting to explain operating costs to their management would be frustrated in describing how, for example, computer processing charges could increase during a period of decreased transaction volume.

In summary, while it might seem desirable to precisely recover expenses monthly (or by other non-annual reporting periods), the disadvantages, unless carefully managed, can far outweigh the benefits.

7.6 CALCULATING CHARGEBACK RATES—BUNDLED COSTS

Returning to the example used in Section 7.4, chargeback rates could be developed by simply dividing each account cost by Average Demand for the coming fiscal year for that account. Figure 7.16 accomplishes this for CPU. Remembering that there is no difference between, say, allocating 10% of the CPU for 1 hour and consuming 6 minutes of CPU cycles, a unit of measurement is cho-

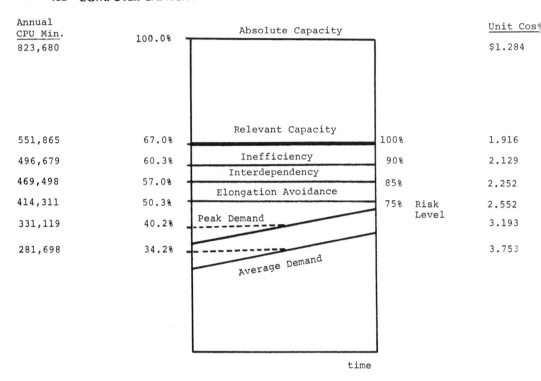

Figure 7.16. Unit Cost of CPU Capacity.

sen that most easily adapts to the computer's resource-accounting package. For IBM users, the package is SMF; for Burroughs users, it is often RAWLOG. The unit of measure these packages provide is minutes or seconds of CPU. At 100% Absolute Capacity, the number of CPU minutes during the fiscal period equals:

$$\text{(Number of CPUs} \times \text{minutes/day)} \times \text{(business days/year)}$$

Assuming the two CPUs in the example used throughout and 1440 minutes/day, if the data center's business week is assumed to be 5.5 days, 52 weeks of business yields 823,680 CPU minutes per year for Absolute Capacity. This is stepped down accordingly for each constraint until, assuming demand is forecast to average 51% of Relevant Capacity (34.2% of Absolute Capacity) during the fiscal year, 281,699 CPU minutes is the basis for calculating the unit CPU charge. This is calculated as $1,057,234 \div 281,699$, or $3.753 per CPU minute.

The other unit costs can be derived in a similar manner. Although in an actual case, efficiency and interdependency constraints would be different in magnitude from one capacity index to the next due to the nature of demand, differences in failure and repair rates between different types of equipment, they are assumed here to be uniform across all chargeout indices for the sake of example. The 9-track unit cost is calculated by first determining the average amount of capacity, i.e., average number of drives during the fiscal period. This is derived from Figure 6.3 as 2 months of 16 drives and 10 months of 32 drives.

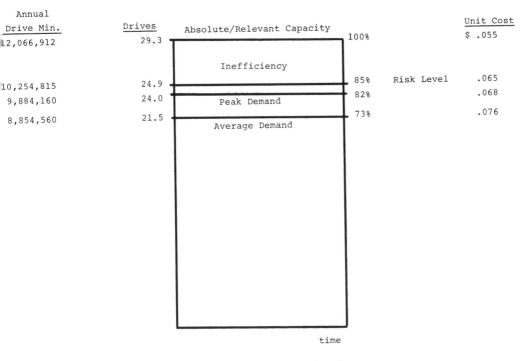

Figure 7.17. Unit Cost of Tape Capacity.

Hence, the average number of drives is 29.3. There is no overhead associated with the operating system, so that Relevant Capacity is equal to Absolute Capacity. Figure 7.17 describes the risk level for this index as 24.9, or 25 drives. It becomes apparent that the form of Figure 7.17 has two separate purposes—one for describing costing scenarios, and one for capacity/demand relationships. The latter would describe the risk level for the first two months as 85% of 16 drives, or 14 drives, and for the last 10 months as 27 drives.

Continuing, the number of minutes in the fiscal period is as before: 1440 × 5.5 × 52, or 411,840. For the full 29.3 drives, Absolute Capacity may be described for costing purposes as 12,066,912 tape-drive minutes. Assuming Peak Demand to be 24 drives, and Average Demand to be 21.5 drives, the average unit cost, or chargeout rate, is $669,189 ÷ 8,854,560, or 7.56¢ per minute of use for each drive. Figure 7.18 provides similar cost rates based on

INDEX	UNIT OF CHARGE	AVERAGE DEMAND	ANNUAL EXPENSE	UNIT COST
CPU	CPU min.	2.82×10^5	$1,057,234	$3.753
9-Track Tape Drives	drive min.	8.85×10^6	669,189	0.076
7-Track Tape Drives	drive min.	1.11×10^6	121,516	0.110
Disk drive	drive min.	1.80×10^7	1,046,376	0.058
Printer	line of print	7.50×10^8	607,450	0.0008
COM	frame	2.19×10^6	142,589	0.065

Figure 7.18. Chargeout Rates—Bundled Costs.

assumed Average Demand forecasts for each of the remaining chargeout indices.

7.7   LIMITATIONS AND BEHAVIORAL ASPECTS OF BUNDLED COSTS

As with any pricing scheme, bundled costs should be used as a chargeout technique only if the limitations to its accuracy are understood and controllable, and if its effects are consonant with corporate objectives regarding user community behavior.

The major advantage of any cost chargeback methodology, and in this specific case of bundled cost chargeback, is that rates and charges are purely a function of expenses and usage. Thus, there is no need for the development of complicated algorithms (which never seem to apply correctly to all jobs) that relate certain types of system activity, such as connect time and I/Os to groupings of data center expenses. Hence, unexpected increases to capacity have minimal effect upon unit cost (only indirect support, i.e., staff services, supervisory, and management expenses, is not incremented along with the hardware), and the data center is able to reconcile capacity and expense variances directly with specific segments of demand that varied from users' forecasts. Further, the fact that cost chargeout has one rate for each type of capacity brings the advantage of being able to prove capacity and expense to chargeout. For example, consider another methodology where a rate r of $1.00 per unit is actually a reflection of two types of capacity, M and N. If broken out separately, let $r_M = \$1.25$ and $r_N = \$.75$ per unit. Users, sensing technical advantage of using M and no cost penalties, convert enough demand from N to M to require unplanned acquisition of more M, resulting in underutilization of N. Unless the data center wishes to change rate structures midway through the year, an action acceptable too few times in a cost analyst's career, it will be forced to undercharge for the additional use of M. It thus has the choice of underrecovering or rejecting user demand. Since cost based chargeout methodologies do not lump M types of capacity into N rates, where $M > N$, they insure against these problems.

The factors that potentially limit accuracy of a bundled cost chargeback methodology are, obviously, the adherence of actual expenses to budget and of actual demand to the annual projection. By holding demand variances to zero for the moment, that is, by assuming that average demand is exactly as forecast, it is apparent that the effect of expense variances on unit cost is minimal. Depreciation does not vary from projections. Equipment that is not depreciated is either under continuous lease, which does not vary in monthly liability, or is subject to lease renewal. This latter category is usually limited in scope and highly predictable during the budget-planning process. The same is usually true of items in the supply budget. Labor expense variations result primarily from variations in staff levels (as opposed to variations in expected individual salary levels). This does not occur in the absence of demand increases or special projects. Special projects requiring significant levels of unforecast staff support do not occur in well-managed organizations. Where they do occur, the error to the chargeout rate is relatively small since nonoperating staff is, as a rule, much smaller than the operations staff and total staff expenses are generally only about one-third the total expense.

The overall affect upon average unit cost of demand variances is, in general, not that large due to the relatively small segment sizes by which I/O equipment is acquired and due to the relatively large size of total I/O costs in relation to total CPU costs. I/O capacity can be increased in relatively small percentages—adding 8 drives to 32 is an increment of 25 percent compared to, say, acquiring a second CPU, an increment of 100%. Hence, each I/O risk level can be managed such that it is always close to peak demand. Restated, increases to peak demand are met with similar size increases to capacity. Hence, variances from projections of annual peak I/O demand do not significantly affect average I/O demand as a percent of capacity. For example, if peak demand for tape drives is 30, and this happens to be associated with an average tape demand of 27 drives, if peak demand rises to 40 drives, unless the character of the entire workload changes (in practice, a remote possibility), average demand will similarly rise by the same percentage to 36 drives. The ratio of average demand to total capacity, the chargeout point, tends not to change much for I/O gear. (An exception to this is if the I/O equipment is dedicated to specific applications. In that case, however, we are unconcerned since dedicated equipment is not subject to chargeout rates but, rather, is charged separately). Thus, the direct portion of the I/O accounts, equipment, operators, and direct supplies, varies in proportion to capacity levels for I/O equipment. While this entity varies from one organization to the next, it generally comprises on the order of 60% to 80% of the total chargeout account. In the example used in the preceding sections, a 25% increase in 9-track tape drive capacity (drives, operators, tapes, and cleaning agents) would result in a 9% decrease in unit cost. The problem one encounters, however, is that such variances usually are not quantified or even perceived to exist until well into the fiscal period when chargeout rates are already fixed. The result is the requirement to credit/debit each user proportionate to his contribution to total demand for each capacity (chargeout) index in order to avoid over/under recovery of expenses.

The CPU expense account, on the other hand, does not necessarily vary at all with demand. A variance of demand from, say, a projection of 60% to an actual of 50% need not affect the number or size segments of CPU capacity required, the number of operators, etc. Although it is an extreme example, the surcharge to users required to reattain full expense recovery would be the full $10 \div 60$, or 16.7%. But since the CPU expense account usually comprises about 20% to 40% of the total expense, the error here would be on the order of only about 3% to 7%. The reader will note in coming sections that unbundled cost chargeout can alleviate this problem somewhat by reducing the scope and therefore magnitude of the accounts against which these variance percentages are applied.

In general, since the base of demand at the beginning of a fiscal period, plus forecast changes during the period, is large with respect to unexpected changes to demand, variances of projected unit cost from actual are minimal. What variances do occur are best handled by direct credits or surcharges at infrequent but prespecified intervals—annually, semiannually, etc. The alternative to surcharges or credits is chargeout rates which vary monthly. The problems with that approach were discussed previously.

A second risk associated with bundled cost chargeout, or, for that matter, any cost chargeout scheme, is related to intrusions into the risk level. Such intrusions can be due to variances in demand projections, as previously discussed, or planned trading of service levels for processing cost advantages. Recalling discussions of Chapter 3, in real (nonvirtual) systems, penetration of the risk level merely results in added service risk. But in virtual systems, there is the added element of job elongation. While elongation has no affect upon CPU chargeout by itself, it can have profound affects upon I/O usage and, therefore, I/O chargeout. As jobs begin to elongate (e.g., as a job that used to execute for 1 hour and consumed a given number of CPU cycles now, because of contention for CPU cycles, requires 1½ hours to complete execution), allocation of I/O drives is extended over a longer elapsed time than otherwise would be required. Since the computer's job- or resource-usage accounting system cannot differentiate between bona fide I/O allocation and time spent in allocation due to delays in acquiring CPU cycles, the utilization it records differs from (is larger than) demand. As a result, the "cost" calculated for chargeout, the product of recorded usage times unit cost, would ordinarily be larger than actual demand costs. In planning to avoid such an overrecovery of expenses, the analyst, after forecasting the resultant increase to average utilization would accordingly calculate lower unit cost chargeout rates for I/O devices.

It is important to also understand that elongating I/O allocation, i.e., stretching allocation along the horizontal axis, has a tendency to increase the number of I/O drives required to service peak loading periods. Delays in releasing drives for other applications requires that additional I/O drives be acquired. Hence, the calculation of the return of decreasing CPU processing costs has as many degrees of freedom (is as multidimensional a consideration) as the number of device classes (CPU plus types of I/O) devices). Thus, not only is accuracy of chargeout threatened when risk levels are penetrated, but the entire economics of production beyond the risk level is a complex, nonlinear issue that should be thoroughly explored during the chargeout planning cycle if the annual demand projection shows transition to that production state is a reasonable possibility.

The third risk associated with bundled cost chargeout relates to the assumption inherent in bundling—that staff services, materials assembly, software maintenance, capacity/performance planning, etc., are used roughly in the same proportions among various members of the user community and from one application to the next. The degree of chargeout inaccuracy and, perhaps as important, the level of complaints about the chargeout methodology, rises in direct proportion to the disparity between actual usage of these services and the users' assumptions. Hence, a good understanding of the usage of these services is required prior to selecting bundled costs as a chargeout methodology.

Since cost-based chargeout methodologies serve the objective of merely grouping and passing on costs, they do no consciously attempt to alter user resource consumption patterns but, instead, allow the user to tailor his processing behavior to data center expense patterns. Thus, if the data center finds it can offer one type of I/O facility cheaper than another competitive facility, economics will transfer control of growth of both facilities to the user community. While this would seem to make management of capacity growth simpler and seem to be of particular benefit to internal corporate data centers and other not-for-profit organizations, where cost transfer is often the desired policy, there are several other implications. Systems managers will assign programmers to convert from current devices to newly introduced, cheaper equipment; potentially, this can conflict with other systems development schedules and affect the payback of conversion to the new equipment. Strategic corporate systems decisions, such as building large on-line data base–oriented information systems, moving from a large, centralized data processing facility to small, distributed ones, etc., may be affected by the high exposure this method gives to corporate expenses. Finally, in a cost-sensitive environment, the method has the potential of allowing misrepresentation of cost data input to dedicated-facility versus utility decisions. This can most often occur when the format of the decision is merely to state equipment, staff, and supplies of the proposed dedicated facility and then to compare the associated components of dedicated facility expenses with anticipated utility charges. In such cases, it is not always obvious that services included in utility charges, staff services, service-risk avoidance, back-up, and so on are provided to the same degree or are even missing entirely from the proposed new facility. While this would be the result of faulty or biased cost accounting and improper choice of the format for presentation of the decision data, it is an inherent structural fault of bundled cost chargeout that permits this situation to occur. This can be avoided by a slight change in methodology— unbundled cost chargeout.

7.8   UNBUNDLED COST CHARGEOUT

A somewhat more precise method of determining costs of computer processing is to unbundle, or separate, supportive services from core processing services and then to chargeout each service separately. Pursuing this approach obviously implies that there is sufficient knowledge about current usage of each service to forecast demand for it during the coming fiscal period. The first time this is attempted, users have little, if any, idea of their future use of staff services. The initial forecast, although crude, is best developed from historical records of staff service usage by the various members of the user community.

Figure 7.19 begins the conversion of the bundled CPU account of Figure 7.11 to an unbundled account. Note how the process of building the cost base for each resource or chargeout index is identical to the process taken for the bundled cost methodology. Indeed, the only reason Figure 7.19 differs from Figure 7.1 is that we are assuming we have carried forward previous sections' analyses of direct terminal usage; direct and supervisory labor; the role of budgeting and costing, production management, and data center management labor; and the allocation of computer operations and data center management supply expenses.

	ANNUAL EXPENSE
EQUIPMENT	
CPU	$582,000
Add'l Core—Lease	96,000
Add'l Core—Add'l Use	10,020
Card Reader/Punch Allocation	6,000
Terminals and Data	
Comm.—Direct	6,800
Subtotal	$700,820
LABOR	
Console Operators	114,530
Supervisors	69,394
Budgeting and Costing	4,862
Production Management	4,730
Data Center Management	
Direct	5,204
Subtotal	198,720
SUPPLIES	
Direct	—
Computer Operations	6,478
Data Center Management	
Direct	750
Subtotal	7,228
Total	$906,768

Figure 7.19. CPU Account (Partial Unbundled).

Appendix D provides the partial unbundled accounts for the other five indices.

The issues at hand are to determine how to calculate costs for usage of the support facilities and how to transfer the costs for these types of capacity through chargeout.

The methodology is basically the same as was used to develop computer capacity cost rates:

1. Categorize capacity into distinct classes
2. Select an appropriate, easy to count unit of measure
3. Forecast average demand during the fiscal period
4. Collect budgeted cost data and
5. Divide.

The capacity classes have been given as organizational units in the budget: materials assembly, capacity/performance planning, tape library services, etc. If the analyst determined that some organizational unit provided one service that varied radically from its other offerings, particularly in terms of the effort or resources expended providing one unit of the service, then the existence would be recognized within that organization of distinct service classes. Separate cost accounting and, hence, separate chargeout, would then be developed

SERVICE	UNIT OF MEASURE	ANNUAL DEMAND
Tape Library	Tapes Stored per Month	300,000
Materials Assembly	Jobs Setup	60,000
Bursting and Decollating	Outputs Burst/Decollated	50,000
Messenger Services	Packages Delivered	150,000
Capacity/Performing Planning	Man-hours	1,400
Software Maintenance and Development	Man-hours	7,000

Figure 7.20. Support Services.

for each service. For the sake of example, the simple case of one service per organizational unit is assumed. Figure 7.20 lists each service; an index of count, or unit of measure; and an assumed annual demand.

The first four services are characterized by success criteria that are well defined, jobs are either setup or not, delivered or left behind. And the resources consumed per occurrence are relatively invariant (the exception being that one job that always creates 40 boxes of output to be delivered to the next county). Hence, the services are structured to facilitate the development of cost rates based on units of output that can be individually charged out. The final two services, however, are not so conveniently structured. The demands they satisfy vary widely in requirements and resources expended. For example, the systems maintenance analyst's task is orders of magnitude more difficult for installing a new operating system than for troubleshooting a job that has failed to successfully complete. Therefore, the latter two services are best charged out, and therefore unit costs are best calculated, according to man-hours rather than units of output.

The remaining organizational expenses are recognized as indirect costs and allocated as follows for the sake of example. Production management and computer operations supplies are split equally among the nine types of resources in the operating area: CPU, tapes (subdivided into 9-track and 7-track), disk, printer, COM, bursting and decollating, materials assembly, the tape library, and messenger services. Since the example deals with three staff areas of small but very unequal size, staff management, labor, and supplies expenses will be allocated in proportion to the number of people staffing capacity/performance planning, software maintenance and development, and budgeting and costing; this proportion is 1:5:2. Data-center-management labor and supplies are, as before, allocated equally to the operations and staff areas. Within these two areas, allocations are in the same manner as production and staff management. It should be remembered that these allocations are matters of judgment, as were the allocations of indirect expenses in the section describing bundled costs. Acceptable accounting practices permit a variety of allocation schemes, as long as each is rational and supportable. What is required is that the method selected additionally most closely reflects the manner in which business is conducted. Figure 7.21 summarizes the allocations of the current example.

The last step required prior to developing unit costs for the categories listed in Figure 7.20 is to allocate the remaining nonchargeable organizational

Figure 7.21. Indirect Expense Allocation Expense Category.

Account Allocated Towards	Prod. Mgt. Labor	Computer Ops. Supplies	Staff Svcs. Mgt.- Labor	Staff Svcs. Mgt.- Supplies	Data Center Mgt. Labor	Data Center Mgt. Supplies	Budgeting and Costing	Total
CPU	4730-	6478-			5204-	750-	4863-	22004-
9-Track Tape	4625-	5758-			4606-	667-	4322-	19578-
7-Track Tape	506-	720-			578-	83-	540-	2447-
Disk	4730-	6478-			5204-	750-	4861-	22023-
Printer	4731-	6478-			5204-	750-	4862-	22025-
COM	4730-	6478-			5204-	750-	4862-	22039-
Tape Library	4731-	6478-			5204-	750-	4861-	22024-
Materials Assembly	4730-	6478-			5203-	750-	4862-	22023-
Bursting/Decollating	4731-	6477-			5203-	750-	4862-	22023-
Messenger Services	4731-	6477-			5203-	750-	4861-	22022-
Capacity + Performance Planning			7096-	2562S-	5859-	844-	7293-	23604-
Software Maint. and Develop.			35978-	10262S-	29470-	4218-	36462-	118053-
Budgeting & Costing			14191-	5050-	11708-	1688-	-	33637-
Total	49575-	58300-	56765-	20220-	93665-	13500-	87510-	373515-

170

	ANNUAL EXPENSE	
EQUIPMENT		
—	—	
Subtotal		—
LABOR		
Analysts	$54,873	
Staff Services Management	14,191	
Data Center Management	11,708	
Subtotal		$80,772
SUPPLIES		
Staff Services Management	5,050	
Data Center Management	1,688	
Subtotal		6,738
Total		$87,510

Figure 7.22. Budgeting and Costing Account.

expense: budgeting and costing. Since this component is direct support to the data center manager, its expense will be allocated in the identical manner— 50% to staff functions, 50% to the operating chargeout indices, etc. Figure 7.22 and the indicated column of Figure 7.21 summarize this process.

Figure 7.23 describes the process of calculating unit costs for the six unbundled services by selecting the tape library as an example.

With demand assumed to be 300,000, the cost for a tape stored for one month equals $112,088 ÷ 300,000, or $0.374. The accounts for the remaining services are provided in Appendix E. The bursting and decollating, messenger services, and materials assembly unit costs are calculated for each unit of demand in the same manner.

While the capacity/performance planning and software maintenance and development unit costs are calculated in the same manner, their chargeout is

	ANNUAL EXPENSE	
EQUIPMENT		
—	—	
Subtotal		—
LABOR		
Clerks	$90,064	
Production Management	4,731	
Data Center Management	5,204	
Budgeting and Costing	4,861	
Subtotal		$104,860
SUPPLIES		
Computer Operations	6,478	
Data Center Management	750	
Subtotal		7,228
Total		$112,088

Figure 7.23. Tape Library Account.

	ANNUAL EXPENSE	
EQUIPMENT		
CPU	$582,000	
Add'l core—Lease	96,000	
Add'l core—Add'l Use	10,020	
Card Reader/Punch Allocation	6,000	
Terminals and Data		
Comm.—Direct	6,800	
Subtotal		$700,820
LABOR		
Console Operators	114,530	
Supervisors	69,394	
Budgeting and Costing	4,862	
Production Management	4,730	
Data Center Management		
Direct	5,204	
Subtotal		198,720
SUPPLIES AND SERVICES		
Direct	—	
Computer Operations	6,478	
Data Center Management		
Direct	750	
Capacity/Performance Planning	6,765	
Software Maintenance and Development	47,957	
Subtotal		61,950
Total		$961,490

Figure 7.24. CPU Account (Final—Unbundled).

handled differently. To understand this, we need to remember capacity/performance planning provides forecasting and measurement services for the computer center as well as directly for the user. For purposes of illustration, it will be assumed the split is 50% to the data center and 50% directly to users. The software maintenance group is the same, but its proportion of effort spent troubleshooting and otherwise providing direct support to the user base is somewhat less. It will be assumed the division is 70% to the site and 30% to the user. The meaning of this is that while the support services have been unbundled, it is recognized that normal business requires that the computer center be the biggest subscriber of some services. In order to treat their expense as an indirect cost incurred by the data center, the appropriate proportion of expense, 50% of capacity performance planning and 70% of software maintenance and development in the example, is allocated to the major processing index accounts—CPU, tapes, disk, and printer. This is shown for the CPU in Figure 7.24 and for the remaining chargeout indices in Appendix F.

Figure 7.25 summarizes the complete set of unbundled cost rates.

7.9 LIMITATIONS AND BEHAVIORAL ASPECTS OF UNBUNDLED COSTS

The advantages of unbundled costing are similar to those of bundled costing—direct relationship of chargeout to expenses and usage, limitation of rate vari-

INDEX	UNIT OF MEASURE	PROJECTED UNIT COST
CPU	CPU minute	$3.410
9-Track Tape	Drive-minute	0.063
7-Track Tape	Drive-minute	0.088
Disk	Drive-minute	0.053
Printer	Line of Print	0.0006
COM	Frame	0.060
Tape Library	Tapes Stored per month	0.374
Materials Assembly	Jobs Setup	0.467
Bursting and Decollating	Outputs Burst/Decollated	0.586
Messenger Services	Packages Delivered	1.338
Capacity/Performance Planning	Man-hours	38.655
Software Maintenance and Development	Man-hours	39.148

Figure 7.25. Summary—Unbundled Rates.

ances if capacity variances occur during the year, and the ability to adapt to changes in customer usage preferences for certain types of capacity without threatening full recovery.

While the differences in limitations between bundled and unbundled cost chargeback would seem small, their effect can be quite large. Both methods have essentially the same limitations—recovery problems upon intrusion into the risk zone and upon large variances between budgeted and actual expenses or between projected demand and actual usage. The behavior of users, however, can differ sharply from one method to the other.

The immediate effect of unbundling noncore processing and staff costs is to reduce the apparent cost of core processing, i.e., of utilizing the major capacity indices (in the example used throughout, CPU, tape, disk, and printers). The resulting impulse for any user working under a small to medium margin is immediately to eliminate all nonessential services. These generally include non-crucial systems maintenance and capacity/performance planning. The effect of eliminating the former can be a decrease of service and performance in the near term, as procedures and libraries are updated less frequently and as data sets and data bases are reorganized or backed-up less frequently. The effect of eliminating the latter is a decrease in service and performance over the long term, as both software and hardware become untuned, resulting in both an effective decrease in capacity (the untuned capacity is capable of less processing than tuned capacity) and an increase in utilization (since untuned software results in unnecessary logic and data manipulations). When the data center attempts to reduce its chargeout rates by eliminating capacity planning activities and costs, the service problem is exacerbated since there would remain no rational or well-managed techniques for determining capacity levels necessary to meet expected user service targets. Indeed, there would be sharply reduced capability even to determine what those service targets will be. These factors of cost and service risk place responsibility on senior management to become active in the decision to trade service for lower computer processing costs or to remove the added expense factors from the capacity/cost decision process. Removing the costs from the decision process is difficult to do well since it involves distorting the accounting process by, for example, assigning some items as corporate, rather than data processing, overhead. True values for return on capacity acquisition and on automating functions then become difficult to determine. It also becomes difficult to exercise control over these "hidden" data processing services and their costs.

An unexpected benefit of the unbundled cost structure is that it explicity states the costs of noncore processing services in the utility environment and thereby forces questions regarding the existence of similar services in proposed dedicated facility alternatives. This automatically prompts senior, nontechnical managers to ask questions regarding the effect of any absence of these services or service risk in proposed dedicated alternatives. More about this topic in the next chapter.

7.10 ALLOCATION PRICING

The previous two methodologies merely segregated data center expenses by capacity category and transferred these costs to the user, i.e., adopted a not-for-profit, or zero-margin, approach to pricing. A simple extension of this is to increase any or all rates to achieve a desired margin. Thus, if the desired margin is 12%, the unbundled CPU rate would be $3.819, the print rate $0.0007, the software maintenance rate $43.846, and so on. This assumes the corporation has no bias toward any particular capacity (chargeout) index. If, instead, it was deemed appropriate to encourage the planning process, it might adopt a zero (or even negative) margin for capacity/performance planning and correspondingly increase the margin on some or all of the other indices to maintain the overall target margin (in this discussion, 12%).

As a pricing scheme, this methodology has many of the benefits and risks of costing. The benefits include the ability to link capacity, expense, and profit variances to specific demand variances and the ability to adapt to changes in customer usage preferences for certain types of capacity without having to implement major changes in the rate structure. Risks include that of major variances of actual demand or expenses from forecasts, intrusion into the risk zone, etc. A further risk, particularly when allocation is used as a basis for pricing, is that it is generally an unfamiliar way of charging to most purchasers of data processing services. Hence, there is the risk that users will not perceive their charges to be reflective of the services they have received, regardless of how well developed the rate schedule may be. This can lead to unwarranted accusations that services cost too much, are not of sufficiently high quality given the prices charged, and so on.

7.11 CPU–I/O PRICING

This chargeback methodology is described as a pricing technique because its structure cannot reflect a complete direct relationship to the cost of acquired capacity. Although there can be a direct relationship developed between

INDEX	UNIT OF CHARGE	ANNUAL DEMAND	ANNUAL EXPENSE	UNIT COST
CPU	CPU min.	2.82×10^5	$1,057,234	$3.753
9-Track Tape	I/O	0.96×10^9	669,189	0.0007
7-Trach Tape	I/O	0.08×10^9	121,516	0.0015
Disk	I/O	1.74×10^9	1,046,376	0.0006
Printer	I/O	7.50×10^8	607,450	0.0008
COM	frame	2.19×10^6	142,589	0.065

Figure 7.26. CPU–I/O Pricing.

charges for CPU usage and data center expenses, unless the vendors have begun billing the data center for I/Os or EXCPs, rather than for units of equipment, the data center cannot directly pass its expenses on in the form of charges per per I/O. Some conversion of its costs to unit EXCP charges is necessary. Furthermore, the margin, that is the difference between planned total chargeout and expense, may be greater than zero. Hence, the charges are prices, not pure costs.

The actual unit prices are calculated by grouping equipment, labor, and supply expense items for the fiscal period according to chargeout index, CPU minutes (or seconds), or I/Os and then by dividing by expected activity during the fiscal period. This is similar to the procedure followed for the costing methodologies described earlier. In practice, I/Os are segregated and charged according to capacity type: tape I/Os, disk I/Os, and printer I/Os. Using the cost accounts developed earlier for the bundled cost methodology, Figure 7.26 is the CPU-I/O pricing version of Figure 7.19. Demand is, as before, assumed for the sake of example.

This scheme for chargeback has the advantage of format, i.e., it is in the language the programmer, usually the immediate purchaser of computer services, is accustomed to seeing and in which he is used to communicating. Hence, the programmer is apt to relate to the data center in a more favorable manner than if communication was carried out in the language of non–data processing heathens. Since hostility tends to rise in an organization, there can be pressure to "give them what they want," to charge in whatever framework makes the user happy. In an independent service bureau, this approach has some merit.

Since this chargeout methodology is not directly linked to capacity, there are problems when, during the fiscal period, the nature of the workload changes with respect to activity per unit of capacity, e.g., when the average daily number of EXCPs per disk drive changes. These changes can be as a result of natural evolution of demand as new applications are developed, or as a result of an attempt to compromise the pricing algorithm.

Example 7.2

Paralleling Chapter 2's Example 2.1, the programmer has initially blocked his records at 500 characters each, resulting in a per-job cost of

$$(310 \div 60) \times \$3.753 + 10,000 \times 0.0006 \text{ (assuming disk I/Os)}$$

yielding $19.39 + $6.00 = $25.39, or $7261.68 annually. Understanding that his charges are based on the number of I/Os attributable to his program, he reblocks his data into 1000-character records. This translates to a charge of

$$(305 \div 60) \times \$3.753 + 5000 \times 0.0006$$

or $19.08 + $3.00 = $22.08, for an annual charge of $6314.24, a reduction of 13%.

Most of this difference is linked to the EXCP charge, even though there is no quantitative change in either the program functioning or the final output. Moreover, there is no change to the amount of expense the data center must suffer to provide the required capacity. The algorithm simply is prone to being compromised. Another limitation is that the algorithm is insensitive to variations within even the most stable workloads.

Example 7.3

Job B processes immedialely upon completion of Job A. Each takes precisely 60 elapsed minutes and 10.0 minutes of CPU time. Job A executes 100 disk EXCPs and Job B 100,000, although both require the space of a full disk drive. What can be observed about the price of executing each job?

Job A is charged $37.59 while Job B receives a $97.53 bill. Since the cost to the data center for running each job obviously identical (they both require identical capacity), the data center is discouraging the use of high-activity files, such as on-line data input systems, systems that perform a large number of sorts, etc., and is encouraging the development of large-size, seldom-accessed data banks. This is somewhat counter to a number of types of automation efforts.

A second observation is that because the cost to the data center of executing each job is the same, Job B, in effect, is subsidizing Job A by absorbing a greater share of the costs. Hard feelings sometimes result when Job B's owners discover this.

In summary, since the adoption of CPU-I/O pricing results in an uneven burden of processing costs and discourages certain types of automation that might otherwise be beneficial, an analysis of the effect of this chargeout scheme is required prior to its selection, particularly in the not-for-profit corporate data center.

7.12   THROUGHPUT PRICING

Just as there were a number of variations of accounting for demand using the throughput method, there are several ways to price according to throughput. Two will be discussed here.

The first is derived from the multiprogramming level; it merely charges per hour of processing time, regardless of which resources are used. This technique is a favorite of certain cost accountants because it requires absolutely no knowledge of data processing. Its results reflect that expertise.

The method requires the analyst to estimate the number of elapsed (wall-clock) hours of processing that will take place during the fiscal period and divide that sum into total expenses. The result is an hourly rate to be applied to all jobs. So, for our example where total annual expenses are $3,865,354, if the analyst forecasts the multiprogramming level to average 10, the number of elapsed hours would then be $24 \times 10 \times 5.5 \times 52$, or 68,640, and the cost per elapsed hour would be $56.31. That would be the charge for the job that used one CPU second and one-tenth of a disk drive for an hour as well as for the job that used 15 minutes of CPU and five disk drives for an hour. This method, although still used by some data centers, is a relic from the days when computers processed only one job at a time. It is accurate only for non-multiprogramming environments.

A second throughput-oriented pricing scheme is based on the kernal or standard job concept. One of its several variations counts the number of kernals, those unitized measures of CPU time to EXCPs. If the kernal consisted of 1 CPU second and 100 EXCPs, the methodology would count the actual number of each attributable to a job, divide by 1 and 100, respectively, to determine the number of kernals "consumed," and multiply by the rate per kernal. This rate would be previously developed by estimating the number of CPU seconds and EXCPs expected during the fiscal period and dividing into the respective cost accounts. If this seems nothing more than an obfuscation of CPU-I/O pricing, it is because that is exactly what it is. It is this feature that promotes the existence of the next variation, which, for lack of a better term, is referred to as "service bureau pricing."

Service bureaus typically charge for time-sharing services in terms of work units, which are similar to kernals, and in terms of connect hours. Connect hours refers to the elapsed time during which the programmer is logged on, i.e., the computer recognizes a terminal in the network is capable of transmitting or receiving data. When done properly, rates for this pricing scheme are determined by developing cost accounts for both computer gear and data communications equipment, forecasting usage as before, and dividing. In practice, some computer equipment costs are included in the connect time rate to reflect CPU used in polling and to help reduce the compute rates. The kernal rates are often termed billing units, work units, compute units, etc. Occasionally, CPU-I/O rates will be substituted for kernal rates, but, in general, the method leaves users with absolutely no knowledge of what they have used or how to reduce future billings. Hence, some data centers find this method to be the preferred chargeout scheme.

The kernal method shares the same behavioral characteristics as the CPU-I/O method. It tends to be somewhat more insensitive to variances from one job to another, however, since it deals in groupings of CPU and I/O activity. For example, if the kernal is measured to be 1 CPU second and 100 EXCPs, if one job uses 100 CPU seconds and 10,000 EXCPs, it is charged for 100 kernals. The job using 50 CPU seconds and 10,000 EXCPs is probably also charged for 100 kernals (unless the analysts compromises the system by defining "partial kernals," a conflict of terms). But, since this is a pricing, not costing scheme, this may be of little consequence unless the user community becomes upset when jobs they perceive to consume different resources receive the same charge.

7.13   PENALTY CHARGES

The final approach to pricing discussed here relates to a group of techniques used to radically modify customers' usage patterns. This is most often accomplished by charging premiums through increasing unit prices, either according to time of day or according to type of usage.

The first alternative, placing premiums according to time of day, is common to many industries and needs little explanation. Here the data center attempts to limit the difference between peak and average demand by increasing unit prices during the period when peak demand occurs. For example, if CPU time is generally priced at $3.753 per minute, the data center might charge $4.50 during the peak shift. This has the effect of discouraging nonessential use during the peak and reduces the overall level of capacity required. (That is, since the amount of capacity acquired is a function of peak, not average, demand, discouraging usage during peak periods reduces the required segment size, in the case of CPUs, or number of segments, in the case if I/O gear.) At the same time, surcharging peak periods has the effect of increasing revenues from the segments of the user community that are most responsible for the final decision on capacity sizing. The intent is to eliminate the increase to unit cost caused by the acquisition of larger capacity segments. Figure 7.27 describes the problem.

Here, it is assumed peak and average demand are 75% and 50% respectively. If the size capacity required to service the peak costs $100, average unit cost is $2.00. If, on the other hand, half the capacity (CPU) could be acquired for $75, then average unit cost would be $1.50. The methodology under discussion attempts to preserve the cheaper $1.50 rate for those users that are outside the peak.

There are problems with this approach. One is that the process of considering demand beneath the average is an unlimited, recursive process. For example, if consideration of the left most, peak half of Figure 7.27 is omitted, the secondary

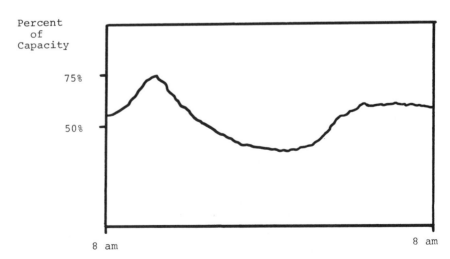

Figure 7.27. Demand Profile.

peak on the right side becomes a primary peak and the peak-average argument continues, ad infinitum. A more politically oriented problem occurs when attempts to discourage usage during peak periods are too successful. Here, old peaks disappear and new ones are formed at a different time of day if users have acted to avoid penalty charges. But when the new peaks are formed (that is, when the old peaks have shifted as they follow the applications to their new time slots and as new applications appear for processing), then penalty charges, at least in theory, also move in time accordingly. As a result, the user whose demand pattern has changed to avoid surcharges can again encounter them as a direct result of his efforts, whereas no effort to use an off-peak time slot could have resulted in penalty avoidance. Therefore, unless carefully managed, this type of penalty algorithm can be self-defeating. (This problem is more likely to occur in nontime-critical, batch processing shops.)

The second type of penalty charging scheme is used to discourage usage, not during specific time frames, but rather of certain types of devices. This would occur most often in a corporate data center that is trying to effect some type of strategic change in its data processing structure. For example, it may occur as a result of decisions to encourage distribution of processing functions, where each corporate user would assume direct responsibility for his immediate computer processing needs. The corporation might retain centralized CPUs to act as a communications switch, enabling any part of the corporation to access the data it needed from any other part of the corporation. Here, one would probably surcharge the use of tape drives and printers while minimizing the charges for CPU cycles and, probably, disk drive usage. It should be recognized that enacting these types of surcharges are no more than a cost-accounting approach to implementing a managerial decision and would not be used in an environment free of organizational constraints.

There are as many ways to implement this approach as there are demand-accounting schemes. One is based on the Allocation Method. Here, the analyst develops resource expense accounts, such as the bundled accounts of Appendix C, and volumes such as those of Figure 7.18. He or she then determines what overall increase in processing cost will cause users to want to establish their own, cheaper facility and adjusts unit costs accordingly. This may be done by merely increasing unit costs, e.g., allowing the 9-track tape drive unit cost to rise from, say, $0.076 to $0.095 and overrecovering, or by subsidizing CPU and disk annual expenses with the other annual expense indices. An example of the subsidy approach is to assign an annual expense to the 9-track tape index of $836,423 and reduce the CPU index to $890,000. This results in a tape drive price of $0.095 per minute and a CPU of only $3.156. If desired, and if done correctly, this approach can still result in a zero profit.

A second approach to charging penalties for usage is a variation of the kernal method. Based on the kernal demand-accounting method and the so-called Two-Tier Pricing Method, this approach relies upon determining average utilization as a function of standard units of CPU utilization, and then establishing one blanket price for CPU usage without tape drives and printers (as an example) and a second blanket price if the CPU is used in conjunction with those devices. For example, suppose the analyst determined that the average job used 10% of the available CPU cycles for 10 minutes. Then, if the risk zone were at 70% of Relevant Capacity, capacity would, under this accounting scheme, be measured to be 7 kernals high. At 286 business days per year and 1440 minutes per day, capacity is then equal to 286×144 or 41,184 kernals per year.

Since the intent of this scheme (and this specific example) is to discourage all usage of tapes and printers within the centralized computer facility, the kernals are priced according to whether the application makes no use at all of tapes and printers (with the exception of nondiscretionary systems, not applications functions, such as printing of job control and termination information, SYSOUT, etc.) or whether it makes some use, minor or major. Thus, the application requiring 10 minutes of CPU and executing 10^2 tape EXCPs receives the same charge as the application requiring 10 minutes of CPU and 10^5 EXCPs. Hence, the user is rewarded not for merely reducing his tape or printer usage, but for eliminating it entirely or distributing the function to his own site.

If pricing schemes involving usage penalties are adopted, the analyst may encounter several obstacles, although allocation penalty pricing has the potential for offering a fewer number of problems. In all such schemes, if the data center operates as a nonprofit organization, as do most corporate and academic installations, usage penalties disturb the ratio of charges from one resource or chargeout index to the next. That is, in nonprofit organizations, chargeback is a zero-sum game. Since each application has a different mix of resource usage, subsidizing one resource with another will result in the pricing scheme being advantageous to some applications and increasing the chargeout to others. It is important organizationally to know which users will be adversely affected and what their reaction is likely to be prior to convincing the corporation to adopt the candidate pricing algorithm. Zero-sum situations have the added problem that the subsidy derived by surcharging the "undesirable" resource indices decreases as one is successful in their elimination. Therefore, if the CPU expense account were reduced in year 1 by penalizing printer usage and if the strategy were successful and no printers remained in year 2, the charges (mainly CPU) to the remaining users would then increase. This is one of the best ways known to mankind of alienating a loyal customer base.

Kernal and other, similarly based Two-Tier Pricing Methods bring the added problem of not being able to directly prove charges to specific levels of resource usage. Hence, users are faced with the added difficulty of not being able to understand how to control charges, given their existing use of "desirable and undesirable" resources.

7.14 SUMMARY

Chargeback, then, is a function of corporate or data center objectives, and no single chargeback method is the correct choice for all environments. The recognition of the difference between pricing and costing is essential to relating the objectives to the chargeback process and the establishment of an accurate cost base, from which either cost or price chargeback can be effected.

Cost chargeback, essentially price equals cost, can be bundled or unbundled, depending on the homogeneity with which services are distributed among the user community. Unbundled services refers to breaking out staff support services, capacity/performance planning, and systems maintenance from the core processing services of CPU, tape, etc. Because the data center is, itself, usually the largest user of support services, the degree to which these services can be unbundled is somewhat limited. Since these services are generically different from the core processing services and present distinct expenses to the corporation, a pure cost approach to computer chargeback would favor the unbundled methodology. Price chargeback can be developed as a function of the Allocation Demand Accounting Method, of throughput methods, or of whatever methodology is in conformance with generally accepted accounting practices and with the data center's overall strategic objectives.

While the preceding discussion has centered on the technical and accounting ramifications of alternative chargeback methodologies, organizational considerations require a full analysis of the probable distribution of expenses among the various members of the user community. Practically, this should be completed prior to the analyst seeking the corporate blessing of the proposed algorithm. This is particularly important for the case where a chargeback methodology already exists and an alternative is being proposed. In such cases, it is not uncommon for costs to be displaced enough to significantly affect the return on new projects or the profitability of computerized services the corporation offers. While this is not to suggest that chargeback methodologies be selected on the basis of their effect on the return or profitability of a few select users, it would be irresponsible to provide management with partial data to make an organizationally sensitive decision.

8
UTILITY VERSUS DEDICATED–FACILITY DECISIONS

The economic, organizational, and technical control issues associated with deciding between establishing computer utilities and establishing dedicated or distributed facilities are discussed in this chapter. Economic issues presented include: standard bottom-line comparisons as well as the treatment of unutilized capacity; the implications of imbalances between peak and average demand in relation to capacity segment size; and economies of scale.
Control issues discussed include control over discretionary versus nondiscretionary processing and the economic implications of alternative methods of accommodating discretion. Technical-control issues discussed include problems of nonstandardization of hardware, software, and input/output requirements of applications.

8.1 DEFINITION OF TERMS

One of the more confusing aspects of utility versus nonutility decisions are the terms themselves. Throughout this chapter, the following definitions will be observed:

Utility. Any segment of capacity, computer or otherwise, designed for general use, i.e., for a variety of uses or users.

Dedicated Facility. A segment of capacity set aside for a particular purpose, e.g., one specific application or a specific set of highly related functions.

Distributed Facility. A utility or dedicated facility geographically separated from other capacity segments.

There are a number of variations of computer facilities, resulting in the possibility of confusion if attempting to classify a particular facility.

Example 8.1

XYZ uses two computers for processing 5 applications. What are the possible classifications?

If the applications are freely mixed between the two systems, then this clearly is a dual-machine utility servicing the entire demand base. If, on the other hand, there is a policy of scheduling and processing only user A's application on one system and only user B's applications on the other, then these represent two dedicated facilities. There are a number of further variations that can cause confusion unless one maintains that a facility cannot be managed as a utility in some respects and as a dedicated facility in others.

For example, if A's applications are segregated to CPU 1 and B's to CPU 2, and if both CPUs can address and freely access all I/O devices, then XYZ has not two dedicated facilities but rather, a utility with sharply defined scheduling preferences. The reasoning behind this relies on three points. One is that in such instances organizational pressures generally result in one CPU serving as back-up for the other. That is, if A's CPU fails, he will press to have his critical jobs transferred to B's CPU. It then becomes apparent that CPU 2 is the primary machine for one set of work and the secondary machine for another set. Furthermore, unless the CPUs are very lightly utilized, these conditions will result in some of B's noncritical work being delayed so that A's critical work can be accommodated. This is the classic case of the utility mode of operation with stabilized production scheduling and a well-defined contingency plan in case of problems.

The second point is that CPU costs generally comprise only a small percentage of the total computer processing expense, as we saw in Chapter 6. Hence, there are no major economic reasons for separately costing and charging out each CPU; that is, their costs would be averaged and their chargeout rates calculated identically as in a utility. This is especially true for the case where both CPUs are utilized at roughly the same rate, i.e., the differences are no more than 10% to 20%. It is doubtful that, in any case, usage spreads would remain larger than this since the resulting low utilization levels would raise questions regarding the wisdom of maintaining two CPUs of that size without sufficient demand. The final point is that if some equipment is utility in nature, then management and operational staff are also utility in nature and not dedicated to specific users' devices. This is especially true when I/O gear, representing the vast majority of devices, and where setup staff are not dedicated to specific users.

If there is no distinction of data center management according to users, no large-scale distinction of equipment according to users, and no distinction of chargeout rates, then the facilities are not dedicated.

Example 8.2

Company C has four computers and a community of four users within the corporation. Each computer runs only the demand of one user, and each user directly manages the operating staff of its computer, although all users share the tape library owned by user A and the equipment to smooth power fluctuations (uninterruptable power supply, or UPS) purchased by user B. Each user has negotiated back-up arrangements for its critical applications with the other users. How should the facilities be classified?

Were we to ignore the fact that there are separate managements on the computer floor(s), this case would seem to be a four-computer utility with sharply defined, static scheduling preferences. Even though I/O might not be shared between CPUs, because each computer system services certain applications and provides general back-up in a multiuser environment whenever a primary system fails, and because each shares support of facilities and equipment, it is difficult to distinguish their purpose from that of a utility, even though they may be in separate but nearby locations. Rather, this is a case of distributed data processing management, where little if anything in the equipment or other functioning is changed from the utility, but the perception of dedication is achieved through the creation of four overlapping managements. In an environment where lines of business interrelate, and therefore where applications interrelate, passing data sets from one user area to another, this arrangement is exceedingly difficult to coordinate and manage well.

Example 8.3

Company D also has four computers but they service two user areas. Each user has two computers servicing its demand (10 applications for user A and three applications for user B), and each set of two computers is completely independent of the other. Except for recovery from disasters such as floods or fires, critical applications are backed up by the second computer at each facility, i.e., the user manages priorities within his own shop. Are these dedicated facilities?

With three applications, user B must have one system that services one application and one system that services two. This satisfies the criterion that each segment services one specialized function or a very limited number of related functions. If each system is totally separate from the other (I/O is nonsharable, etc.), user B is said to have two dedicated facilities. If the two CPUs share I/O, operations staff, and management, then, because the three applications represent a limited set of related needs, user B is said to have one dedicated dual-machine facility.

User A, on the other hand, supports a fairly large number of applications (that are probably not very highly related). This lends a "general-purpose" flavor to user A's operation and qualifies that facility as a utility. The demand set may service a single broad segment of the corporation but because the uses are of a general-purpose nature across that segment, the equipment also must be regarded as general purpose.

8.2 DECISION CRITERIA

The reasons for entering a utility versus dedicated-facility decision process are either organizational or economic. Organizational issues center about control over the production process and service. Where there are complaints about the servicing of applications, such as slow response time for on-line applications, poor turnaround of batch submissions, or insufficient allocation of resources for development or maintenance, it is necessary first to determine whether the problems are real or whether they camouflage other issues.

If they are real, it is then necessary to determine whether the problems are capacity problems and are subject to the techniques outlined in Chapter 3, or whether they concern work methods or efficiency and are subject to the methods of Chapter 4. In the latter case, one is faced with the choice of launching an improvement effort, replacing the management, or throwing hardware at the problem.

But sometimes the "service problems" are issues that camouflage production or development problems in other line areas under the control of other managers. This situation is often characterized by a multitude of statements to the effect that the other line operation could better serve or penetrate the marketplace if only the data center did not deliver output late (even though input from that other line operation might generally be late), or that systems would not be implemented 12 years behind schedule if testing turnaround were faster. Solving this type of service issue by addressing the root causes—problems in the other production areas—is often organizationally quite difficult, particularly if there are more than just a few areas requiring attention. In such cases, distribution or dedication is sometimes considered for the sole purpose of compartmentalizing and localizing all the factors of production related to each group of services or end products. If all the factors of production, including data processing, are placed under one point of corporate responsibility, then service problems, costs of production, and development of new systems for each service or product line can be addressed with one manager.

The economic reasons for entering the utility and dedicated-facility decision process are self-evident—the decision process seeks to determine which alternative offers the cheaper means of production at a given level of risk. Since dedicated facilities managed by the user area do not have to deal with the extra set of management required for a general-purpose utility, the lines of communication are shorter and the planning function and responses to day-to-day production issues can be handled more effectively. In such cases, where dedication is supported on the grounds of increased service, injecting economics into the decision process implies that the users be able to articulate and quantify their expectations of increased service attributable to their direct management of the data processing operation, and further, that they be able to quantify the economic benefit of the service increment and compare that benefit to the incremental cost of dedication. This is to say that the incremental cost of dedication should be treated as any other investment—by determining the return expected from the investment and comparing it to alternative investment opportunities, as outlined in Chapter 6.

Several scenarios call for decisions between dedicated and utility alternatives to data processing operations. Either the corporation is establishing new facilities and is attempting to define its initial direction; the corporation currently employs the utility approach, is not completely satisfied, and is examining alternatives; or, the converse, the corporation is somewhat dissatisfied with its current dedicated approach and is evaluating the utility alternative. Whatever the circumstances, the decision process is based on consideration of three factors:

- The characteristics of demand
- Uncertainty of demand projections and the associated risk with various size capacity segments
- The incremental cost of one approach as compared to the other.

8.3 DEMAND CONSIDERATIONS

Sizing capacity is obviously a function of peak demand requirements, i.e., the risk level for any type of capacity should be positioned somewhere above peak demand, as in Figure 8.1. Stated another way, the size capacity selected for a facility, whether utility or dedicated, is determined in such a manner that the risk point is sufficient to accommodate peak demand plus projected growth. Extrapolating from earlier discussions of Chapter 2, demand, in this specific case, peak demand, defines the amount of capacity the operations staff must be

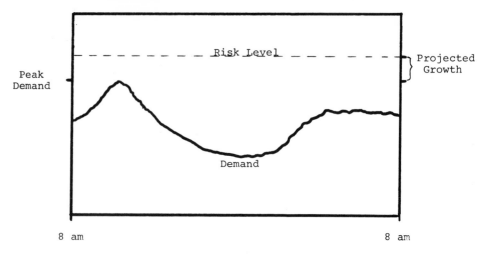

Figure 8.1. Sizing Capacity.

prepared to allocate to guarantee being able to service applications or jobs adequately for a given percentage of the time. So, if the variance of some set of applications, A, is such that 50% of the time it requires a daily peak of 2 units of capacity, 25% of the time a peak of 3 units, 15% a peak of 4 units, and 10% a peak of 5 units, then guaranteeing adequate resources to A for 90% of the time requires the availability of capacity of 4. Accommodating variances of this sort is identical for all capacity types: CPU, tape drives, disk drives, manpower, etc. Utility versus dedicated-facility trade-offs require analysis of the interre-

Job	Time	50th Percentile Utilization	Utilization Plus 2σ	Demand Including Cyclical Fluctuations
Input Capture	8 am	0	0.0	0
"	9 am	5	6.0	8
"	10 am	6	7.2	10
"	11 am	7	8.4	11
"	Noon	16	19.2	27
"	1 pm	18	21.7	30
"	2 pm	7	8.4	12
"	3 pm	6	7.2	10
"	4 pm	5	6.0	8
"	5 pm	5	6.0	8
"	6 pm	7	8.4	12
"	7 pm	15	18.0	25
"	8 pm	24	28.8	40
"	9 pm	9	10.8	15
FM	10 pm	55	60.0	71
RPG	11 pm	6	7.0	8
"	Midnight	0	0	0
"	1 am	0	0	0
"	2 am	0	0	0
"	3 am	0	0	0
"	4 am	0	0	0
"	5 am	0	0	0
"	6 am	0	0	0
"	7 am	0	0	0

Figure 8.2. Statement of Demand.

lationship of this type of variance across multiple sets of applications. Before considering the problem in this complexity, a simpler example of demand sizing is examined.

Example 8.4

In Example 2.5, demand was assumed to be flat for the 9 AM to 10 PM period. Here, assume a more realistic case, that of Figures 8.2 and 8.3, where transactions peak from 12 noon to 2 PM and again from 7 PM to 9 PM. The broken line represents normal (50th percentile) utilization. Each day's transaction volume varies, resulting in variations in resources consumed. Using CPU consumption as the key or critical resource, these variations are measured and a coefficient of variation $C_v = \mu/\sigma$ calculated. (More reference to this statistic later.) For simplicity, assume the Input Capture job averages 9.9% ($\mu = 9.9$) and peaks at 24% with uniform standard deviation of 10% of the average for each hour ($\sigma_i = 0.1\mu_i$). Then, for 95% confidence in being able to provide sufficient resources, it can be calculated that peak utilization during the critical on-line (9 AM– 10 PM) portion of the day is 28.8% (24% × 1.20). For purposes of capacity sizing, the peak would be read off the 10 PM–11 PM time frame as 60%. However, recognizing that the example considers the needs of a retail business, and recognizing also that there are sharp cyclical variations in transaction volumes for retail concerns, the analyst takes the business volume during the time of year the values of 60% and 28.8% were derived, compares that volume to anticipated (or historical) volume during the peak season, and adjusts the statement of demand accordingly.

This adjustment usually is based on historical trend data, on an analytical model that might be available, or perhaps on a regression indicating that a $Y\%$ change in trans-

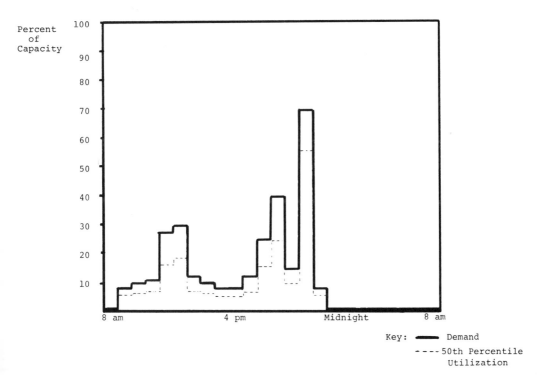

Figure 8.3. Statement of Demand.

action volume translates to an $X\%$ change in CPU time requirements, disk require- ments, etc. If, for example, the analysis indicated 39% expected business increase would produce an 18.5% increase in the File Maintenance's (FM's) CPU requirements, overall peak demand then would be 71%. This process is the way in which the demand profile of Example 2.5 was developed and how the hypothetical DEF-10 CPU was selected as the appropriate size CPU.

The peak during the on-line portion of the day would be 40% with a secondary on- line peak occurring around 1 PM. The importance of secondary peaks should become apparent as the discussion continues.

Summarizing, the selection of hardware dedicated to one application is purely a function of peak demand and its variance, taking into account cyclical (especially seasonal) fluctuations.

In a multiapplication dedicated facility, the required capacity size is deter- mined by adding the profiles of demand to each other, taking into account the variance of each application, the degree to which the peaks and valleys of each application complement or reinforce each other, and the degree of covariance among the applications.

Example 8.5

An application exists with the same CPU profile as that of Example 8.4, Figure 8.2. A credit authorization system (AUTH), its purpose is to handle inquiries against cus- tomers' credit cards to determine whether retail sales and cash advances will exceed individual credit limits. A related system, DDA, is profiled in Figure 8.4. Its function is to handle inquiries against customers' checking accounts and to post checks and pay- ments. The two systems communicate via a commonly accessed data base. What size capacity segment(s) (in this case we are discussing only CPU requirements) should be acquired?

It is important to first note that the utilization and demand numbers given in Figures 8.2 through 8.4 are percents and therefore relative to some base capacity size. The exercise, then, is to determine capacity needs relative to this base. Assume, for the sake of example, that the next larger machine has a relative size of 1.5, the next smaller machine a relative size of 0.75, and that the risk point for the larger of the two machines is at 75% and at 70% for the smaller machine.

Before proceeding, the analyst needs to know which columns of Figures 8.2 and 8.4 to add to give a total of demand. If both applications business cycles reinforce each other, for instance, if they both peak during November and December, and, if the user is not willing to impose degraded response times on his customer base, the analyst then sums rightmost columns. In this case, we note there are three periods of interest: noon until 2 PM, where combined demand rises to around 80%; 8 PM to 9 PM, where demand rises to 60%; and 10 PM to 11 PM, where demand rises to 71%.

One equipment alternative is, obviously, one 1.5 size machine. This reduces peak demand from 80% to $80 \div 1.5$ or 53.3%, well under the service-risk point. It also allows $(75 - 53.3)/53.3$, or a 40.7% growth to the current demand base before the next service risk point is reached. The drawback to this option (referred to later as Alternative 1) is its failure to provide back-up in the event of system failure.

A second alternative is to process the two applications on one 1.0 size machine. With the intrusion of the risk zone only five points, this option implies limited, perhaps 10%,

Job	Time	50th Percentile Utilization	Demand
On-Line	8 am	0.0	0
"	9 am	14.7	20
"	10 am	7.3	10
"	11 am	22.1	30
"	Noon	36.8	50
"	1 pm	36.8	50
"	2 pm	29.4	40
"	3 pm	7.3	10
"	4 pm	7.3	10
"	5 pm	11.0	15
"	6 pm	7.3	10
"	7 pm	11.0	15
"	8 pm	14.7	20
"	9 pm	7.3	10
"	10 pm	0.0	0
"	11 pm	0.0	0
"	Midnight	11.0	15
"	1 am	14.7	20
"	2 am	7.3	10
"	3 am	5.9	10
"	4 am	17.9	30
"	5 am	8.9	15
"	6 am	3.0	5
"	7 am	0.0	0

Figure 8.4. Statement of DDA Demand.

response degradation during some portion of the peak season. The number of instances and duration of intrusions into the risk zone can usually be estimated by the analyst using regressions of historical transaction data. As with the previous alternative, this option does not address the issue of back-up.

Beyond these two alternatives are those dedicating an entire machine to a single application. Because in these cases the applications are on separate CPUs, the processing of one does not interfere with the processing of the other. Hence, the issue of whether seasonal peaks reinforce each other is meaningless, and the sizing of each machine is a function of the peak seasonal requirements of the individual applications. One of these alternatives is two 0.75 machines. This would result in on-line peak demands of 50% ÷ .75 = 66.7% and 71 ÷ .75 = 94.7%, respectively. Assuming the evening authorization file maintenance (FM) could be elongated with no effect on its own deadline requirements and with no critical effect on the scheduled processing of DDA jobs that depend on the AUTH FM for input, peak demand for that system is read off Figure 8.2 as 40%. This capacity alternative then is associated with on-line peaks of 66.7% for DDA and 40 ÷ .75, or 53.3%, for AUTH. (It should be noted that proceeding with the analysis under the assumption there is no penalty for elongating the AUTH FM implies the analyst knowingly alters the formal statement of demand.) A variation of this alternative, one 0.75 machine and one 1.0 machine, avoids the elongation of the AUTH FM. Both of these options provide degraded backup in the event of system failure and can accommodate some volume growth, although this is limited to only about 12% of the base for DDA.

The final alternative is two 1.0 machines, which can accommodate much greater growth (25/.50, or 50%, for DDA on-line, limited growth for the AUTH FM, and 87.5% for AUTH on-line) and provide slightly degraded back-up. Remember that all the shared machine approaches assumed reinforcement of seasonal peaks and an unwillingness to give one application processing (service) priority over the other.

The decision process for selecting the best of the five alternatives centers about creating a payoff matrix, weighing the economic benefit of decreased equipment and staff costs associated with the one machine approaches against the economic (marketing) benefits of consistently acceptable response time and of back-up. These latter benefits are often difficult to quantify and this sometimes results in the circumvention of the decision process. In these instances, something akin to worst case analyses are often used, where the alternative that is the safest (offers the least risk to service) is selected. Here, economics are, for all intensive purposes, removed from the analysis.

In creating the decision matrix, some assumptions regarding operating expenses and service penalties must be made for the sake of example. Let the annual operating expense for a 0.75 configuration be $850,000; $1,000,000 for a 1.0 size configuration; and $1,250,000 for a 1.5 size configuration. For the single-machine alternatives, costs would be allocated on the basis of average demand. Since DDA averages 11.7% for the 50th percentile and AUTH averages 7.9%, DDA would be assigned (11.7/19.6) $\times$ $1,000,000, or $597,000, for Alternative 2, AUTH (7.9/19.6) $\times$ $1,000,000 or $403,000 and so on for the remaining alternatives.

Hypothetical penalties for degraded service are shown in Figure 8.5. In an actual case, these penalties would be calculated by the marketing areas, taking into account any penalty fees that may be incurred, business losses during capacity outages (or insufficiencies), future business losses due to customer dissatisfaction, etc. Total penalties/losses are added to the processing (data center) expense in Figure 8.6 and summed. At the same time, this figure relates cost to service risk as a function of capacity size. In an actual case, the qualitative terms "low" and "medium" would be replaced by specific service values, such as meeting response objectives 90% of the time, providing 20-second response time 10% of the time, and so on. These values would be calculated using the capacity and reliability evaluation techniques of Chapters 3 and 4.

As a final step, the incremental costs per application of each decision, i.e., the differ-

a)   DDA

Capacity Alternative	Expected Service Penalties due to Seasonal Peaks (000)	Expected Service Losses due to Capacity Outages (000)	Total Penalties/Losses (000)
1	$ 0	$ 5	$ 5
2	$10	$10	$20
3	$ 0	$ 5	$ 5
4	$ 0	$ 5	$ 5
5	$ 0	$ 0	$ 0

b)   AUTH

Capacity Alternative	Expected Service Penalties due to Seasonal Peaks (000)	Expected Service Losses due to Capacity Outages (000)	Total Penalties/Losses (000)
1	$ 0	$40	$ 40
2	$115	$50	$165
3	$ 0	$10	$ 10
4	$ 0	$10	$ 10
5	$ 0	$ 5	$ 5

Figure 8.5. Estimated Penalties/Losses Due to Service Problems.

a) DDA

Capacity Alternative	DDA Capacity	Service Risk	Processing Expense (000)	Expected Penalties/Losses (000)	Total Cost (000)
1	shared	low	$ 746	$ 5	$ **751**
2	shared	medium	$ 597	$20	$ 617
3	.75	low	$ 850	$ 5	$ 855
4	.75	low	$ 850	$ 5	$ 855
5	1.00	low	$1,000	$ 0	$1,000

b) AUTH

Capacity Alternative	AUTH Capacity	Service Risk	Proccessing Expense (000)	Expected Penalties/Losses (000)	Total Cost (000)
1	shared	low	$ 504	$ 40	$ 544
2	shared	medium	$ 403	$165	$ 568
3	.75	low	$ 850	$ 10	$ 860
4	1.00	low	$1,000	$ 10	$1,010
5	1.00	low	$1,000	$ 5	$1,005

Figure 8.6. Annual Expenses Plus Penalties/Losses.

ence in costs between the base alternative, taken here as Alternative 1, and the costs of the other alternatives are calculated in Figure 8.7. The total incremental cost is the sum of the incremental costs per application, $365,000 for Alternative 3, and so on. If the penalties are calculated correctly in Figure 8.5, the lowest cost alternative is chosen. In this case, Alternative 2, one 1.0 machine, would be selected. Apparently, in this example, the penalties for poor service during the DDA seasonal peak are not great enough to offset additional capacity costs. If, as an extreme opposite case, the user believed poor service during the peak season would drive all business elsewhere, the expected penalty would be much greater and the incremental cost of Alternative 2 would be accordingly

a)   DDA

Capacity Alternative	Total Capacity	DDA Capacity	Annual Cost (000)	Incremental Cost (000)	Unit Cost
1	1.50	Shared	$ 751	$ --	1.00
2	1.00	Shared	$ 617	$(134)	.82
3	1.50	.75	$ 855	$ 99	1.14
4	1.75	.75	$ 855	$ 99	1.14
5	2.00	1.00	$1,000	$ 244	1.33

b)   AUTH

Capacity Alternative	Total Capacity	AUTH Capacity	Annual Cost (000)	Incremental Cost (000)	Unit Cost
1	1.50	Shared	$ 544	$ --	1.00
2	1.00	Shared	$ 568	$ 24	1.04
3	1.50	.75	$ 860	$266	1.58
4	1.75	1.00	$1,010	$416	1.86
5	2.00	1.00	$1,005	$411	1.85

Figure 8.7. Comparison of Alternative Costs.

much greater. A mild case of this is indicated by the higher total (and unit) cost for AUTH from Alternative 1 to Alternative 2.

The rightmost column compares the normalized annual costs for each alternative. So, where annual costs for Alternative 2 are $617,000 for DDA, the annual cost and unit cost is $617/$751 or 0.82, 18% lower than the base alternative (Alternative 1).

Note that in the foregoing example AUTH unit costs suffer greater increases than do those of DDA.

It should also be noted that while Example 8.5 concerned itself with just two applications, the treatment of reinforced peaks and common (shared or utility) capacity versus dedicated capacity is the same for larger groups of applications.

Example 8.6

Assume the demand profiles of Example 8.5 hold but the DDA and AUTH seasonal peaks do not coincide. What differences arise?

As we have seen, reinforcement of peaks is an issue only among applications that co-reside in one machine. So, in this example, the removal of seasonal peaks as a factor will affect only Alternatives 1 and 2, the shared-equipment alternatives. Peak demand for these scenarios is calculated by summing the rightmost column of DDA with the center column (the 95th percentile, or whatever other percentile the analyst deems appropriate to maintain a given service objective) of AUTH. Limiting the discussion to CPU, Figure 8.8 is the statement of demand for Alternatives 1 and 2. Figure 8.9 compares peak demand for each alternative (reading values of Figures 8.2 and 8.4 for Alternatives 3 through 5) with corresponding values from Example 8.5 (reinforced seasonal peaks). Note that the change to demand associated with reinforced peaks reduces the capacity requirement enough that Alternative 2 becomes marginally feasible.

Time of Day	DDA	AUTH	Total
8 am	0	0	0
9 am	20	6	26
10 am	10	7	17
11 am	30	8	38
Noon	50	19	69
1 pm	50	22	72
2 pm	40	8	48
3 pm	10	7	17
4 pm	10	6	16
5 pm	15	6	21
6 pm	10	8	18
7 pm	15	18	33
8 pm	20	29	49
9 pm	10	11	21
10 pm	0	60	60
11 pm	0	7	7
Midnight	15	0	15
1 am	20	0	20
2 am	10	0	10
3 am	10	0	10
4 am	30	0	30
5 am	15	0	15
6 am	5	0	5
7 am	0	0	0

Figure 8.8. Statement of CPU Demand.

a) Reinforced
   Seasonal Peaks

Capacity Alternative	Utility (DDA & AUTH Coresident)	Dedicated DDA	Dedicated AUTH
1	.53	–	–
2	.80	–	–
3	–	.67	.95
4	–	.67	.71
5	–	.50	.71

b) Reinforced
   Seasonal Peaks

Capacity Alternative	Utility (DDA & AUTH Coresident)	Dedicated DDA	Dedicated AUTH
1	.48	–	–
2	.72	–	–
3	–	.67	.95
4	–	.67	.71
5	–	.50	.71

Figure 8.9. Comparison of Capacity to Peak Demand Ratios.

These examples, while dealing only with two applications, exhibit the same decision structure as full-scale utility and dedicated-facility considerations. Applications or groups of applications are evaluated in terms of their demand, variances in their utilization, interrelationships and degree of covariance with other applications, costs associated with alternative capacity scenarios, and expected losses/gains that are a function of various service levels associated with each capacity alternative. The capacity/risk analysis techniques are those described in Chapters 2 through 5. The cost/financial techniques are those outlined in Chapters 6 and 7. These techniques, however, must be expanded somewhat to address issues that arise when comparing different capacity alternatives. These issues reflect uncertainty about future service risk arising from uncertainty inherent in growth projections. They further reflect the difference between the accounting techniques for handling unutilized capacity in utilities and those suited to smaller, dedicated facilities.

8.4   TREATMENT OF UNCERTAINTY

Uncertainty in this kind of decision process occurs in three areas. One type of uncertainty relates to economics and the possible availability of future generations of capacity, as when a capacity-realignment decision is deferred in the hope that a faster, cheaper alternative will soon be available. Such uncertainty, however, is generally ignored, lest the decision be deferred forever. The second type of uncertainty relates to organizational structures. Will various business units be reorganized, the management structure changed, and will that change complement a proposed dedication or distribution strategy or conflict with it? Can the capacity strategy be easily adjusted in midstream or after implemen-

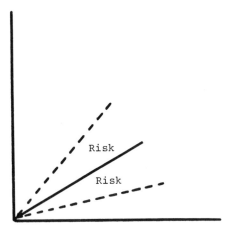

Figure 8.10. Uncertainty of Forecast Demand.

tation, or will there be a choice between capacity dictating organizational structure and the conversion of the corporation's newly converted dedicated facilities into a web of miniutilities? These are valid concerns, and an organization would be going at risk to construct or reorganize any plant capacity, including computer operations, if its future market or business objectives were unclear. This type of forecasting being somewhat outside the purview of this discussion, the third source of uncertainty, uncertainty over the size of future demand, is considered.

Uncertainty of future demand refers to two concerns. First is the uncertainty in the marketplace regarding future transaction volumes and required coding changes to accommodate changing product or service offerings. With respect to the data center, these would translate to changes in existing applications' capacity (especially CPU) requirements. The other concern relates to the emergence of new, previously unforecast applications that may not be the result of strategic marketing plans but of the automation of formerly manual operations. Whichever of the three types of forecasting processes described in Chapter 3 are used, uncertainty changes the resulting demand (or capacity requirement) forecast from the straight line in Figure 8.10 to a cone (dotted lines). These diverge more and more from the straight line the farther into the future one tries to project, i.e., uncertainty increases as target processing scenarios become more distant. And the risk associated with the ability of some specific capacity scenario to process demand is proportional to the distance between the solid and dotted lines. Hence, utility versus dedicated-facility capacity decisions are best made by examining the requirements of the most likely estimates of future demand (solid line) and sensitizing those requirements by both the impact of the requirements at the edges of the cone and by the probability that actual future demand will vary from the straight line and map toward those edges.

Example 8.7

Assume that after lengthy evaluations of marketing plans and their effect upon demand, the most likely growth rate for computer demand (and for the sake of example, the

Growth Rate Number	Annual Growth Rate	Probability of Occurrence
1	10.50%	10%
2	12.75%	15%
3	15.00%	50%
4	17.25%	15%
5	19.50%	10%

Figure 8.11. Table of Growth Rates.

discussion will center about CPU demand, although what follows would apply equally as well to any of the other resource types) is 15% per year, compounded annually. Further assume that the analysis indicates there is a 30% chance of this estimate being in error by 15%, and a 20% chance it may be in error by 30%. Assuming the same demand and capacity alternatives as Example 8.6, what are the implications? Let the useful life of the equipment be 3 years.

Figure 8.11 states the possible growth rates and their probability of occurrence. The process here, is to calculate the size of the different potential future demand states; map them into each capacity alternative, as was done in the previous two examples for the case of no growth; calculate the service risks; receive marketing input on the penalties that could be incurred with degraded service; create a new payoff matrix to determine the magnitude of financial exposure under each alternative; and finally, weight the new payoff matrix by the probability of occurrence of each future demand state to derive the expected incremental cost of each capacity alternative.

Figure 8.12 begins by multiplying third-year growth factors, the annual rate raised to the third power, times peak demand for both the utility (shared) and dedicated environments (again assuming the AUTH FM cannot be excessively elongated without disruption to service). The result is a list of all possible demand scenarios 3 years hence. Since the risk levels are assumed to be at 75% of Relevant Capacity on the large (1.0 and 1.5) machines and at 70% on the smaller (0.75) device, it can be observed that Alternative 2, a shared 1.0 size machine, is totally unsatisfactory under all assumptions. Figure 8.13 converts peak demand to a percentage of capacity for the 1.5 machine of Alternative 1. Here it can be seen that at the end of the 3-year period there is a 65% probability demand will be in the immediate neighborhood of the risk point. Because the calculation of the risk point and the associated degradation of service is not always as precise as one would wish, growth Alternatives 3 and 4 are both treated the same by describing their risk to service as low. Growth Alternative 5, nearly 7 points beyond the risk point, clearly is associated with service degradation during a wider period of the day, and with a high degree of degradation. In order to determine the degree to which growth Alternatives 3 through 5 are a problem, and to evaluate the overall financial

Growth Rate (%)	3 Years Compounded (%)	Shared (Unreinforced Seasonal Peaks)	DDA	AUTH
			(dedicated)	
10.50	34.9	97.1	67.5	95.8
12.75	43.3	103.2	71.7	101.7
15.00	52.1	109.5	76.1	108.0
17.25	61.2	116.1	80.6	114.5
19.50	70.6	122.8	85.3	121.1

Figure 8.12. Alternatives of Peak Demand (Base Capacity = 1.0).

Growth Rate Number	3 Years Compounded (%)	Peak Demand	Service Risk
1	34.9	64.7	–
2	43.3	68.8	–
3	52.1	73.0	Low
4	61.2	77.4	Low
5	70.6	81.9	Medium

Figure 8.13. Alternatives of Peak Demand (Base Capacity = 1.5).

Capacity Alternative 1

Growth Alternative	Expected Service Penalties due to Seasonal Peaks (000)		Expected Service Losses due to Capacity Outages (000)		Total Penalties/Losses (000)
	DDA	AUTH	DDA	AUTH	
1	$0	$0	$5	$40	$45
2	0	0	5	40	45
3	0	0	10	50	60
4	5	30	10	50	95
5	15	120	20	80	235

Figure 8.14. Estimated Penalties/Losses Due to Service Problems.

Capacity Alternative 1

a) DDA

Growth Alternative	Service Risk	Processing Expense (000)	Expected Penalties/Losses (000)	Total Cost (000)
1	–	$746	$ 5	$751
2	–	746	5	751
3	Low	746	10	756
4	Low	746	15	761
5	Medium	746	35	781

d) AUTH

Growth Alternative	Service Risk	Processing Expense (000)	Expected Penalties/Losses (000)	Total Cost (000)
1	–	$504	$40	$544
2	–	504	40	544
3	Low	504	50	554
4	Low	504	80	584
5	Medium	504	200	704

Figure 8.15. Annual Expenses plus Penalties/Losses.

Growth Alternative	Probability of Occurrence	Total Cost (000)	Contribution To Expected Cost (000)
1	10%	$1295	$129.5
2	15%	1295	194.3
3	50%	1310	655.0
4	15%	1345	201.8
5	10%	1485	148.5
		Expected Cost	$1329.1

Figure 8.16. Expected Cost of Capacity Alternative 1.

Growth Alternative	DDA Peak Demand (Base=1.0)	AUTH Peak Demand (Base=1.0)
1	67.5	95.8
2	71.7	101.7
3	76.1	108.0
4	80.6	114.5
5	85.3	121.1

Capacity Alternative	Shared	DDA	AUTH
1	1.50	--	--
2	1.00	--	--
3	--	.75	.75
4	--	.75	1.00
5	--	1.00	1.00
6	--	1.00	1.50
7	--	1.50	1.50

Figure 8.17. Summary of Capacity and Demand Alternatives.

risk to this (one 1.5 machine) capacity alternative, the analyst uses the same marketing data employed in the development of the penalty and cost matricies of Figures 8.5 through 8.7. Figure 8.14 is the resulting hypothetical penalty matrix, and Figure 8.15 presents the related costs for each growth alternative.

Processing expenses are calculated by multiplying the percentage demand each application contributes to total demand by the total ($1.5 million) equipment and staff expense. Figure 8.16 uses this data to calculate the range of cost exposures for this capacity alternative and the expected value of the cost. This latter value is used as a base for calculating the incremental costs of the remaining four capacity alternatives. Using Figure 8.17 as a reference for the capacity segments provided by each alternative and the demand at the end of the third year (base capacity equals 1.0), Appendix G provides the details of the calculations of financial exposure (worst-case total costs) and expected total costs for each capacity alternative. Figure 8.18 calculates the incremental cost of each capacity alternative for the third year. The overall decision regarding which

Capacity Alternative	3rd Year Service Risk	Worst Case 3rd Year Cost (000)	Expected Cost (000)	Incremental Cost (000)
1	Medium	$1,485	$1,329.1	$ --
2	High	1,600	1,432.5	103.4
3	High	2,500	2,315.0	985.9
4	High	2,450	2,254.3	925.2
5	High	2,500	2,332.5	1,003.4
6	High	2,300	2,272.0	942.9
7	Low	2,520	2,507.3	1,178.2

Figure 8.18. Incremental Costs of Alternative Capacity Decisions.

capacity alternative to choose would repeat the process of Figure 8.18 for the first and second years of the investment. Summing these values with their corresponding third year expected costs would provide the final expense data from which the acquisition decision would be made.

The foregoing example is sensitive to two factors: the accuracy of the demand forecast and the accuracy of penalty/loss estimates. With respect to the latter item, the penalty/loss factor, two things may be said. One is that uncertainty associated with this estimate can be treated in the same manner as uncertainty of demand was treated, that is, by using probabilistic errors of estimate. This makes the treatment of the entire capacity selection process somewhat more tedious but no more complicated. The second is that in many cases the penalties for degraded service are not estimated, usually because marketing data are not available or because the data are not adequately communicated across lines of the corporation. In such cases, analyses of the form of Figure 8.18 are performed but with incomplete penalty costs. If one were comparing, for example, Alternatives 5 and 7, a typical conclusion might be to select Alternative 7, stating the belief that the additional service would "be worth the $174.8K incremental expense," but not being able to quantify the added value.

As the discussion illustrates later, the full-utility versus dedicated-facility decision, while somewhat larger in scope than this two application example, employs the same treatment of uncertainty.

8.5   DECISION COSTS

If service and service risk are accurately portrayed in the cost statement for a given capacity alternative, the key decision criterion is the incremental cost, the cost differential between one alternative and another. Before this can be addressed, a discussion is required of the relationship of the cost treatment of unutilized capacity in the utility as opposed to in the dedicated facility.

Maintaining the definitions established earlier in the chapter, the major difference between a utility and a dedicated facility is its purpose: a utility is generalized and a dedicated facility is focused on a limited segment of demand. This has an important implication on the manner in which capacity (specifically, capacity that is not utilized) is considered and, hence, on the way in which costs are defined. Note that this discussion applies primarily to large segment size units of capacity, i.e., CPUs, mass storage devices, etc. The acquisition of small segment size units of capacity primarily I/O devices can be managed to match demand closely and thereby limit the existence of unused capacity.

Figure 8.19 is a capacity/demand chart for a 24-hour operating cycle. Demand is cyclic, peaking at 70% of the risk level and averaging 50%. Hence, excess capacity equals 30% (although other unused capacity also exists during nonpeak hours). Figure 8.20 is this chart projected over a three year time frame to show expected demand growth. For the sake of example, a decreasing rate of growth is assumed with peak demand averaging 80% of the risk level in the first year and increasing to 90% in the second year and 100% in the third. Similarly, average demand is assumed to grow from an average of 60% to 70% and

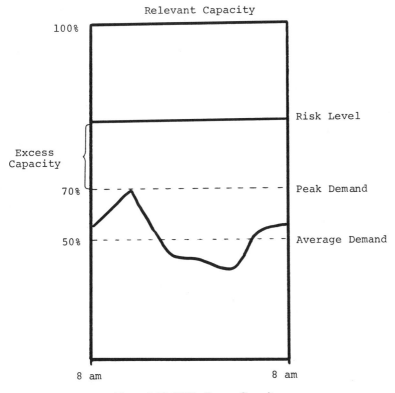

Figure 8.19. Utility Excess Capacity.

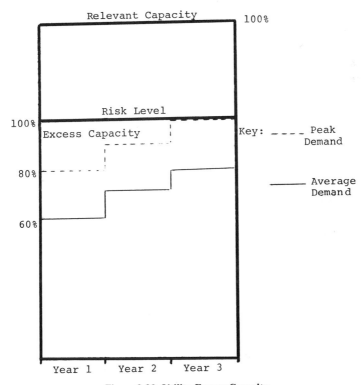

Figure 8.20. Utility Excess Capacity.

80%. Unit costs, as before, are calculated at the point of average demand, 50% in Figure 8.19.

By definition, there is no excess capacity in a dedicated facility. This stems from the fact that dedicated facilities are defined to exist for specific limited sets of demand, such as one application or two highly related applications. Thus, any capacity that is unused is at once an overhead. A utility, on the other hand, is defined as servicing a generalized customer (or application) base. And, just as an electric utility services customers next month whose existence it was unaware of this month, the utility computer center is initially sized to service a generalized base of applications over the declared useful life of the equipment, even though its management may be totally unaware of which new applications will appear, say, 2 years hence. So, when the utility capacity is initially sized and acquired, there is capacity that goes unused according to plan. This differs sharply from the dedicated facility where capacity may go unused because an exact match of available capacity segment size to the waiting application could not be found. For instance, if demand is 3 and capacity is offered by the vendor only in sizes of 1, 2, and 4, capacity size 4 will be selected. The difference between 3 and 4 will go unused and is considered an overhead. The only case when there is excess capacity in a dedicated facility is where larger capacity is acquired because there are indications of future transaction volume changes (and therefore of resource consumption changes), or if there are coding enhancements to the dedicated application(s) planned that will result in resource requirement changes.

Given the period that the corporation may wish to use to account for computer resource usage and bill customers, most often 1 month, dedicated facilities apply 100% of their cost to the application(s) they service. Utilities, on the other hand, apply costs via the rate (unit-cost) approach described in Chapter 7. When developing these rates, the corporation has two alternatives. One is to distribute its costs fully over the immediate fiscal period (fiscal year), as the last chapter described, a methodology that divides expenses for the fiscal period by average demand over the duration of the fiscal period, again, generally 1 year. The second alternative is to also use expenses for each separate annual fiscal period but to divide those expenses by average demand, where the average is calculated from the time the capacity is configured until a new segment of capacity is acquired (i.e., the capacity, taken as a whole, is reconfigured).

For example, in Figure 8.20, capacity becomes saturated after the third year. Presumably, capacity will be added at the start of year 4. Hence, the period the configuration exists in its original state is three years and average demand, accordingly, is calculated as 70%. This type of accounting tends to discount the cost of processing early in the life of the configuration, presumably when dollars are worth more than in later years. Note that it is the existence of excess or unused capacity spanning multiple fiscal periods that makes this type of accounting legitimate. The affect of this accounting technique upon stabilizing unit costs and upon cash flow over the term of the specific configuration is obvious. This complete, the discussion of decision costs is continued.

While incremental cost is perhaps the most important decision criterion, the utility versus dedicated-facility decision considers marginal and average costs. Summarizing the last few examples, in addition to the treatment of costs of unutilized capacity, the cost of a capacity alternative (and therefore its incremental cost compared to another alternative) is a function of several other factors. These include: variations in requirements of individual applications; the degree of covariance among applications; and the difference in relationship of peak demand to average demand between applications, or groups of applications. In addition, there are other costs due to technical and administrative control factors that will be discussed later in this chapter.

Marginal costs are the expenses incurred to produce the next unit. In the context of the computer facility, it is the cost of processing the next job or the cost of processing the next transaction in an existing job. Average unit cost was defined in previous chapters.

Example 8.8

The columns denoting utility demand in Figure 8.21(a) and the solid bars in Figure 8.21(b) describe demand for a two-machine utility that processes 50 applications. CPU demand is expressed as a percent of total relevant capacity of both machines. I/O demand is expressed in numbers of drives that must be allocated. Assume I/O Relevant Capacity is 56. Application X is being developed, and its forecast demand is represented by the crosshatched bars. A decision must be made regarding whether to add this to the utility or to establish a dedicated computer facility. Ignore the costs of establishing the required physical and environmental facilities of a new data center, and assume that the annual cost of running the utility is $2 million and the annual cost of the dedicated

Time	Utility CPU (%)	Utility I/O (drives)	Application X CPU (%)	Application X I/O (drives)	Total CPU (%)	Total I/O (drives)
8 am	30	20	0	0	30	20
9 am	30	20	0	0	30	20
10 am	30	20	0	0	30	20
11 am	40	30	0	0	40	30
Noon	50	40	0	0	50	40
1 pm	60	50	0	0	60	50
2 pm	65	50	0	0	65	50
3 pm	60	50	0	0	60	50
4 pm	55	50	5	5	60	55
5 pm	55	50	10	5	65	55
6 pm	40	40	15	5	55	45
7 pm	40	30	20	5	60	35
8 pm	45	30	20	8	65	38
9 pm	50	30	20	8	70	38
10 pm	55	30	15	8	70	38
11 pm	50	30	15	8	65	38
Midnight	45	30	10	8	55	38
1 am	40	20	5	8	45	28
2 am	35	20	5	8	40	28
3 am	30	20	5	5	35	25
4 am	35	20	0	0	35	20
5 am	40	20	0	0	40	20
6 am	35	20	0	0	35	20
7 am	30	20	0	0	30	20

Figure 8.21(a). Utility Demand.

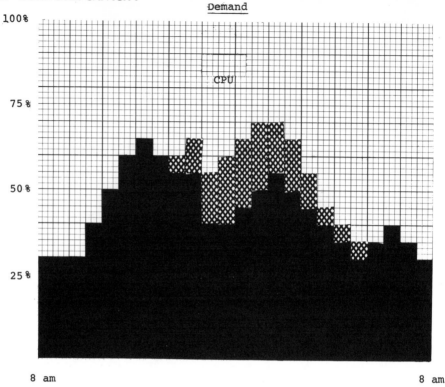

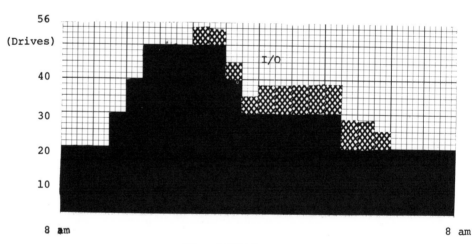

Figure 8.21(b). Demand.

facility would be $750 thousand. What are the changes to average unit cost for the next fiscal period, the incremental costs, and the marginal costs associated with the decision?

It is clear that the addition of Application X to the utility would not reinforce the old peak but instead would create a new peak of 70% at 9 PM. If the risk level associated with the utility's machines is at 75%, there would be no service-risk problem, unless there are segmentation problems spreading the new peak across two machines. For instance, if the original 9 PM demand consisted of two applications, each requiring 50% of one CPU, the addition of Application X requiring 20% of the dual CPU facility (40%

of one CPU) would create a peak that was equal to only 70% but would be an average of 50% and 90%. Clearly, such segmentation would result in service degradation.

Assuming there is no such demand segmentation problem, it can be observed that the current CPU Capacity is sufficient to accommodate the increased demand. Similarly, there are sufficient I/O units. Relevant CPU Capacity, assuming 250 business days per year, can be shown to be a total of 43,200,000 CPU seconds per year for the two CPUs and Relevant I/O Capacity equal to 1.21×10^9 drive seconds. Average unit cost is then 4.67¢ per CPU second (at an average demand of 43.54% + 6.04%, or 49.58%) and 0.14¢ per I/O drive minute (assuming an average demand of 30.83 + 3.38, or 34.21 drives). Since no additional equipment, staff, etc., are required, the marginal cost of running Application X in the utility is zero.

For the dedicated-facility alternative, assume the machine size is 60% that of either of the two utility CPUs. Eight I/O devices are attached. Peak and average CPU demand are then equal to: $2 \times 20\% \div 0.6$, or 66.67%, and $2 \times 6.04\% \div 0.6$, or 20.13%. There are obviously no service-risk problems here. If $600,000 of the total $750,000 is associated with the CPU, unit CPU costs are calculated as:

$$\$600,000/21,600,000 \times 0.2013 = 13.80¢$$

But since a CPU second here is equal to 0.6 CPU seconds on the utility machines, the equivalent or comparable unit CPU cost is:

$$13.80¢/0.6 = 23.00¢$$

4.93 times the utility unit CPU cost. This factor is due to two items: the economy of scale offered by the larger system ($1 million for a capacity of 2.0 versus $600,000 for a capacity of 0.6) and the difference in average demand, the point at which average unit cost is calculated, from 49.58% to 20.13%. Similarly, I/O unit cost can be calculated as 0.20¢ per drive second. Unit costs rising in this manner is indicative of diseconomies of scale, other production inefficiences, or both.

The total cost of processing an Application X in the utility may be calculated to be:

$$6.04/49.58 \times \$1,000,000 + 3.38/34.21 \times \$1,000,000$$

or $221,337, and 100% of $750,000 in the dedicated facility.

From the perspective of the corporation as a whole, the incremental cost of the dedicated alternative is $750,000. If the user's revenue-expense base is isolated from that of the rest of the corporation, his perception of the incremental cost is:

$$\$750,000 - \$221,337$$

or $528,663.

In a true utility, the capacity that would go unused if Application X is dedicated would be taken by another demand increase during the life of the utility. Otherwise, the worth of the CPU and I/O that would remain unutilized would be reflected in higher utility average unit production costs.

Example 8.9

Assume the same demand profile as in the previous example from Figure 8.21 for the utility. Figure 8.22 shows Application X reinforcing the peaks of the existing utility demand. How does this affect the utility versus dedicated decision?

Time	Utility CPU (%)	Utility I/O (drives)	Application X CPU (%)	Application X I/O (drives)	Total CPU (%)	Total I/O (drives)
8 am	30	20	0	0	30	20
9 am	30	20	0	0	30	20
10 am	30	20	5	5	35	25
11 am	40	30	10	5	50	35
Noon	50	40	15	5	65	45
1 pm	60	50	20	5	80	55
2 pm	65	50	20	8	85	58
3 pm	60	50	20	8	80	58
4 pm	55	50	15	8	70	58
5 pm	55	50	15	8	70	58
6 pm	40	40	10	8	50	48
7 pm	40	30	5	8	45	38
8 pm	45	30	5	8	50	38
9 pm	50	30	5	5	55	35
10 pm	55	30	0	0	55	30
11 pm	50	30	0	0	50	30
Midnight	45	30	0	0	45	30
1 am	40	20	0	0	40	20
2 am	35	20	0	0	35	20
3 am	30	20	0	0	30	20
4 am	35	20	0	0	35	20
5 am	40	20	0	0	40	20
6 am	35	20	0	0	35	20
7 am	30	20	0	0	30	20

Figure 8.22(a). Utility Demand.

With demand between the hours of 1 PM to 4 PM varying from 80% to 85% of current demand, there is clearly a service problem. The corporation is faced with two choices. One is to isolate the service problem into debugging by reducing the capacity available for maintenance and development and thereby maintaining sufficient CPU availability for production. This has a cost in terms of delaying returns on projects under development and of reducing the reliability of existing applications requiring maintenance. But since the effectiveness of these activities is difficult to quantify and since poor data center service is sometimes required to explain slipped development schedules, these costs are, in practice, often not quantified. The second choice is to acquire another (third) segment of capacity. This action would only be taken when utility demand was projected to increase beyond Application X to fill the new CPU. From scanning the I/O column, it is clear that additional drives are also required. Ignoring intermittent drive failures, variances in the demand base, etc., assume that two drives are acquired. Hence, the marginal cost of processing Application X in the utility is $500,000 for the additional CPU plus:

$$2 \times \$1,000,000/56$$

or $35,714, for the two I/O drives. As before, cost of developing a dedicated facility is $750,000. The incremental cost of the dedicated facility is then:

$$\$750,000 - \$535,714$$

or $214,286, if the only reason the third CPU was acquired was to keep Application X in the utility. If other applications were also awaiting entry to the utility, $500,000 would be spent anyway by the corporation and it would perceive the incremental cost of dedication to be:

$$\$750,000 - \$35,714$$

Demand

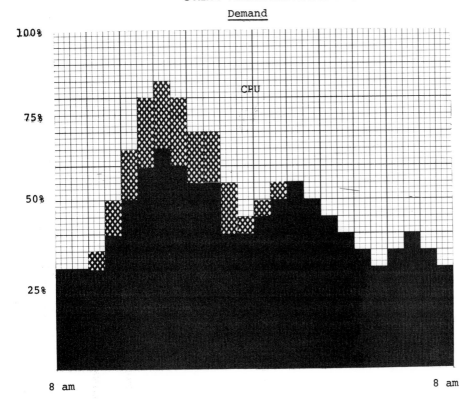

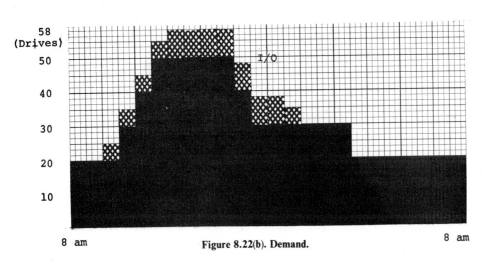

Figure 8.22(b). Demand.

or $714,286. Assuming that the third CPU and additional I/O gear are used to the same degree by future applications as the original equipment was used in Example 8.8, the utility cost for processing Application X would continue to be $221,337 and the user would continue to perceive the incremental cost of dedication to be $528,663.

Example 8.10

Assume the same utility demand profile as that of the previous examples. Application Y is profiled in Figure 8.23. While it is, on average, equal to Application X from before,

Time	Utility CPU (%)	Utility I/O (drives)	Application Y CPU (%)	Application Y I/O (drives)	Total CPU (%)	Total I/O (drives)
8 am	30	20	5	4	35	24
9 am	30	20	5	4	35	24
10 am	30	20	5	5	35	25
11 am	40	30	10	5	50	35
Noon	50	40	10	5	60	45
1 pm	60	50	10	5	70	55
2 pm	65	50	10	5	75	55
3 pm	60	50	10	5	70	55
4 pm	55	50	10	5	65	55
5 pm	55	50	10	5	65	55
6 pm	40	40	10	5	50	45
7 pm	40	30	10	4	50	34
8 pm	45	30	10	4	55	34
9 pm	50	30	10	4	60	34
10 pm	55	30	5	4	60	34
11 pm	50	30	5	4	55	34
Midnight	45	30	5	4	50	34
1 am	40	20	5	4	45	24
2 am	35	20	0	0	35	20
3 am	30	20	0	0	30	20
4 am	35	20	0	0	35	20
5 am	40	20	0	0	40	20
6 am	35	20	0	0	35	20
7 am	30	20	0	0	30	20

Figure 8.23(a). Utility Demand.

note how much more evenly balanced it is across the 24-hour operating cycle—there is relatively little difference between peak and average demand. How does its cost structure compare with that derived in Example 8.8?

As before, the marginal cost of adding this application to the utility is zero—CPU loading does not penetrate beyond the risk point, and there is sufficient I/O capacity. Similarly, since average demand is the same as in Example 8.8, the cost of processing Application Y is $221,337.

The incremental cost of a dedicated facility, however, differs. Here, peak CPU demand is 10% of two 1.0 machines, or 20% of one. Let there be two dedication options available, one from vendor A, the same vendor that supplied the utility equipment and one from vendor B. Vendor A proposes a 0.30 machine with five I/O devices. With peak CPU demand at 67% on the 0.30 machine, there is no service risk due to CPU availability. Assume that there are no tape drive outages. Costs for this system are $300,000. Vendor B proposes a similar capacity configuration costing $225,000 annually. Figure 8.24 summarizes the incremental and annual processing costs for the corporation associated with each alternative.

The Vendor A alternative has an annual operating expense 26% greater than the utility alternative. Assuming the utility computer costs to be 40% of the total corporate expense of providing the services supported by Application Y, the total cost is then $221,337/0.4, or $553,343. Alternative A, then, would add:

$$(\$300,000 - \$221,337)/\$553,343$$

or 14.2%, to the bottom line of the total production costs. If these services were operating at a 15% margin, a Vendor A dedicated decision would essentially remove profitability from the product (service) line.

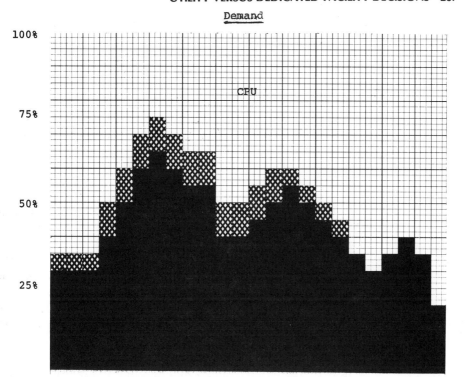

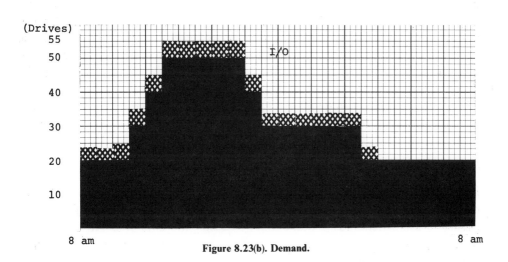

Figure 8.23(b). Demand.

The Vendor B alternative clearly provides ongoing production costs competitive with the utility. The $3,663 annual cost differential would, under the same scenario, translate to only a 0.7% increase in total (computer plus noncomputer) production costs. Clearly, if one considers annual operational expenses and their effect upon profit margins, Vendor B offers an acceptable alternative.

In this example, if the user's bias is to accept Vendor B's proposal, the corporation has two obvious decisions to make. One is whether there is enough demand forecast to replace Application Y's potential utilization of previously acquired utility equipment.

	Alternative		
	Utility	Vendor A	Vendor B
Incremental Cost	$ --	$300,000	$225,000
Annual Processing Costs	$221,337	$300,000	$225,000

Figure 8.24. Cost Comparison.

If there is, the incremental cost of dedication is substantially lowered since the acquisition of Vendor B's equipment either obviates the need to acquire another piece of dedicated equipment (to satisfy another demand increase) or defers the requirement to enlarge the utility. The actual incremental cost of dedication then becomes a function of how quickly the rest of the demand base is growing, the resulting rate at which new equipment must be acquired and becomes heavily loaded, and the time value of money. The second decision the corporation must make is whether there are any special corporate relationships it maintains with Vendor A and the degree to which those relationships will be damaged by the selection of its competitor.

The shape of new segments of demand and the interrelationship between demand segments, then, play important roles in the selection of appropriate size capacity segments and, hence, in the incremental costs of various equipment alternatives. Note that in the previous example, whereas the price of Vendor B's equipment was important to economic viability of dedication, it was the shape of Application Y's demand curve, i.e., the degree of flatness or lack of divergence of peak demand from average demand, that formed the basis for that viability.

Holding equipment demand aside, there are other more subtle factors that often go unrecognized in the utility versus dedicated-facility decision process.

8.6 CONTROL AND TECHNOLOGICAL CONSIDERATIONS

In addition to the equipment-oriented processing services discussed up to this point, all data centers provide supportive services that either facilitate the processing of users' demands or make that processing more reliable. However, since these services play a secondary role to the actual daily execution of jobs, their role is sometimes dismissed as superfluous, and their consideration either scaled down or omitted from evaluations of the service capabilities of proposed dedicated-facility alternatives. The risk of underestimating the effect these factors have upon production centers about the ability of applications to interrelate with each other and the long-term reliability of the production environment.

Recognizing that it is somewhat unwise to allow people to do their own work independently, it is important for management to make sure the analyst structures utility versus dedicated-facility decisions in a manner that compares all services offered by one alternative to all those offered by the other. The analyst can use two methods to accomplish this. One is the use of a highly unbundled costing or pricing structure. As was seen in Chapter 7, unbundling costs, even to a moderate degree, has a pronounced effect upon the articulation of the existence and the expense of support services that already may be provided by the base alternative. And it encourages discussion of the degree to which support services may be beneficial to various equipment (utility or dedicated) alternatives. The second method is simply to create a checklist of support services offered in each alternative. Since a service menu is required for both approaches, the following discussion examines the principal categories of these services.

- **Contingency Planning**
  Relating to conditions that occur in the event of major capacity outages, contingency planning deals with the requirement for insurance or back-up processing facilities for critical applications. In a utility, this is usually accomplished where there is a multi-CPU environment by creating a list of priorities for applications spanning the entire user base. If one CPU fails for more than a short period, actions are taken to suspend processing of those applications at the bottom of the list (usually development and non-critical maintenance) and redistributing those at the top of the list.

  The existence of an adequate contingency plan assumes the existence of the capability to size properly the requirements of the high-priority jobs and establish scheduling scenarios for the most likely cases. In a distributed or dedicated environment, redistribution of workload is made more difficult by geographical and organizational boundaries. Therefore, any comprehensive capacity strategy documents criteria and procedures for invoking back-up and for recovery procedures across all key sectors of capacity and demand.

  It is worth noting that while all contingency planning is based on setting priorities for applications, it is often difficult to get a varied population of users to agree which lines of business within the corporation should receive priority and therefore, which applications should receive top priority. Compounding this is the fact that management may be unwilling to take sides and an agreed-upon, definitive list of application priorities may be unobtainable. In such cases, if the processing environment is a utility, the problem can be circumvented by allowing the utility manager to create his or her own list, which, while imperfect, will be recognized to be better than none. In a dedicated environment, ownership of the contingency problem resides with individual facility and business managers.

  The costs of contingency capacity may take the form of: increased average unit cost (if capacity has been increased to provide for emergencies, average demand will be a lower percent of available capacity); charges received from external data centers for actual usage, provided on a best-efforts basis when outages occur; or insurance premiums plus usage charges when external data centers guarantee a given availability of capacity and a given level of service.

- **Systems Programming Services**

In a utility environment, systems programmers generally provide a large number of services. A great many of these are worthwhile for they facilitate smooth execution of the application base. The services typically required include: maintaining operating systems and keeping them up to date to the extent that the vendor will continue to support the site; updating the operating system to accommodate changes to the hardware configuration; and troubleshooting problems that always seem to crop up as a result of these maintenance and updating activities.

These groups also provide coverage on the data center floor to troubleshoot problems that occur with applications, particularly production, and to install and maintain the software packages users may require, such as data-base management systems, special data access methods, etc.

The costs of systems programming support are sometimes articulated through unbundled costing. However, in practice there is usually insufficient data on the use of each individual type of service rendered to justify separating overall systems programming support into each of its segments. Usually, if there is an indication that these services may in the future be distributed among several users, it would be prudent to initiate some sort of rough internal logging of resources expended and client.

- **Tape Library Services**

While the role of the tape library is decreasing as data processing evolves to on-line shared-disk files, as opposed to batch jobs that pass tapes to each other, batch environments still rely on the tape library as the central means of data exchange. Hence, in any multiuser, multiapplication environment, it is critical that the utility/dedicated-facility analysis recognize the need for controlled storage and exchange of corporate and other business data. For batch shops this is most efficiently addressed by one central tape tracking or control system, and hence, one centralized tape library, if all dedicated facilities, i.e., equipment, are in close proximity. Otherwise, a series of smaller, interrelated facilities, although difficult to manage, are required. As stated, this problem decreases in magnitude as data exchanges become more oriented towards disk or drum storage and are accessed with telecommunications techniques.

- **Materials Assembly/Disassembly Services**

Occasionally, dedicated facility proposals underestimate the degree of preparation required before jobs can be processed. Job control cards may have to be punched, libraries or procedures updated, parameters punched on cards, etc. At the other end of the processing cycle, printed output may have to be physically manipulated, quality/accuracy tests performed, files or catalogues updated, and interaction may be required with users or other applications. In a utility environment, these activities may be somewhat taken for granted, the actual level of manpower not correctly perceived by the user or potential operator of a dedicated alternative. For such items, an assessment by an independent, qualified third party is useful for determining the cost of establishing the equivalent services offered by the utility in a dedicated facility.

- **Scheduling Services**
  In multiapplication, and especially multimachine, facilities, this function: establishes a game plan for the coming day's processing, particularly important where there are large numbers of on-demand jobs or daily variations in an application's processing profile; monitors adherence of actual production status to planned; and adjusts plans, i.e., makes midstream schedule changes as variances begin to threaten individual deadline commitments. These services are obviously not required in one or two application dedicated environments.

- **Messenger Services**
  Charged with the responsibility of meeting preset delivery and input gathering commitments, the messenger services function takes on greater importance in a dedicated, and especially a distributed, environment. As the number of items passed between data centers is added to the normal user-directed delivery schedule, and as that schedule becomes more complex to manage as the number of processing centers increases.

- **Bursting and Decollating Services**
  The final direct production function for applications producing multipart printed output, it is difficult to maintain a centralized, timely bursting and decollating service in a dedicated environment due to the effect of varying input (output from printers) availability times. The effect of these variances is compounded by the nature of the bursting and decollating operation, a mechanical environment with a high degree of manual intervention on machines that process one work order at a time. In large-volume centers, printers with automatic burster/trimmers are an alternative to less cost-efficient (duplicated) distributed bursting and decollating facilities.

- **Capacity Planning Services**
  Well-run, large utilities tend to maintain close contact with marketing and systems areas, inventorying projected future increases to demand and preparing capacity acquisition strategies to insure adequate service levels in the future. While the intent of distribution or dedication is to place processing closer, both geographically and organizationally, to business areas or other responsibility centers, a certain discipline is required to effect reliable forecasting of requirements. Allowing a dedicated-facility financial analysis to omit this capability either recognizes that the applications the proposed facility will service will never change in function (specifically, that no funds will be allocated to further development or to anything other than emergency maintenance/troubleshooting), or else recognizes the introduction of an unspecified level or risk to the viability of the proposed capacity in the mid- to long-term future.

  Recognizing the inefficiencies of establishing little capacity-planning functions wherever in the corporation there are computer processing facilities, the entry of costs into the dedicated-facility financial analysis can either be a direct assignment of staff and other expenses or an allocation from some centralized planning group.

- **Site-Preparation Services**

  These services refer to the actual physical preparation required to establish or maintain a computer center environment. Included are planning and execution of electrical work, plumbing, air conditioning, and, occasionally, reinforcement of the physical plant. These functions are performed in two modes. One is the establishment of new data center facilities, where the costs of such efforts are (or should be) amortized across the useful life of the data center and included in the financial analysis of the proposed facility. Indeed, most such proposals include these factors. But to omit some cost provisions from on-going production costs is to assume the facility will never require any hardware change whatsoever—not a tape drive, a printer, a terminal, or even just the creation of an office on the data center floor. This omission, again, assumes little if any volume growth in the services supported by the applications being processed and no allocation of funds for programmers to enhance applications or develop new applications.

    As with capacity planning services, the financial entry for site-preparation services can be an allocation from a centralized corporate group for small dedicated facilities where dedicating staff would introduce inefficiencies.

- **Financial-Planning Services**

  These types of services can be divided into six classes: (1) developing and administering to annual data center expense and capital budgets; (2) developing and administering cost- or price-oriented chargeout systems; (3) developing unit costs from the budget for use in these chargeback systems; (4) responding to the multitude of questions that always arise when users are presented with their monthly invoices; (5) servicing users' requests for financial analysis of proposed new facilities; and (6) performing lease versus purchase analyses.

    When not resident in the data center organization, these services can also appear financially as allocations from centralized corporate financial-planning groups.

- **Environmental Services**

  Differing somewhat from the primarily labor-intensive services discussed so far, environmental services include the cost of electrical power, amortization of such physical plant items as air conditioning, uninterruptable power equipment, and floor space, and security factors including amortization of access-control mechanisms and security personnel expenses.

While not necessarily complete, the preceding list is intended to be a general indication of the types of services that may exist in one alternative, although their costs may not be differentiated from the overall cost of processing, and may not exist or be comparable in another alternative.

Often, in an actual decision scenario, it is useful to have the level and costs of these services presented in tabular form, as in Figure 8.25. The use of this type of structure is helpful in minimizing the risk of buying less servicing, direct processing, and support than would at first appear. This is particularly useful in the absence of fully unbundled cost comparisons. In addition to insuring proper comparison of the degree of existence of certain services, it is incumbent upon the reviewer of utility versus dedicated-facility decisions to determine the degree of standardization necessary to enable applications run in different data centers under different management structures to interrelate. Although there is a broad scope to these primarily technological concerns, two areas generally deserve the most attention.

One area relates to the requirement for data centers to provide mutual backup. A point of concern here is the degree of standardization of operating systems, which refers not only to the type of operating system selected, but also to the details, that is, the options selected, for each operating system on each dedicated machine. Although two applicatons may process under one type of operating system, for example, IBM's MVS, user A's application may require options that have not been included in user B's copy of that operating system. Such concerns about compatibility extend to technical conventions for naming data sets and programs, organization of system libraries and procedures, programming languages supported in specific data centers, software packages supported, procedures for file recovery and back-up, etc. These problems are often minimized by the creation of centralized systems programming groups to attend to the various dedicated facilities. The usual objection to this centralized approach, however, is in the area of service. But as with processing service, difficulties with systems programming service are either management problems or staff-size (capacity) problems. Both can be addressed with performance contracts, and both will not necessarily be solved, in the global sense, by dedication.

The second type of technological concern relates to the requirement for applications (and therefore individual dedicated data centers) to exchange data. In a batch-processing environment, the exchange medium is generally tape. Here, it is critical that technical compatibility be maintained for such things as file-naming conventions and tape-label formats. On the engineering side, if two tape drives do not have similar tolerances for their read/write heads, one will not be able to read the data the other has written. Hence, in a dedicated envi-

Service	Alternative 1 Staff/Cost	Alternative 2 Staff/Cost	Alternative 3 Staff/Cost		Alternative M Staff/Cost
1) full backup	xx/yyy	xx/yyy	xx/yyy	• • •	xx/yyy
2) systems programming	xx/yyy	xx/yyy	xx/yyy	• • •	xx/yyy
3) performance measurement	xx/yyy	xx/yyy	xx/yyy	• • •	xx/yyy
•	•	•	•	• • •	•
•	•	•	•	• • •	•
•	•	•	•	• • •	•
M) hardware planning	xx/yyy	xx/yyy	xx/yyy	• • •	xx/yyy

Figure 8.25. Capacity Alternative Decision—Support Services Comparison.

ronment, it is extremely important to insure all vendor engineers conform to uniform maintenance procedures.

Example 8.11

The K Corporation has a large utility data center, comprised of three very large CPUs, 160 disk drives, 84 tape drives, two high-speed printers, and four very high speed printers. The demand base consists of 125 applications, 100 of which are divided among five major user areas. Unhappy with the users' perceptions of the level and cost of service the utility is providing, management is entertaining proposals for dedication. How should the decision process be structured?

Using CPU as the critical resource, let each utility machine be associated with a base capacity of 2. Total capacity is then 6 and demand is given in Figure 8.26. Demand is stated in terms of CPU requirements, the critical resource since that is the most expensive element of capacity to acquire and since CPU is available only in relatively very large segments. Costs for alternative facilities presented later will also reflect the expense of the other (I/O) classes of capacity. The analysis required to determine the size of I/O capacity for each capacity alternative is identical to the CPU analysis and, so, will be omitted. Assume the total cost of the entire utility, including equipment, staff, supplies, software packages, etc., is $9 million annually.

In Figure 8.26, peak utilization is recognized to vary daily and, over any time period—say, 1 month—an average and standard deviation may be calculated. Assuming a normal distribution, 90% confidence for the statement of peak demand calls for a value of $\mu + 1.5\sigma$. This is calculated as shown for each user grouping of demand and for the composite (utility). Note the role that variance plays in the determination of peak demand.

In order to select capacity segments for each demand grouping, assume that machines are available in relative sizes of 2.0, as stated in the base capacity configuration, 1.25, 1.0, 0.75, and 0.50 and that the risk point for each machine is at 80%. Converting demand from a percent of the utility (base equals 6.0) to a more usable number, the peak demand values of Figure 8.26 are multiplied by 6. These are given in Figure 8.27 for each dedicated-facility scenario.

At once the significance of C_v, the indicator of demand variances, on capacity selection becomes apparent. Users 2 and 4, who on average have the same peak requirements (see Figure 8.26) cannot be accommodated by the same size CPUs. User 4 can be

	Peak Utilization			Peak Demand	Average Demand
	Avg.	Std. Dev.	C_v	(90% Confidence)	
User 1	12.0	2.0	.17	15	10
User 2	11.5	2.3	.20	16	10
User 3	11.0	.7	.06	12	10
User 4	11.5	1.0	.09	13	10
User 5	15.0	3.3	.22	20	9
Remainder	7.0	.8	.11	8	6
Utility	63.5	5.0	.08	70	55

Figure 8.26. Statement of Demand.

	Peak Demand	Average Demand
User 1	90	60
User 2	96	60
User 3	72	60
User 4	78	60
User 5	120	54
Remainder	48	36

Figure 8.27. Statement of Demand (Base = 1.0).

placed within the 80% limit on a 1.0 size machine, but user 2, with the higher C_v, requires at least the 1.25 size machine.

Beginning the process of comparing costs, if the utility's chargeout methodology is fully bundled, utility costs, assuming full chargeout, are calculated by multiplying the total annual expense of the utility by the percent of total average demand attributable to each user. These are calculated as:

User 1	$1,636,364
User 2	1,636,364
User 3	1,636,364
User 4	1,636,364
User 5	1,472,727
Remainder	981,817
Total	$9,000,000

(For the sake of simplicity of the example, costs are left lumped according to CPU demand. An actual calculation would be more detailed.)

The exercise now turns to separating these values into allocations of equipment, supplies, operating staff, and support. The separation of operating staff enables the comparison of coverage at individual workstations between dedicated alternatives and the utility. Differences indicate either substandard or excess staffing postures. The separation of support is in accordance with the earlier discussion of comparing levels of non-core processing services. Turning to the service of back-up, it is noted that the triplex utility offers internal back-up, that is, when one machine fails, critical applications are transferred to another CPU, I/O drives assumed being shared or switchable between CPUs. In the dedicated environment, this obviously requires that each facility consist of at least two CPUs. Hence, User 4 cannot be placed on one 1.0 size CPU but, rather, his demand, if back-up is deemed valuable, must be segmented into two equal parts and placed on two 0.50 size CPUs. Obviously, issues such as the desirability of processing half of demand during periods of capacity outages and the ability to split demand into two equal segments, affect the final CPU selection.

Financial analyses of alternative capacity scenarios; tradeoffs between penalties and losses resulting from system outages versus the incremental cost of smaller, redundant segments of capacity; and the incremental cost of dedication are performed as before.

Hence, the utility versus dedicated-facility decision process is one with concerns regarding many indirect services in addition to core production capabilities. The final issue discussed related to the evaluation of alternative processing scenarios is that of economies of scale.

8.7   ECONOMIES OF SCALE

Economy of scale refers to the lowering of unit production costs as a function of increasing output or plant (capacity) size. Stated differently, if, in the long run, unit cost in a plant that has been expanded continues to slope downward, then, in this context, increasing economies of scale have been realized. Conversely, since it is clear that increasing economies of scale cannot be realized forever, an upward slope of the average unit cost is an indicator of decreasing returns to scale. This is reflected by Figure 8.28.

There are two ways in which economies of scale are realized. One is by economies of agglomeration and the other by economies of specialization. "Economies of agglomeration," roughly translated, refers to increasing returns to scale resulting from gathering various segments of demand into a fewer number of larger segments. The larger demand segments can be serviced by a small number of large segments of capacity rather than by many more smaller capacity segments. This enables the lowering of unit costs by taking advantage of the cost/performance benefits of more productive hardware, such as 10,000-line-per-minute printers rather than, say, 2000-line-per-minute printers and of operating-staff savings associated with the smaller number of large capacity devices. A further advantage obtainable through agglomeration of demand is increased efficiency of the uses of manpower. While there have been relatively recent experiments with despecialization of labor (most notably, that of the Swedish auto manufacturer Volvo), the creation of relatively large labor pools enables the worker to maintain concentration on a specific task and obviates the need for employees to move from one workstation (such as the master console)

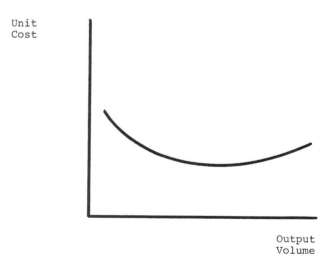

Figure 8.28. Changing Economies of Scale.

to another (tape stations, job setup, etc.). As an additional benefit, the resulting gain in efficiency eliminates some delays where application processing is suspended, awaiting the allocation of a peripheral resource. Thus, employee specialization can avoid an artificial inflation of the statement of hardware demand. A variation of this strict approach to manpower allocation is assignment of staff to specific workstations with periodic rotation to other workstations.

"Economies of specialization" refers to the provision of facilities or services critical to the production process but too costly for each producer to maintain in the small quantities it alone requires. The mechanics for providing these services are specialization of function, where in data processing, one production center may, for example, maintain an extensive tape library that accommodates the needs of smaller, adjacent production centers.

Increasing returns to scale do not continue at a constant rate and, in fact, the change may at some point become negative. A major cause of diseconomies of scale is insufficient managerial control. In large, complex organizations where there is considerable delegation of authority, the maze of bureaucratic procedures that can exist and the large degree of coordination among various organizational units can become a constraint to effective allocation of computer hardware resources. Causes of diseconomies of scale are referred to as deglomerative forces. Where these forces exist, marginal costs become greater than average unit costs, creating upward pressure on unit cost, the primary symptom of diseconomies of scale.

Even where resource allocation is not ineffective, there may exist the perception of ineffectiveness. Because it is difficult to measure effectiveness and managerial control and even more difficult to quantify inefficiencies resulting from such deglomerative problems, it is difficult to identify the point at which a firm optimizes the economy of scale of one of its computer operations. Therefore, although it is true that economies of scale are a determinant of the structure a firm ought to establish for its computer operation (or, for that matter, any other operation), no precise way exists to quantify the factors contributing to the decision process that determines the optimal structure. One can only isolate those entities affecting the outcome and deal with them in a manner that is more qualitative than quantitative. How, then, does one determine where economies of scale are possible?

While it is true that the full value of economies of scale is realized only when demand, or output volume, is great enough to warrant the establishment of a large, diversified production facility, the inherent structure of data processing is such that compromises are possible which permit a degree of dedication. An example is that of the tape library, given previously, where several small dedicated production centers may share the support facilities of another center. This permits dedication of hardware and operating staff while retaining centralized control over a data exchange facility. Similar scenarios are easily visualized for such functions as bursting and decollating, systems programming, capacity planning, guard and other security services, environmental services (air conditioning, power), etc. These scenarios are of utility support organizations servic-

MODEL	CAPACITY	COST	CAPACITY/COST
3X31	0.25	0.50	0.50
3X32	0.50	0.75	0.67
3X33	1.00	1.00	1.00
3X34	2.00	1.50	1.33
3X35	3.00	1.75	1.71

Figure 8.29. Equipment Generation N.

ing dedicated (or utility) production facilities. Organizationally separate, the support functions would be billed on a contract or per-usage basis to each dedicated or utility production facility that they service, and the charges would be entered into that facility's chargeout system. When that chargeout system is based upon unbundled costs, the contribution to unit cost of each support service is made visible and may easily be compared to contributions of proposed dedicated support functions of equal caliber. This assumes that the services provided by the utility support function have been accurately documented, both in terms of function and manpower expended, and that it can be shown that the staffing for the proposed dedicated alternative will provide roughly the same quality of services. In this manner, the incremental economies of scale for support functions can be evaluated.

Similarly, economies of scale for hardware can be determined by comparing the cost of computing devices for various large- and small-scale alternatives. While this topic has been covered in earlier examples dealing with different size configurations, it is important to complete the discussion by maintaining the distinction between economies of scale and price/performance characteristics of different generations of equipment. When a vendor introduces a line of equipment of varying capacity sizes and costs, such as those in Figure 8.29, the larger devices offer greater economies of scale. When the next generation of equipment with similar functions is offered by that same vendor, it is incorrect to state, for example, that because device 4X31 provides the same price/performance ratio as device 3X33, yet is only one-fifth its size, that there are no economies of scale associated with the larger 3X33 device. Economy-of-scale comparisons and analyses must be kept within equipment lines. Finally, it is difficult to make comparisons between specialized minicomputers and general-purpose computers (Figure 8.31).

MODEL	CAPACITY	COST	CAPACITY/COST
4X31	0.20	0.20	1.00
4X32	0.40	0.35	1.14
4X33	0.80	0.60	1.33
4X34	1.60	0.95	1.68
4X35	2.50	1.25	2.00

Figure 8.30. Equipment Generation N + 1.

	CPU CAPACITY	I/O CAPACITY	COST
Vendor X			
Model 3X31	10	10	0.50
Vendor D			
Model P70	11	2	0.10

Figure   8.31.   Minicomputer—General-Purpose Computers: A Comparison.

While CPU capacity is greater on Vendor D's cheaper machine, I/O capacity is significantly smaller. A composite capacity is impossible to calculate (unless, of course, it can be shown that 8 I/O units of Vendor X's equipment will never be used, in which case questions are raised regarding why Vendor X's more expensive equipment was selected). Furthermore, there may be other factors—vendor support, maintenance, software availability—that differ and cannot be quantified. Hence, economy-of-scale analyses must not only be kept within equipment lines but also must apply only to equipment with similar functions or purposes.

8.8   SUMMARY

The alternative processing scenarios available to a corporation can be either general-purpose facilities, known as utilities, or facilities dedicated to restricted segments of demand. Either case can be centralized or distributed to different locations, and either can be serviced by a utility or dedicated management structure, although the latter presents some problems.

The decision process for determining whether the computer hardware structure should be dedicated or utility is an involved procedure centering about three major factors: current demand; future changes to demand and existing uncertainty regarding the size and timing of those changes; and costs.

Factors of demand include normal peak daily requirements, the size of variances to these peaks, the probability or frequency with which a given size variance occurs, and the degree to which both normal peaks and variances are caused by the interrelationships between applications. These interrelationships can either be due to predecessor/feeder relationships or to reinforcement of peak usage periods due to coincidental output deadlines.

Anticipated increases in future demand are added to the profile of current demand for each alternative capacity scenario. Uncertainties in the timing and size of these increases complicate the equipment selection process either by adding risk that demand will be too large to be processed on the proposed hardware without unacceptable service degradation or by adding the risk that the timing of the acquisition of the hardware will be less than optimal.

Finally, the issue of costs relates not only to the usual concerns of marginal and incremental costs of alternative decisions and of annual and average unit costs, but also to the risk that the stated costs of one alternative may not be directly comparable to those of another alternative. This situation arises in cases where noncore processing services, such as back-up and technical assistance, are not articulated well enough to determine whether they exist in equivalent levels in each alternative processing scenario. Economies of scale are either economies of agglomeration or economies of specialization. The former type refers to the grouping of demand into large segments that can take advantage of better price/performance hardware and that bring sufficient volume to justify large, multifunction organizations. Economies of specialization refers to specialization of function such that services essential to the production process, but too costly for any one data center to provide in the small volume it alone requires, are produced en masse by some one data center and sold to the other corporate users.

9
COMMUNICATING ISSUES

*Recognizing that correct data is only about 25% of what is required
to facilitate decisions, this chapter addresses methods of communicating capacity/demand and cost issues between the data center and senior
management.*

9.1 INTRODUCTION

The most valuable commodity in any organization is the attention of senior
management. With it, any problem can be solved, and without it no major
decisions can ever be approved. But, as textbooks on the subject of organization
will agree, that attention is a scarce resource, and as with any other scarce
resource it should be used sparingly and effectively if it is to be available whenever decision approvals are required. Using management's attention sparingly
implies that they receive a minimal amount of information from the data center.
Indeed, the more numbers communicated, the greater the chance of misinterpretation or confusion. As a rule, no information need be offered unless it
directly pertains to specific actions that are being sought.

Using management's attention effectively implies that communications are
concise and in a language with which the intended audience is already fully
familiar. Put more bluntly, few people outside the world of data processing
enjoy speaking "computerese." If forced to converse in that manner, most non-data processing managers will either misinterpret the data they receive, lose
confidence in managers they perceive cannot communicate in the language they
and their peers accept, or simply lose interest and fail to make any decision.

There are generally two classes of communications to management. One is
some sort of monthly or other cyclic set of indices that describes either production or budgetary data. (Since the presentation of budgetary data is generally
understood, it is set aside for the purposes of this discussion.) Usually, the purpose of such production indicators is little more than to let management know
that the data center still exists and that no disasters have recently occurred. The
other class of communications is associated with impending changes or decision
processes. The presentation of this second class is key to the establishment of
an effective dialogue between the data center and senior management.

9.2 DATA PRESENTATION

It is important to recognize the difference between management's concerns and
the concerns of the data center. Management abhors an absence of data, and

rightly so. Without brief monthly indices, it would be impossible for them to obtain quick glances of the business-as-usual state and of overall progress in meeting key objectives. But aside from waving hello, little value accrues to the data center by providing these statistics. Since it often cannot escape the burden of providing them, however, the data center ought to use the opportunity to encourage management to ask the questions it wishes them to pose and to respond to certain types of indices that the data center will use when it asks management to approve capacity acquisition decisions. Once this type of dialogue is established, dialogues during decision-making sessions will be much simpler and far more effective.

In selecting data, there are two options: to publish everything or to publish only key indicators. Since management's production concerns generally are units of output, plant utilization, service, and unit cost, those are the key indicators they should ordinarily receive and nothing else. Other data can be provided on request (a rarity) or in response to specific problems that arise. Note how this approach to communicating with management follows the two-tier concept of separating capacity/demand issues from tuning issues. Capacity/demand issues are reserved for concerns of management, whereas tuning concerns are directed toward the technical staff. Each has access to the other's data when desired.

The key indicators are provided according to the availability of the data. Units of output has no meaning in a multiapplication environment since the output, processed data, is intangible and rarely spread homogeneously across the application base. For example, if one application produced one report and another application produced another 10, no direct comparison of the size or significance of the two outputs could be made. Hence, no statement regarding the total number of units of output can be made. This is particularly true where the primary result of each application is the updating of a large number of dissimilar records or the processing of highly different transactions.

For the case of a facility dedicated to one application, a count of transactions processed or records updated might have some meaning. However, one must be careful to distinguish between results (output) from the data center and transactions arriving indirectly from other work areas. The former, if in a form conducive to measurement, might be representative of output. The latter is often broken down or grouped into intermediate transactions of different sizes and different computer-resource requirements. Counts of these items, again, if in a form conducive to measurement, can have little meaning to a corporate front office that evaluates information mainly in relation to the goods or services it perceives it is marketing. Hence, units of output is often an index that is impossible to formulate well. Besides, if computer processing is, in fact, supportive of the processing of some item for another node of the corporation, the unit of ouput for that item will be counted as part of that nodes' monthly index.

One choice of data to publish is utilization statistics on the analysts' 10 favorite classes of equipment and staff, as the Throughput Method of demand accounting suggests. But, as described in earlier chapters, this approach tends to be somewhat confusing and does not always relate directly to plant (capacity) utilization. A second choice is to follow the Allocation Method and publish the demand statistic as described by the Critical Resource Concept. As with the statement "The mill is at 80% capacity," while this does not describe the entire environment, it provides a picture of the most critical element and provides an idea of the state of the plant, that is, the data center, under normal business conditions. Unusual conditions are either not of significant duration or fall into one of two categories. One is the emergency of which management, if it has been alert, is already cognizant; the second is the case of persistent data center problems that tend to become known throughout the corporation regardless of the type of index published.

Figure 9.1 offers a tabular format that can be used to communicate production indices. The first row states the capacity level that existed during the reported month. This is useful for comparing the states of different data centers and for interpreting relative movements of the statistic. (For example, if demand dropped by 33%, was a third system added that month?) The service statistic is merely the accumulation of performance against service criteria specified in each demand contract that the data center maintains with its user community.

Since capacity chargeout rates probably should remain fixed during the fiscal period (see Chapter 7), a monthly unit cost statistic has little meaning. If budgetary variances are treated separately as budget items (rather than as production-cost items), the only factors that could be reflected in a varying unit-cost statistic are variances due to changing average demand, since monthly average unit cost would vary inversely to average demand, and to variances due to efficiency. I.e., the unit cost of utility capacity varies inversely with the amount of

	JAN	FEB	MAR	APR	MAY	JUN	JUL	AUG	SEPT	OCT	NOV	DEC
Relevant* Capacity	1.4	1.4	1.4	1.4	1.4	1.4	2.0	2.0	2.0	2.0		
Average Demand	68%	69%	71%	72%	70%	74%	51%	54%	53%	57%		
Peak Demand	81%	83%	85%	80%	85%	92%	66%	67%	68%	74%		
Performance Effectiveness Factor	96%	97%	96%	96%	97%	95%	99%	98%	97%	99%		
Service Indices:												
DPD Controlled	97%	98%	97%	98%	98%	96%	97%	96%	98%	96%		
Overall	96%	95%	96%	97%	97%	95%	96%	95%	97%	94%		

*In terms of 2 IBM 3033 Central Processing Units

Figure 9.1. Table of Production Indices.

	JAN	FEB	MAR	APR	MAY	JUN	JUL	AUG	SEPT	OCT	NOV	DEC
Relevant* Capacity	1.4	1.4	1.4	1.4	1.4	1.4	2.0	2.0	2.0	2.0		
Average Demand	68%	69%	71%	72%	70%	74%	51%	54%	53%	57%		
Peak Demand	81%	83%	85%	80%	85%	92%	66%	67%	68%	74%		
Efficiency	96%	97%	96%	96%	97%	95%	99%	98%	97%	99$		
Standard Unit Cost	1.00	1.00	1.00	1.00	1.00	1.00	1.00	1.00	1.00	1.00		
Variance Between 100% Capacity and 85% Risk Level	.18	.18	.18	.18	.18	.18	.18	.18	.18	.18		
Efficiency Variance	.00	.00	.00	.00	.00	.01	.00	.00	.00	.00		
Difference Between Risk Level and Average Demand	.29	.27	.23	.21	.25	.17	.19	.12	.14	.06		
Average Unit Cost	1.47	1.45	1.41	1.39	1.43	1.36	1.37	1.30	1.32	1.24		

* In terms of 2 IBM 3033 Central Processing Units

Figure 9.2. Table of Production Indices.

capacity available for productive purposes. Figure 9.2, which attempts to show these items, can be confusing to someone who only sees the chart once a month. Furthermore, the chart, even if understood, offers no information beyond the statistics of average demand and monthly efficiency. Both of these conditions are to be avoided if managements' attention is to be preserved for future needs. Figure 9.2, then, while adhering to the correct language and ostensibly the proper indices, is clearly a case of providing excessive and superfluous data. For this reason, Figure 9.1 omits cost data and includes an efficiency statistic.

When tables of statistics are not effective for dealing with certain management styles, pictures can be more appropriate. Figure 9.3 offers a method of graphing demand trends. The solid line represents actual demand and the dashed line represents the current forecast. To keep the chart simple, only three items are shown relative to Relevant Capacity: peak demand, average demand, and the risk level. These items are expressed in a manner that is consistent with the Critical Resource Concept, again, for purposes of simplicity. Often an accompanying paragraph or two explaining the major reasons for change from last month to the current month adds credibility by giving the perception of having control and of understanding the data. In the example given in Figure 9.4, the graph fosters the perception of control and lack of bias by establishing feedback to report on the permanency of changes to demand, by fully disclosing the data center's (site's) contribution to the demand problem, and by challeng-

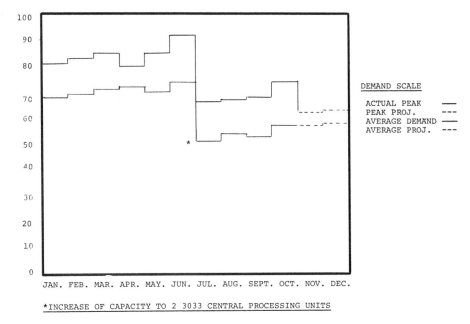

Figure 9.3. Data Processing Division Capacity Chart.

ing the validity of its own statistics (efficiency) when they exceed accepted tolerance limits. Figure 9.5 is similar to Figure 9.2 in that it provides information that can be quickly understood. (Here, the solid and dashed lines have the same meaning as before and the dotted lines denote the original forecast.) The idea is to provide management with a comparison of the actual capacity/demand position of the data center with what was originally forecast. While noble in

```
Attached are the October production indices and
capacity/demand chart.

Increases from the site and MTG account for the
entire change in peak demand and three of the
four point change to average demand.  The
site half of the increase arose in the operations
area and in systems programming.  In next month's
report, we will comment whether these increases
were temporary and, if not, whether they can
be managed out of the peak.  At that time, we
will also report on whether the MTG user antici-
pates that increase to be permanent.

Efficiency, the complement of CPU downtime plus
production re-runs, was again reported by the
site to be 99%, well outside the 2% tolerance
limit of the 95% objective.  This would indicate
either problems in the manner in which the
statistics is compiled or that the sites objective
of 95% was set too low.  We will address this
issue with the site in January.
```

Figure 9.4. Explanation of Indices.

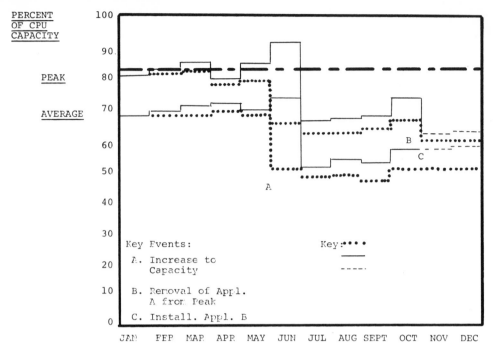

Figure 9.5. Data Processing Division Capacity Chart.

purpose, the analyst's excessive enthusiasm has resulted in ignoring the difference in requirements between reporting business-as-usual statistics and presenting data in support of specific decisions required to address a particular problem.

Suppose, for the sake of example, that Figure 9.3 evolved into Figure 9.6 several months later. Demand now varies significantly from earlier projections, and the current projection has demand penetrating the risk zone within several months. Now is the time for gaining management's attention with a warning that a decision must be made either to permit degrading the servicing of computer demand or to allocate funds for a major capacity acquisition. The kinds of communication required to effect decisions are merely an elaboration of the communications dealing with the business-as-usual state.

Remembering that management would rather not deal with either degraded service or commitments of funds, it is important to continue to limit the flow of data to as little as the audience wishes to see. Since presentations dealing with service and financial matters are usually more effective in the form of face-to-face meetings rather than the impersonal submission of indices, the presentation can often be structured by layering the data and sensing when the audience will accept no more. Further, if the data center wishes to maintain the audience's attention, it is important to keep the entire presentation in the language with which management is most comfortable. *This implies avoiding all use of technical jargon.*

The data prepared to facilitate the decision should anticipate three questions:

- What happened?
- What is the best alternative solution?
- How much will it cost?

The first question, "What happened?", is the most important since it opens the presentation, states the issue management is being asked to consider, and provides reference data for them to understand the business and organizational factors that led to the need for a decision. The chart in Figure 9.6 is a good starting point since it states the issue succinctly: the corporation will run short of computer capacity during month x. But this diagram presents only peak and average demand. A slightly more detailed chart, such as in Figure 9.7, is required to describe a typical 24-hour operating cycle for the data center. The first column indicates the time of day, here expressed in 1-hour intervals, and the second column provides the raw usage statistic, expressed in CPU minutes. The third column converts the second column into a percentage of Relevant Capacity. It may be observed the site has a Relevant Capacity of 12 (i.e., 391.42/0.5436). The histogram to the right converts column 3 into graphical format and provides an easy-to-read picture of the capacity/demand state. With the risk point assumed at 80%, the equipment complex is nearly saturated.

The value of a 24-hour chart, such as the one in Figure 9.7, is that it surfaces questions regarding which applications constitute the peak, and therefore which applications take joint responsibility for the need to augment capacity. Atten-

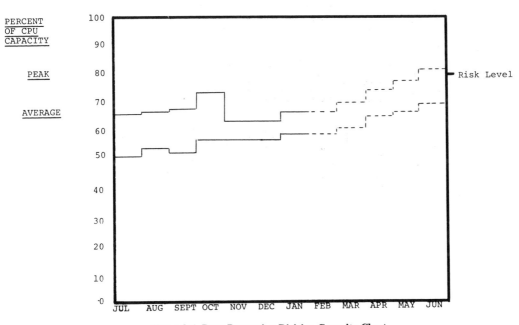

Figure 9.6. Data Processing Division Capacity Chart.

WORK OF FEBRUARY 1980

GRAPH OF AVERAGE CPU USED FOR ALL JOBS   BY ALL USERS

INTERVAL	AMOUNT	PERCENT
0800-0900	391.42	54.36%
0900-1000	422.50	58.68%
1000-1100	475.47	66.04%
1100-1200	551.85	76.65%
1200-1300	504.94	70.13%
1300-1400	512.92	71.24%
1400-1500	525.68	73.01%
1500-1600	541.51	75.21%
1600-1700	542.10	75.29%
1700-1800	531.47	73.82%
1800-1900	547.83	76.09%
1900-2000	475.76	66.08%
2000-2100	469.78	65.25%
2100-2200	453.27	62.95%
2200-2300	392.02	54.45%
2300-0000	399.65	55.51%
0000-0100	307.21	42.67%
0100-0200	317.07	44.04%
0200-0300	352.28	48.93%
0300-0400	406.61	56.47%
0400-0500	387.45	53.81%
0500-0600	410.17	56.97%
0600-0700	432.25	60.04%
0700-0800	401.04	55.70%
AVERAGES	448.01	62.22%

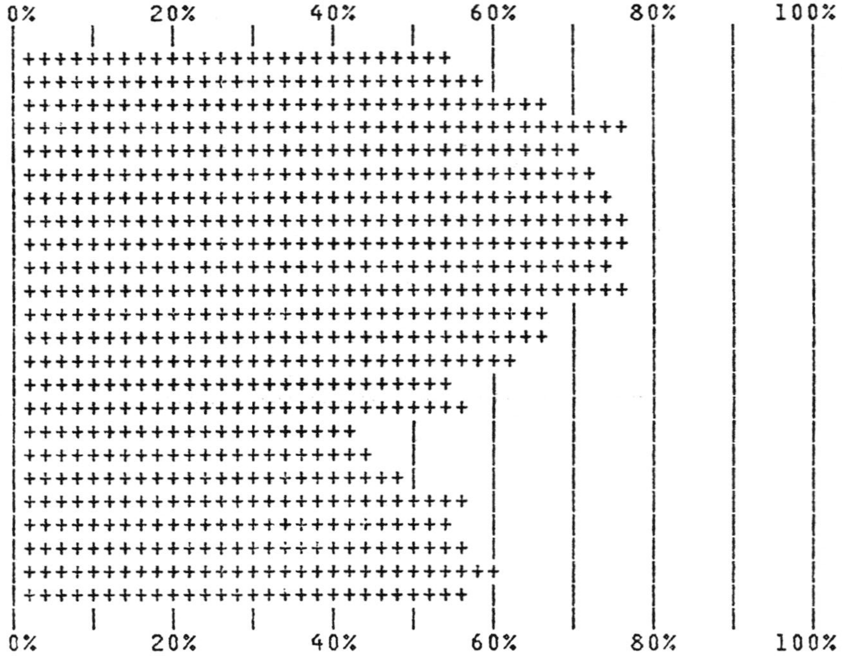

Graph scale: 0%   20%   40%   60%   80%   100%

Figure 9.7.

tion is then focused on the management of this subset of demand to determine whether the business requirements of some applications are such that their processing either can be deferred to periods of lighter production (2200 to 0300 in the example) or the capacity required be reduced. As an aside, Figure 9.8 provides an example of how this format can also be used to also address minor capacity issues such as I/O equipment. A final point of reference, Figure 9.9 is a tabular equivalent of a pie chart describing the share of total demand accounted for by each major user group.

With the issue having been stated that capacity will soon be in short supply, an explanation is required that either states that the targeted saturation date is as previously forecast, i.e., the request for new capacity should come as no surprise to the corporation, or that there has been a variance to the previous forecast. Figure 9.10 hypothesizes a case where there, in fact, has been a variance from the forecast. The solid line represents the trend of actual demand over the last, say, 3 years. The lower dotted line represents the demand prediction the data center manager presented to his management last year. Based on the slope of all but the last few months, his forecast merely extends the previous growth rate into the future. However, the temporary surge of demand during those last few months turned out to be indicative of continued future growth, as described by the upper dotted line. Thus he explains, he is now back before management to seek capacity relief many months ahead of his earlier expectations.

These methods of describing capacity and demand are generally sufficient to state issues and describe what conditions have changed. The uncertainty that the data center manager faces as he seeks a capacity-acquisition decision relates to the extent to which his superiors will believe the data he has presented as well as to what users' perceptions are with regard to the amount of computer capacity they need and the rate at which their usage is growing. Hence, whenever possible, data such as the information in Figure 9.6, Figure 9.7, and those following should be derived from the computer's own job-accounting system. And if at all feasible, the actual formatted output should be computer-generated because, while managers may challenge other managers, they often are reluctant to attack a faceless computer, its manufacturer, and what they perceive to be a massive data base. As a result, data prepared by hand and printed by computer can have greater credibility than computer-generated data that has been manually typed. In addition, the ability to return rapidly with reordered or supplemental data helps foster the perception that the capacity-acquisition decision is based on a foundation of broad and well-ordered data.

Reinforcing the data provided by Figure 9.10, Figures 9.11a and 9.11b offer computer-generated quarterly growth trends for two users identified in Figure 9.9. The purpose of charts such as these is to provide supplemental data on the reasons for the variance in demand growth trends if it appears there is resistance to previously supplied data. If the discussion goes further, it is likely to occur at a lower level of detail, and users will be told to verify that the data presented is accurate. Figure 9.12a continues the 24-hour operating cycle approach down to the application level while Figure 9.12b provides a record of resource con-

WORK OF FEBRUARY 1980

GRAPH OF AVERAGE NUMBER OF TAPE DRIVES USED FOR ALL JOBS BY ALL USERS

INTERVAL	AMOUNT
0800-0900	40.25
0900-1000	34.99
1000-1100	39.43
1100-1200	43.16
1200-1300	42.62
1300-1400	42.94
1400-1500	41.33
1500-1600	40.62
1600-1700	38.43
1700-1800	40.70
1800-1900	44.31
1900-2000	41.91
2000-2100	40.55
2100-2200	44.22
2200-2300	45.29
2300-0000	46.52
0000-0100	51.73
0100-0200	57.12
0200-0300	51.98
0300-0400	43.56
0400-0500	40.60
0500-0600	49.43
0600-0700	52.99
0700-0800	54.19

| AVERAGE | 44.54 |

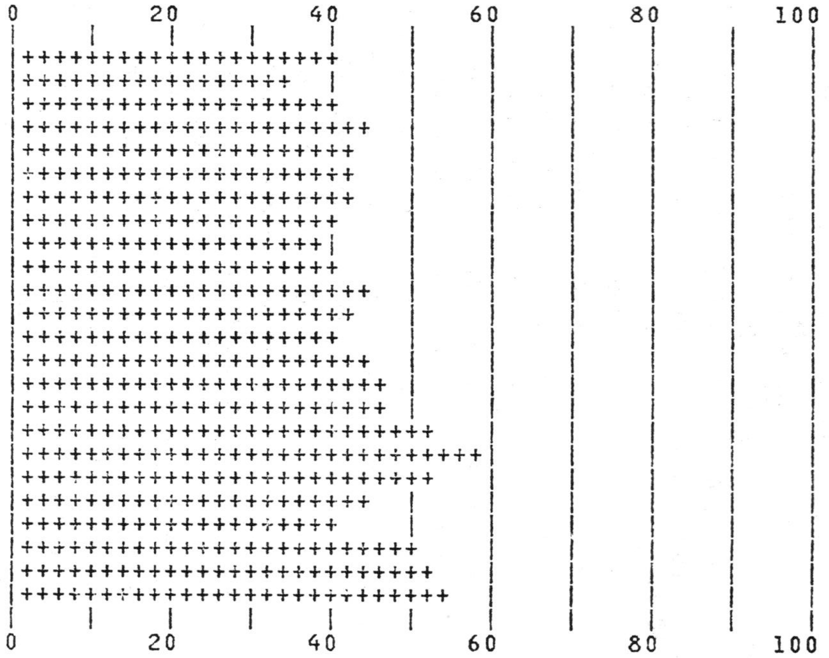

Figure 9.8.

UTILIZATION ANALYSIS:

RANKING OF USER GROUPS FOR COMBINED PRODUCTION AND DEBUGGING

CPU TIME   (MINUTES)

	SMOOTHED VALUE	% OF UTILITY	ACCUMULATED PERCENTAGES
OSHG USER TOTALS	1233.47	22.01%	22.01%
PPSG USER TOTALS	1203.84	21.48%	43.49%
CNTL/MSG USER TOTALS	1190.45	21.24%	64.73%
PUG USER TOTALS	648.31	11.57%	76.30%
MTG USER TOTALS	466.62	8.33%	84.63%
CUG USER TOTALS	462.78	8.26%	92.89%
HRD USER TOTALS	209.26	3.73%	96.62%
GENL AUD USER TOTALS	68.06	1.21%	97.83%
CORP BKG USER TOTALS	51.77	0.92%	98.75%
ADMIN GR USER TOTALS	22.75	0.41%	99.16%
CSG USER TOTALS	22.68	0.40%	99.56%

Figure 9.9.

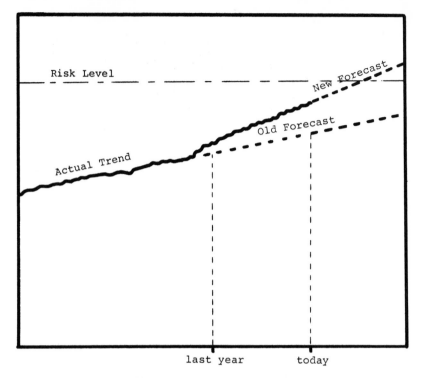

Figure 9.10. Peak Demand Trend.

sumption each time each job within an application is processed. The purpose of these charts is not to directly convey resource usage statistics to senior management, but rather to make them aware that the data center's information base is extraordinarily detailed and is based on the unbiased job-accounting system of a third party (usually the equipment vendor). A further purpose is to quickly convince any user to support the resource usage conclusions at which the data center has arrived.

The foregoing structures for presenting data are generally sufficient to support the need for capacity acquisitions under a variety of organizational environments. The remaining two requirements, selecting the optimal alternative solution and determining the costs involved, are addressed with the same techniques relating to service and capacity as were described in Chapters 4 through 8.

9.3 SUMMARY

Implementing a capacity decision is as much as a function of the ability to communicate issues to senior management as it is a function of correct technical problem solving. Decision data that is communicated to senior, nontechnical managers is best received when the information is presented in nontechnical language and in small, concise packages. Whether the presentation is in a tab-

CPU RESOURCES OF MAJOR USERS
AS PERCENT OF CAPACITY
AS OF 12/79 (DEMAND=57%)
MTG

BAR CHART OF CPUOVHD

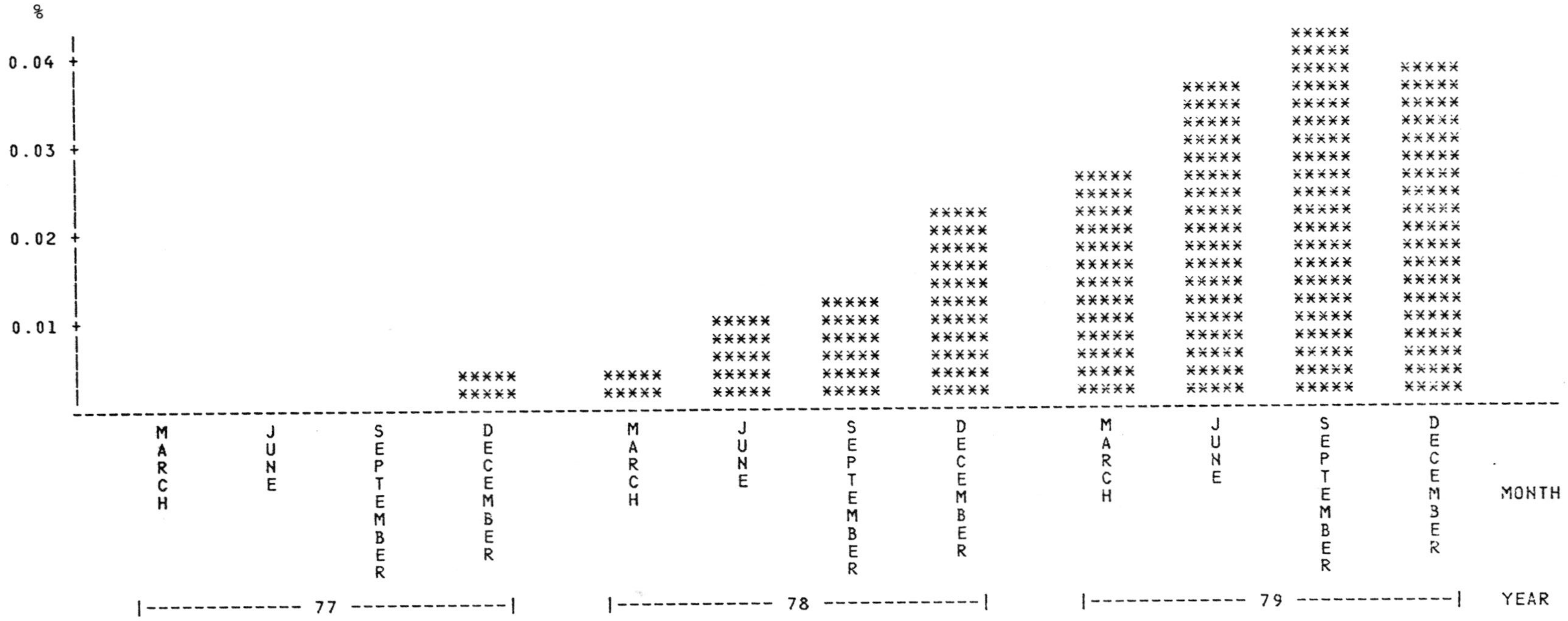

Figure 9.11(a).

CPU RESOURCES OF MAJOR USERS
AS PERCENT OF CAPACITY
AS OF 12/79 (DEMAND=57%)
FINPLNG, CSG, CNTL, CORP/CTL

BAR CHART OF CPUOVHD

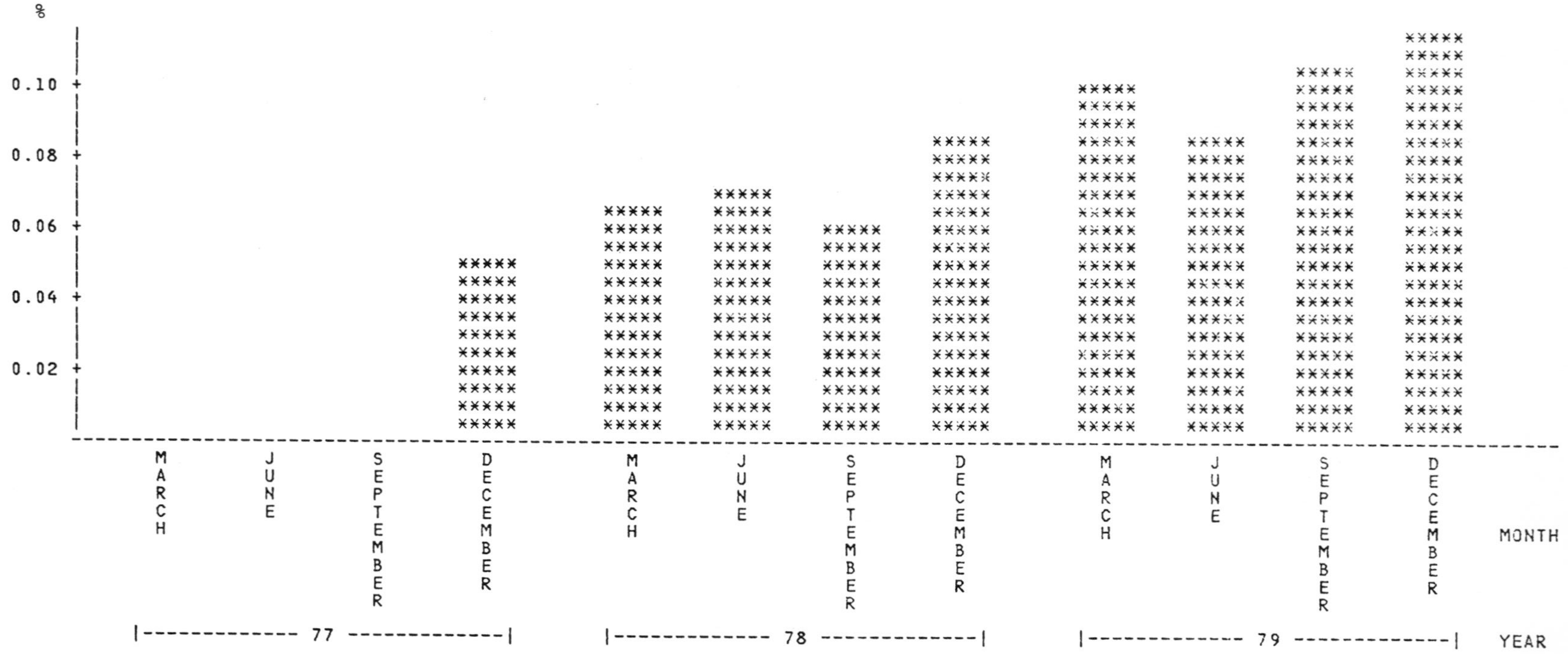

Figure 9.11(b).

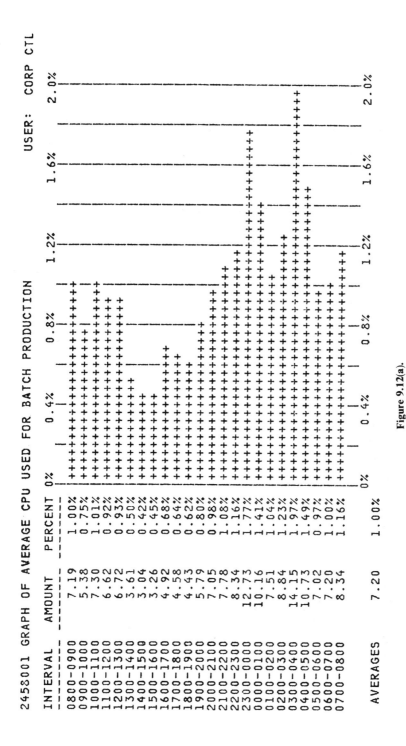

Figure 9.12(a).

APPLICATION: 2458001 CCIF
CATEGORY: BATCH PRODUCTION

USER: CORP CTL

JOB NAME	DBG CL	CPU	DATE RUN	START	ELPSD MINS	ACTUAL CPU MINS	PERCENT	CORE (KB)	TAPE DR	MTS	FLGS
RELAVR03		2	02/08/80	2257	40	0.65	1.62%	0196	02	004	#
RELAVR03		2	02/08/80	2338	39	0.58	1.49%	0196	02	004	#
RELAVR03		2	02/09/80	1550	48	0.67	1.40%	0196	02	003	#
RELAVR03		2	02/09/80	1642	35	0.64	1.83%	0196	02	004	#
RELAVR03		2	02/09/80	1718	32	0.65	2.03%	0196	02	004	#
RELAVR03		2	02/09/80	1754	38	0.66	1.74%	0196	02	004	#
RELAVR03		2	02/12/80	0836	28	0.60	2.14%	0264	02	004	#
RELAVR03		2	02/12/80	0939	39	0.63	1.62%	0264	02	004	
RELAVR03		2	02/12/80	1020	42	0.64	1.52%	0264	02	004	
RELAVR03		2	02/12/80	1106	43	0.65	1.51%	0264	02	004	
RELAVR03		1	02/14/80	0526	34	0.61	1.79%	0280	02	004	#
RELAVR03		1	02/14/80	0601	52	0.62	1.19%	0260	02	004	#
RELAVR03		1	02/16/80	0859	58	0.64	1.10%	0264	02	004	
RELAVR03		2	02/17/80	1046	24	0.59	2.46%	0264	02	004	
RELAVR03		1	02/20/80	0836	76	0.97	1.28%	0264	02	003	
RELAVR03		1	02/20/80	1654	49	0.56	1.14%	0280	02	004	
RELAVR03		1	02/20/80	1743	30	0.53	1.77%	0280	02	003	#
RELAVR03		1	02/21/80	0605	46	0.61	1.33%	0260	02	003	#
RELAVR03		1	02/21/80	0705	24	0.55	2.29%	0260	02	004	
RELAVR03		1	02/23/80	1013	45	0.65	1.44%	0264	02	004	#
10 JOBS ON 3033:			<MEAN>	0140	44	0.63	1.44%	247	2.0	3.8	
146.2 RUNS/YR			<S.D.>	5:25	14	0.12	0.34%	34	0.0	0.4	

Figure 9.12(b).

ular or graphical format, the terminology used should be matched to that which the senior manager receives from other parts of the corporation, usually demand as a percent of capacity, units of output (if applicable), and efficiency. If appropriate, unit cost data can be added. While the reporting of monthly business-as-usual statistics is limited to small numbers of key indices, information packages supporting requests for decision approvals are usually larger and stratified to anticipate various levels of management's concerns.

APPENDIX A

DATA PROCESSING SERVICE AGREEMENT
FOR THE
ACCOUNT INQUIRY SYSTEM (AIS)

The Account Inquiry System of the Customer Services Division, referred to as the User herein, and the Data Processing Division (DPD) are committed to meet the input/output times and the other specifications contained in this agreement.

_____	_____	_____	_____
Charles Brown, V.P.	**Date**	**John Smith, V.P.**	**Date**
Customer Services Division		**Data Processing Division**	

DPD SERVICE PACKAGE

- DPD provides to each User the following total service package to ensure an efficient, timely mode of operation:
  - Job Setup and Control
  - Library-Tape Storage and Maintenance
  - Disk Space Management
  - Back-up Contingency Planning
  - Manpower Planning
  - Computer Hardware Planning
  - Computer Software Planning
  - Capacity/Performance Planning
  - Internal Systems Support
  - Resource Usage Monitoring
  - Monthly Application Costing
  - Protection Services:
    - Site Security
    - Fire
    - Power/Air Conditioning

Timeliness Commitments

User is committed to assure that input will be serviceable and timely on 95% of the days that jobs are run. Input deadlines are specified on Attachment 1.

DPD is committed to assure that no more than 5% of the output deadlines are missed because of problems (hardware problems, handling errors, etc.); i.e., DPD-controlled output timeliness is guaranteed to be at least 95%.

Quality Control

DPD will make its best efforts to assure that the quality of output meets or exceeds the standards set in the Operations Run Book. Among the defects that the utility will attempt to eliminate are:

- Incomplete Output
  - Missing Documents
  - Incomplete Data
- Invalid Output
  - Illegible Printing
  - Skewed Printing
  - Illegible Carbon Copies and Overlays
  - Output on Invalid Forms
  - Form not burst and trimmed properly

Attachment 1

INPUT/OUTPUT SPECIFICATIONS

The User and DPD agree to measure and report on the following critical inputs/outputs:

INPUT	DELIVERY TO DPD	OUTPUT	DELIVERY TO USER
New Account Tape	4:00 PM	Financial Update Report	8:00 AM
Account Status Tape	4:00 PM	Account Status Report	8:00 AM
Parameter Revision Cards	8:00 AM	Exception Report	9:00 AM

In the case of forecasted late input availability, the User will notify the DPD Production Manager 1 hour prior to the above required input arrival times. Notification of pending late arrival of output shall be made by the DPD Production Manager to the User's Production Manager at least 1 hour prior to the required output delivery deadline. DPD shall be responsible for pickup and delivery of all input and output.

The User agrees to make his best efforts to contact DPD's materials assembly/disassembly (MAD) area within 2 hours of receipt of output believed to be incorrect. DPD will inspect the output to verify the defect and determine its cause. At the request of the User, DPD will rerun the job whether or not a quality failure has been committed.

Performance Reports

User agrees to send a daily report assessing the quality and timeliness of DPD outputs to DPD's Production Manager. The Production Manager will compare this to his records and resolve the differences with a User Representative. Before publishing the monthly service index statistics, DPD's Service Agreements Coordinator will contact both the Production Manager and the User Representative to confirm the agreed-upon timeliness and quality figures for the month.

Among the statistics shown will be: total days output was late, primary reasons for lateness (user, application program, DPD problems, etc.), and timeliness percentages. Comments on these statistics should be sent to DPD's Service Agreements Coordinator.

Revisions

Revisions to this agreement will be considered in anticipation of, or subsequent to, any of the following:

- Significant growth in the capacity requirements, number of transactions processed or volume of printed output. "Significant growth," unless defined elsewhere in this contract, is an increase of 20% over the volumes and capacity shown in Attachment 2.
- Relocation of the application to another DPD site.
- Failures to meet contracted timeliness/quality criteria.
- Addition of new jobs.

If any of these factors causes the overall output timeliness to fall below 95% for 3 consecutive months, this agreement may be suspended at the written request of the User or DPD. However, if output timeliness falls below 95% because of DPD problems, DPD may not suspend the agreement. If the agreement is suspended, DPD and the User will continue to make their best efforts to meet the contracted deadlines until revised agreement is completed or until the suspension of the existing agreement is lifted.

This contract remains in effect between the signing departments despite changes of personnel.

Attachment 2

Statement of AIS Computer Demand

JOB NAME	CPU MIN.	TAPE DRIVES	DISK DRIVES	ELAPSED TIME (MIN.)
AIS on-line	60	1	2	480
AISJOB1	10	0	2	60
AISJOB2	10	0	2	60
AISJOB3	10	0	2	60

APPENDIX B

DATA PROCESSING SERVICE AGREEMENT
FOR
PROVIDING COMPUTER RESOURCES FOR TESTING

The Data Processing Division (DPD), and Users A,B,C, and D, referred to herein as the User, are committed to meet the service and volume specifications described in this document.

_____	_____	_____	_____
Ralph Ferra, V.P.	Date	John Smith, V.P.	Date
User A		Data Processing Division	
_____	_____		
Mary Houseman, V.P.	Date		
User B			
_____	_____		
Carol Jones, V.P.	Date		
User C			
_____	_____		
Harold White, V.P.	Date		
User D			

Service Committment

DPD will provide testing resources as categorized in Table 1, *Testing Job Classification*, and Table 2, *Level of Service*. The User agrees that any increase in resource requirements is subject to equipment availability and vendor delivery schedules, and that users will provide quarterly updates to their requirement forecasts.

When contention for the same disk file exists between jobs, the requests shall be honored in the sequence the jobs are received subject to priority constraints. When a job is delayed because of contention by a previously submitted job, one of the jobs shall be cancelled by the operator who will indicate on the job request card (JRC) why the job was cancelled. If the cancelled job is rerunable, the job will be rerun, and the reason for the delay will be indicated on the log-out entry and the JRC. If a job is not rerunable, the reason will be indicated on the log-out entry and JRC. For both cases, the job causing the cancellation will be indicated on the log-out entry.

Definitions

Definitions for Table 1, *Testing Job Classifications*, are as follows:

1. **Turnaround Category** This is the classification of service for work to be completed based upon the listed resource requirements as shown in Table 1. All testing jobs must have the turnaround category indicated on the Job Request Card (JRC).
2. **Submission Time** The time when a job is logged in by DPD.
3. **Turnaround Time** This category is based upon the time required to process the job from DPD "log-in" to "log-out" time.
4. **CPU** The number of CPU minutes that may be requested for a turnaround category.
5. **Elapsed Time** The amount of time required by the job from the time of "initiation" until "termination." This time is usually independent of time the job is on the input/output queues.
6. **Private Disks** Disk packs that are required to be specifically mounted for a particular job in a turnaround category. Permanently mounted packs are not in this category.
7. **Tapes** The number of tape drives that are required for a turnaround category.
8. **Print Page Volume** The maximum number of pages that can be printed for a turnaround category.
9. **Bursting/Decollating** Bursting and/or decollating service available for a turnaround category.

Table 1   Testing Job Classifications

TURNAROUND CATEGORY	SUBMISSION TIME	TURNAROUND TIME	CPU (MIN.)	ELAPSED TIME	PRIVATE DISKS	TAPES	PRINT-PAGE VOLUME	BURST/ DECOL.
1	8 AM–6 PM	1 hr.	3	30	0	0	100	No
2	8 AM–6 PM	2 hrs.	6	30	0	0	300	No
3	8 AM–5 PM	1½ hrs.	3	35	1	3	300	No
4	8 AM–5 PM	2 hrs.	10	60	3	5	500	No
5	8 AM–5 PM	3 hrs.	5	45	4	5	500	Yes
6	8 AM–5 PM	3 hrs.	5	60	4	6	1000	No
7	8 AM–5 PM	4 hrs.	5	60	4	6	1000	Yes
8	Up to 5 PM	Overnight	20	120	4	6	2000	Yes
9	5 PM–8 AM	24 hrs.	30	120	4	6	2000	Yes
10	Scheduled	Scheduled	>30	>120	>4	>6	>2000	Yes

Table 2   Level of Service

TURNAROUND CATEGORY	NUMBER OF JOBS REQUIRED TO MEET TURNAROUND TIME	JOBS REQUIRED TO MEET TURNAROUND TIME (%)	MAXIMUM FAILURE LEVEL (*) (HOURS)
1	200	95	2
2	150	95	2
3	80	95	4
4	30	95	8
5	10	90	8
6	20	95	8
7	10	90	8
8	10	98	4
9	5	80	12
10	20	95	24

*For each turnaround category, this column specifies the longest time that jobs in that turnaround category can be delayed.

APPENDIX C

7-Track Tape Drive Account (Final-Bundled)

	ANNUAL EXPENSE
EQUIPMENT	
Tape Drives—Rental	$54,000
Tape Drives—Add'l. Use	3,000
Card Reader/Punch Allocation	667
I/O Channel (0.7)	9,450
Terminals and Data Comm.—Direct	374
Terminals and Data Comm.—Allocation	561
Subtotal	$68,052
LABOR	
Operators	14,040
Supervisors	7,804
Tape Library	10,007
Materials Assembly	2,958
Messenger Services	2,227
Capacity Planning	753
Software Maintenance and Development	3,861
Budgeting and Costing	1,357
Production Management	1,053
Staff Services Management	1,577
Data Center Management	
Direct	1,158
Staff Contribution	1,301
Subtotal	48,096
SUPPLIES	
Tapes	267
Cleaning Agents	33
Computer Operations	3,243
Staff Services Management	1,262
Data Center Management	
Direct	375
Staff Contribution	188
Subtotal	5,368
Total	$121,516

Disk Drive Account (Final-Bundled)

	ANNUAL EXPENSE	
EQUIPMENT		
Disk Drives—Rental	$432,000	
Disk Drives—Depreciation	327,886	
I/O Channels (8)	108,000	
Card Reader/Punch Allocation	6,000	
Terminals and Data Comm.—Direct	—	
Terminals and Data Comm.—Allocation	5,100	
Subtotal		$878,986
LABOR		
Materials Assembly	26,617	
Messenger Services	20,039	
Capacity Planning	6,776	
Software Maintenance and Development	34,746	
Budgeting and Costing	12,209	
Production Management	9,473	
Staff Services Management	14,191	
Data Center Management		
Direct	10,420	
Staff Contribution	11,708	
Subtotal		146,179
SUPPLIES		
Computer Operations	12,972	
Staff Services Management	5,050	
Data Center Management		
Direct	1,502	
Staff Contribution	1,687	
Subtotal		21,211
Total		$1,046,376

Printer Account (Final-Bundled)

	ANNUAL EXPENSE	
EQUIPMENT		
Printers—Rental	$45,600	
Printers—Depreciation	35,715	
Printers—Add'l. Use	4,740	
Burster/Decollator—Rental	6,000	
Card Reader/Punch Allocation	6,000	
I/O Channels (2)	27,000	
Terminals and Data Comm.—Direct	3,400	
Terminals and Data Comm.—Allocation	5,100	
Subtotal		$133,555
LABOR		
Operators	58,500	
Supervisors	70,070	
Bursting and Decollating	57,330	
Materials Assembly	26,618	
Messenger Services	20,040	
Capacity Planning	6,777	
Systems Maintenance and Development	34,745	
Budgeting and Costing	12,210	
Production Management	9,473	
Staff Services Management	14,192	
Data Center Management		
Direct	10,421	
Staff Contribution	11,708	
Subtotal		332,084
SUPPLIES		
Flatpack	120,000	
Ribbons	600	
Computer Operations	12,971	
Staff Services Management	5,050	
Data Center Management		
Direct	1,502	
Staff Contribution	1,688	
Subtotal		141,811
Total		$607,450

COM Account (Final-Bundled)

	ANNUAL EXPENSE	
EQUIPMENT		
COM unit	$66,000	
Subtotal		$66,000
LABOR		
Operator	19,656	
Messenger Services	9,907	
Budgeting and Costing	6,036	
Production Management	4,683	
Data Center Management		
Direct	5,152	
Subtotal		45,434
SUPPLIES		
Film and Developer	24,000	
Computer Operations	6,413	
Data Center Management		
Direct	742	
Subtotal		31,155
Total		$142,589

APPENDIX D

9-Track Tape Drive Account (Partial-Unbundled)

	ANNUAL EXPENSE	
EQUIPMENT		
Tape-Drives—Rental	$175,200	
Tape Drives—Add'l. Use	6,250	
Card Reader/Punch Allocation	5,333	
I/O Channels (5.3)	71,550	
Terminals and Data Comm.—Direct	3,026	
Subtotal		$261,359
LABOR		
Operators	112,320	
Supervisors	62,435	
Budgeting and Costing	4,322	
Production Management	4,205	
Data Center Management Direct	4,626	
Subtotal		187,908
SUPPLIES		
Tapes	2,133	
Cleaning Agents	267	
Computer Operations	5,758	
Data Center Management Direct	667	
Subtotal		8,825
Total		$458,092

7-Track Tape Drive Account (Partial-Unbundled)

	ANNUAL EXPENSE	
EQUIPMENT		
Tape Drives—Rental	$54,000	
Tape Drives—Add'l. Use	3,000	
Card Reader/Punch Allocation	667	
I/O Channel (.7)	9,450	
Terminals and Data Comm.—Direct	374	
Subtotal		$67,491
LABOR		
Operators	14,040	
Supervisors	7,804	
Budgeting and Costing	540	
Production Management	526	
Data Center Management Direct	578	
Subtotal		23,488
SUPPLIES		
Tapes	267	
Cleaning Agents	33	
Computer Operations	720	
Data Center Management Direct	83	
Subtotal		1,103
Total		$92,082

Disk Drive Account (Partial-Unbundled)

	ANNUAL EXPENSE	
EQUIPMENT		
Disk Drives—Rental	$432,000	
Disk Drives—Depreciation	327,886	
I/O Channels (8)	108,000	
Card Reader/Punch Allocation	6,000	
Terminals and Data Comm.—Direct	—	
Subtotal		$873,886
LABOR		
Budgeting and Costing	4,861	
Production Management	4,730	
Data Center Management Direct	5,204	
Subtotal		14,795
SUPPLIES		
Computer Operations	6,478	
Data Center Management Direct	750	
Subtotal		7,228
Total		$895,909

Printer Account (Partial-Unbundled)

	ANNUAL EXPENSE	
EQUIPMENT		
Printers—Rental	$ 45,600	
Printers—Depreciation	35,715	
Printers—Add'l. Use	4,740	
Card Reader—Punch Allocation	6,000	
I/O Channels (2)	27,000	
Terminals and Data Comm.—Direct	3,400	
Subtotal		$122,455
LABOR		
Operators	58,500	
Supervisors	70,070	
Budgeting and Costing	4,862	
Production Management	4,731	
Data Center Management Direct	5,204	
Subtotal		143,367
SUPPLIES		
Flatpack	120,000	
Ribbons	600	
Computer Operations	6,478	
Data Center Management Direct	750	
Subtotal		127,828
Total		$393,650

COM Account (Partial-Unbundled)

	ANNUAL EXPENSE	
EQUIPMENT		
COM Unit	$66,000	
Subtotal		$66,000
LABOR		
Operator	19,656	
Budgeting and Costing	4,862	
Production Management	4,730	
Data Center Management Direct	5,204	
Subtotal		34,452
SUPPLIES		
Film and Developer	24,000	
Computer Operations	6,478	
Data Center Management Direct	750	
Subtotal		31,228
Total		$131,680

APPENDIX E

Materials Assembly Account

	ANNUAL EXPENSE	
EQUIPMENT		
—	—	
Subtotal		—
LABOR		
Clerks	$106,470	
Production Management	4,730	
Data Center Management	5,203	
Budgeting and Costing	4,862	
Subtotal		$121,265
SUPPLIES		
Computer Operations	6,478	
Data Center Management	750	
Subtotal		7,228
Total		$128,493

Bursting and Decollating Account

	ANNUAL EXPENSE	
EQUIPMENT		
Burster/Decollators—Rental	$ 6,000	
Subtotal		$6,000
LABOR		
Operators	$57,330	
Production Management	4,731	
Data Center Management	5,203	
Budgeting and Costing	4,862	
Subtotal		72,126
SUPPLIES		
Computer Operations	6,477	
Data Center Management	750	
Subtotal		7,227
Total		$85,353

Messenger Services Account

	ANNUAL EXPENSE	
EQUIPMENT		
—	—	
Subtotal		—
LABOR		
Clerks	$90,064	
Production Management	4,731	
Data Center Management	5,203	
Budgeting and Costing	4,861	
Subtotal		$104,859
SUPPLIES		
Computer Operations	6,477	
Data Center Management	750	
Subtotal		7,227
Total		$112,086

Capacity/Performance Planning Account

	ANNUAL EXPENSE	
EQUIPMENT		
Terminal (1) and Data Comm.	$ 3,400	
Subtotal		$3,400
LABOR		
Analyst	27,105	
Staff Services Management	7,096	
Data Center Management	5,854	
Budgeting and Costing	7,293	
Subtotal		47,348
SUPPLIES		
Staff Services Management	2,525	
Data Center Management	844	
Subtotal		3,369
Total		$54,117

Software Maintenance and Development Account

	ANNUAL EXPENSE
EQUIPMENT	
Terminals (5) and Data Comm.	$ 17,000
Subtotal	$17,000
LABOR	
Analysts	138,983
Staff Services Management	35,478
Data Center Management	29,270
Budgeting and Costing	36,462
Subtotal	240,193
SUPPLIES	
Staff Services	12,625
Data Center Management	4,218
Subtotal	16,843
Total	$274,036

APPENDIX F

9-Track Tape Drive Account (Final-Unbundled)

	ANNUAL EXPENSE	
EQUIPMENT		
Tape Drives—Rental	$175,200	
Tape Drives—Add'l. Use	6,250	
Card Reader/Punch Allocation	5,333	
I/O Channels (5.3)	71,550	
Terminals and Data Comm.—Direct	3,026	
Subtotal		$261,359
LABOR		
Operators	112,320	
Supervisors	62,435	
Budgeting and Costing	4,322	
Production Management	4,205	
Data Center Management Direct	4,626	
Subtotal		187,908
SUPPLIES AND SERVICES		
Tapes	2,133	
Cleaning Agents	267	
Computer Operations	5,758	
Data Center Management Direct	667	
Capacity Planning	6,012	
Software Maintenance and Development	42,628	
Subtotal		57,465
Total		$506,732

7-Track Tape Drive Account (Final-Unbundled)

	ANNUAL EXPENSE	
EQUIPMENT		
Tape Drives—Rental	$54,000	
Tape Drives—Add'l. Use	3,000	
Card Reader/Punch Allocation	667	
I/O Channel (.7)	9,450	
Terminals and Data Comm.—Direct	374	
Subtotal		$67,491
LABOR		
Operators	14,040	
Supervisors	7,804	
Budgeting and Costing	540	
Production Management	526	
Data Center Management Direct	578	
Subtotal		23,488
SUPPLIES AND SERVICES		
Tapes	267	
Cleaning Agents	33	
Computer Operations	720	
Data Center Management Direct	83	
Capacity/Performance Planning	752	
Software Maintenance and Development	5,328	
Subtotal		7,183
Total		$98,162

Disk Drive Account (Final-Unbundled)

	ANNUAL EXPENSE	
EQUIPMENT		
Disk Drives—Rental	$432,000	
Disk Drives—Depreciation	327,886	
I/O Channels (8)	108,000	
Card Reader/Punch Allocation	6,000	
Terminals and Data Comm.—Direct	—	
Subtotal		$873,886
LABOR		
Budgeting and Costing	4,861	
Production Management	4,730	
Data Center Management Direct	5,204	
Subtotal		14,795
SUPPLIES AND SERVICES		
Computer Operations	6,478	
Data Center Management Direct	750	
Capacity/Performance Planning	6,765	
Software Maintenance and Development	47,956	
Subtotal		61,949
Total		$950,630

Printer Account (Final-Unbundled)

	ANNUAL EXPENSE	
EQUIPMENT		
Printers—Rental	$ 45,600	
Printers—Depreciation	35,715	
Printers—Add'l. Use	4,740	
Card Reader/Punch Allocation	6,000	
I/O Channels (2)	27,000	
Terminals and Data Comm.—Direct	3,400	
Subtotal		$122,455
LABOR		
Operators	58,500	
Supervisors	70,070	
Budgeting and Costing	4,862	
Production Management	4,731	
Data Center Management Direct	5,204	
Subtotal		143,367
SUPPLIES AND SERVICES		
Flatpack	120,000	
Ribbons	600	
Computer Operations	6,478	
Data Center Management Direct	750	
Capacity/Performance Planning	6,764	
Software Maintenance and Development	47,956	
Subtotal		182,548
Total		$448,370

COM Account (Final-Unbundled)

	ANNUAL EXPENSE	
EQUIPMENT		
COM unit	$66,000	
Subtotal		$66,000
LABOR		
Operator	19,656	
Budgeting and Costing	4,862	
Production Management	4,730	
Data Center Management Direct	5,204	
Subtotal		34,452
SUPPLIES AND SERVICES		
Film and Developer	24,000	
Computer Operations	6,478	
Data Center Management Direct	750	
Subtotal		31,228
Total		$131,680

APPENDIX G

Expected Cost of Capacity

		Capacity Alternative 2 (One 1.0 machine)			
GROWTH ALTERNATIVE	SERVICE RISK	PROBABILITY OF OCCURRENCE (%)	EXPECTED PENALTIES/LOSSES (000)	TOTAL COST (000)	CONTRIBUTION TO EXPECTED COST (000)
1	High	10	$300	$1,300	$ 130.0
2	High	15	350	1,350	202.5
3	High	50	400	1,400	700.0
4	High	15	600	1,600	240.0
5	High	10	600	1,600	160.0
				Expected Cost	$1,432.5

		Capacity Alternative 3 (Two 0.75 machines)			
GROWTH ALTERNATIVE	SERVICE RISK	PROBABILITY OF OCCURRENCE (%)	EXPECTED PENALTIES/LOSSES (000)	TOTAL COST (000)	CONTRIBUTION TO EXPECTED COST (000)
1	High	10	$400	$2,100	$ 210.0
2	High	15	500	2,200	330.0
3	High	50	600	2,300	1,150.0
4	High	15	800	2,500	375.0
5	High	10	800	2,500	250.0
				Expected Cost	$2,315.0

Expected Cost of Capacity

Capacity Alternative 4(DDA on 0.75 machine, AUTH on 1.0 machine)

GROWTH ALTERNATIVE	SERVICE RISK	PROBABILITY OF OCCURRENCE (%)	EXPECTED PENALTIES/LOSSES (000)	TOTAL COST (000)	CONTRIBUTION TO EXPECTED COST (000)
1	High	10	$260	$2,110	$ 211.0
2	High	15	265	2,115	317.3
3	High	50	380	2,230	1,115.0
4	High	15	590	2,440	336.0
5	High	10	600	2,450	245.0
					Expected Cost $2,254.3

Capacity Alternative 5 (Two 1.0 machines)

GROWTH ALTERNATIVE	SERVICE RISK	PROBABILITY OF OCCURRENCE (%)	EXPECTED PENALTIES/LOSSES (000)	TOTAL COST (000)	CONTRIBUTION TO EXPECTED COST (000)
1	High	10	$100	$2,100	$ 210.0
2	High	15	200	2,200	330.0
3	High	50	350	2,350	1,175.0
4	High	15	450	2,450	367.5
5	High	10	500	2,500	250.0
					Expected Cost $2,332.5

Expected Cost of Capacity

Capacity Alternative 6 (DDA on 1.0 machine, AUTH on 1.5 machine)

GROWTH ALTERNATIVE	SERVICE RISK	PROBABILITY OF OCCURRENCE (%)	EXPECTED PENALTIES/LOSSES (000)	TOTAL COST (000)	CONTRIBUTION TO EXPECTED COST (000)
1	—	10	$10	$2,260	$ 226.0
2	—	15	10	2,260	339.0
3	Low	50	20	2,270	1,135.0
4	Medium	15	30	2,280	342.0
5	High	10	50	2,300	230.0
					Expected Cost $2,272.0

Capacity Alternative 7 (Two 1.5 machines)

GROWTH ALTERNATIVE	SERVICE RISK	PROBABILITY OF OCCURRENCE (%)	EXPECTED PENALTIES/LOSSES (000)	TOTAL COST (000)	CONTRIBUTION TO EXPECTED COST (000)
1	—	10	$5	$2,505	$ 250.5
2	—	15	5	2,505	375.8
3	—	50	5	2,505	1,252.5
4	—	15	10	2,510	376.5
5	Low	10	20	2,520	252.0
					Expected Cost $2,507.3

INDEX